D1353122

Praise for *Just Mercy*

'*Just Mercy* should be read by people of conscience in every civilized country in the world to discover what happens when revenge and retribution replace justice and mercy. It is as gripping to read as any legal thriller, and what hangs in the balance is nothing less than the soul of a great nation.' —Desmond Tutu, Nobel Peace Laureate

'Every bit as moving as *To Kill a Mockingbird* ... A searing indictment of American criminal justice and a stirring testament to the salvation that fighting for the vulnerable sometimes yields.' —David Cole, *New York Review of Books*

'[*Just Mercy*] makes a powerful case for reform of the US criminal justice system ... [Bryan Stevenson] doesn't indulge in self-pity or self-righteousness. He just tells stories, real stories — some of which will make you gasp at the inhumanity of humankind ... [He] is one of those individuals who manages to see the "better angels of our nature" and, amid all the horrifying accounts of injustice, he finds grace, dignity, humanity.' —Raymond Bonner, *Financial Times*

'Our American criminal justice system has become an instrument of evil. Bryan Stevenson has labored long and hard, and with great skill and temperate passion, to set things right. Words such as important and compelling may have lost their force through overuse, but reading this book will restore their meaning, along with one's hopes for humanity.' —Tracey Kidder, Pulitzer Prize–winning author of *Mountains Beyond Mountains*

'Unfairness in the justice system is a major theme of our age ... This book brings new life to the story by placing it in two affecting contexts: Stevenson's life work and the deep strain of racial injustice in American life ... You don't have to read too long to start cheering for this man. Against tremendous odds, Stevenson has worked to free scores of people from wrongful or excessive punishment, arguing five times before the Supreme Court ... The book extols not his nobility, but that of the cause, and reads like a call to action for all that remains to be done ... The message of the book, hammered home by dramatic examples of one man's refusal to sit quietly and countenance horror, is that evil can be overcome, a difference can be made. *Just Mercy* will make you upset and it will make you hopeful ... Bryan Stevenson has been angry about [the criminal justice system] for years, and we are all the better for it.' — Ted Conover, *The New York Times*

'Powerful, profoundly affecting ... [*Just Mercy*] documents, in a measured, anecdotal way, the inside story of the policy of mass incarceration, the barely credible inhumanity that has seen young boys kept in solitary confinement for years and decades, and the evidence of institutional racism at the heart of the American justice system.' — *The Observer*

'Not since Atticus Finch has a fearless and committed lawyer made such a difference in the American South. Though larger than life, Atticus exists only in fiction. Bryan Stevenson, however, is very much alive and doing God's work fighting for the poor, the oppressed, the voiceless, the vulnerable, the outcast, and those with no hope. *Just Mercy* is his inspiring and powerful story.' — John Grisham

'[Bryan Stevenson] has done as much as any other living American to vindicate the innocent and temper justice with mercy for the guilty ... [*Just Mercy* is] a work of style, substance and clarity. Mixing commentary and reportage, he adroitly juxtaposes triumph and failure, neither of which is in short supply, against an unfolding backdrop of the saga of Walter McMillian, an innocent black Alabaman sentenced to death for the 1986 murder of an

18-year-old white woman ... Stevenson is not only a great lawyer, he's also a gifted writer and storyteller. His memoir should find an avid audience among players in the legal system — jurists, prosecutors, defense lawyers, legislators, academics, journalists — and especially anyone contemplating a career in criminal justice.' — *The Washington Post*

'Stevenson's contributions to social justice have been remarkable. But his efforts, on top of his continuing legal practice, to provide this inside glimpse of the criminal justice system are priceless.' — *The Seattle Times*

'Bryan Stevenson is one of my personal heroes, perhaps the most inspiring and influential crusader for justice alive today, and *Just Mercy* is extraordinary. The stories told within these pages hold the potential to transform what we think we mean when we talk about justice.' — Michelle Alexander, author of *The New Jim Crow*

'From the frontlines of social justice comes one of the most urgent voices of our era. Bryan Stevenson is a real-life, modern-day Atticus Finch who, through his work in redeeming innocent people condemned to death, has sought to redeem the country itself. This is a book of great power and courage. It is inspiring and suspenseful. A revelation.' — Isabel Wilkerson, author of *The Warmth of Other Suns*

JUST MERCY

BRYAN STEVENSON is the executive director of the
Equal Justice Initiative in Montgomery, Alabama,
and a professor of law at New York University Law
School. He has won relief for dozens of condemned prisoners, argued five times before the Supreme Court, and won national acclaim for his
work challenging bias against the poor and people
of color. He has received numerous awards, including the MacArthur Foundation "Genius" Grant.

www.eji.org

Just Mercy

A Story of Justice
and Redemption

Bryan Stevenson

SCRIBE

Melbourne • London

Scribe Publications
2 John St, Clerkenwell, London, WC1N 2ES, United Kingdom
18–20 Edward St, Brunswick, Victoria 3056, Australia

First published by Scribe 2015
Reprinted 2016 (twice), 2017, 2018 (twice), 2019
This edition published 2020

This edition published by arrangement with Spiegel & Grau, an imprint of
Random House, a division of Random House LLC, a Penguin Random House
Company, New York

Just Mercy is a work of nonfiction. Some names and identifying details
have been changed.

Text design by Caroline Cunningham
Printed and bound in the UK by CPI Group (UK) Ltd, Croydon CR0 4YY

Scribe Publications is committed to the sustainable use of natural resources
and the use of paper products made responsibly from those resources.

9781912854790 (UK paperback)
9781925849745 (Australian paperback)
9781925113570 (e-book)

Catalogue records for this book are available from the National Library of Australia
and the British Library

scribepublications.co.uk
scribepublications.com.au

In memory of Alice Golden Stevenson,

my mom

Love is the motive, but justice is the instrument.

—Reinhold Niebuhr

Contents

Just Mercy

Introduction

Higher Ground

I wasn't prepared to meet a condemned man. In 1983, I was a twenty-three-year-old student at Harvard Law School working in Georgia on an internship, eager and inexperienced and worried that I was in over my head. I had never seen the inside of a maximum-security prison—and had certainly never been to death row. When I learned that I would be visiting this prisoner alone, with no lawyer accompanying me, I tried not to let my panic show.

Georgia's death row is in a prison outside of Jackson, a remote town in a rural part of the state. I drove there by myself, heading south on I-75 from Atlanta, my heart pounding harder the closer I got. I didn't really know anything about capital punishment and hadn't even taken a class in criminal procedure yet. I didn't have a basic grasp of the complex appeals process that shaped death penalty litigation, a process that would in time become as familiar to me as the back of my hand. When I signed up for this internship, I hadn't given much thought to the fact that I would actually be meeting condemned prisoners. To be honest, I didn't even know if I wanted to be a lawyer. As the miles ticked by on those rural roads, the more convinced I became that this man was going to be very disappointed to see me.

I studied philosophy in college and didn't realize until my senior year that no one would pay me to philosophize when I graduated. My frantic search for a "post-graduation plan" led me to law school mostly because other graduate programs required you to know something about your field of study to enroll; law schools, it seemed, didn't require you to know anything. At Harvard, I could study law while pursuing a graduate degree in public policy at the Kennedy School of Government, which appealed to me. I was uncertain about what I wanted to do with my life, but I knew it would have something to do with the lives of the poor, America's history of racial inequality, and the struggle to be equitable and fair with one another. It would have something to do with the things I'd already seen in life so far and wondered about, but I couldn't really put it together in a way that made a career path clear.

Not long after I started classes at Harvard I began to worry I'd made the wrong choice. Coming from a small college in Pennsylvania, I felt very fortunate to have been admitted, but by the end of my first year I'd grown disillusioned. At the time, Harvard Law School was a pretty intimidating place, especially for a twenty-one-year-old. Many of the professors used the Socratic method—direct, repetitive, and adversarial questioning—which had the incidental effect of humiliating unprepared students. The courses seemed esoteric and disconnected from the race and poverty issues that had motivated me to consider the law in the first place.

Many of the students already had advanced degrees or had worked as paralegals with prestigious law firms. I had none of those credentials. I felt vastly less experienced and worldly than my fellow students. When law firms showed up on campus and began interviewing students a month after classes started, my classmates put on expensive suits and signed up so that they could receive "fly-outs" to New York, Los Angeles, San Francisco, or Washington, D.C. It was a complete mystery to me what exactly we were all busily preparing ourselves to do. I had never even met a lawyer before starting law school.

I spent the summer after my first year in law school working with a juvenile justice project in Philadelphia and taking advanced calculus courses at night to prepare for my next year at the Kennedy School. After I started the public policy program in September, I still felt disconnected. The curriculum was extremely quantitative, focused on figuring out how to maximize benefits and minimize costs, without much concern for what those benefits achieved and the costs created. While intellectually stimulating, decision theory, econometrics, and similar courses left me feeling adrift. But then, suddenly, everything came into focus.

I discovered that the law school offered an unusual one-month intensive course on race and poverty litigation taught by Betsy Bartholet, a law professor who had worked as an attorney with the NAACP Legal Defense Fund. Unlike most courses, this one took students off campus, requiring them to spend the month with an organization doing social justice work. I eagerly signed up, and so in December 1983 I found myself on a plane to Atlanta, Georgia, where I was scheduled to spend a few weeks working with the Southern Prisoners Defense Committee (SPDC).

I hadn't been able to afford a direct flight to Atlanta, so I had to change planes in Charlotte, North Carolina, and that's where I met Steve Bright, the director of the SPDC, who was flying back to Atlanta after the holidays. Steve was in his mid-thirties and had a passion and certainty that seemed the direct opposite of my ambivalence. He'd grown up on a farm in Kentucky and ended up in Washington, D.C., after finishing law school. He was a brilliant trial lawyer at the Public Defender Service for the District of Columbia and had just been recruited to take over the SPDC, whose mission was to assist condemned people on death row in Georgia. He showed none of the disconnect between what he did and what he believed that I'd seen in so many of my law professors. When we met he warmly wrapped me in a full-body hug, and then we started talking. We didn't stop till we'd reached Atlanta.

"Bryan," he said at some point during our short flight, "capital punishment means 'them without the capital get the punishment.' We can't help people on death row without help from people like you."

I was taken aback by his immediate belief that I had something to offer. He broke down the issues with the death penalty simply but persuasively, and I hung on every word, completely engaged by his dedication and charisma.

"I just hope you're not expecting anything too fancy while you're here," he said.

"Oh, no," I assured him. "I'm grateful for the opportunity to work with you."

"Well, 'opportunity' isn't necessarily the first word people think of when they think about doing work with us. We live kind of simply, and the hours are pretty intense."

"That's no problem for me."

"Well, actually, we might even be described as living less than simply. More like living poorly—maybe even barely living, struggling to hang on, surviving on the kindness of strangers, scraping by day by day, uncertain of the future."

I let slip a concerned look, and he laughed.

"I'm just kidding . . . kind of."

He moved on to other subjects, but it was clear that his heart and his mind were aligned with the plight of the condemned and those facing unjust treatment in jails and prisons. It was deeply affirming to meet someone whose work so powerfully animated his life.

There were just a few attorneys working at the SPDC when I arrived that winter. Most of them were former criminal defense lawyers from Washington who had come to Georgia in response to a growing crisis: Death row prisoners couldn't get lawyers. In their thirties, men and women, black and white, these lawyers were comfortable with one another in a way that reflected a shared mission, shared hope, and shared stress about the challenges they faced.

After years of prohibition and delay, executions were again taking place in the Deep South, and most of the people crowded on death row had no lawyers and no right to counsel. There was a growing fear that people would soon be killed without ever having their cases reviewed by skilled counsel. We were getting frantic calls every day from people who had no legal assistance but whose dates of execution were on the calendar and approaching fast. I'd never heard voices so desperate.

When I started my internship, everyone was extremely kind to me, and I felt immediately at home. The SPDC was located in downtown Atlanta in the Healey Building, a sixteen-story Gothic Revival structure built in the early 1900s that was in considerable decline and losing tenants. I worked in a cramped circle of desks with two lawyers and did clerical work, answering phones and researching legal questions for staff. I was just getting settled into my office routine when Steve asked me to go to death row to meet with a condemned man whom no one else had time to visit. He explained that the man had been on the row for over two years and that they didn't yet have a lawyer to take his case; my job was to convey to this man one simple message: *You will not be killed in the next year.*

I drove through farmland and wooded areas of rural Georgia, rehearsing what I would say when I met this man. I practiced my introduction over and over.

"Hello, my name is Bryan. I'm a student with the . . ." No. "I'm a law student with . . ." No. "My name is Bryan Stevenson. I'm a legal intern with the Southern Prisoners Defense Committee, and I've been instructed to inform you that you will not be executed soon." "You can't be executed soon." "You are not at risk of execution anytime soon." No.

I continued practicing my presentation until I pulled up to the intimidating barbed-wire fence and white guard tower of the Georgia Diagnostic and Classification Center. Around the office we just called it "Jackson," so seeing the facility's actual name on a sign was jarring—it sounded clinical, even therapeutic. I parked and found my way to the prison entrance and walked inside the main building with its dark corridors and gated hallways, where metal bars barricaded every access point. The interior eliminated any doubt that this was a hard place.

I walked down a tunneled corridor to the legal visitation area, each step echoing ominously across the spotless tiled floor. When I told the visitation officer that I was a paralegal sent to meet with a death row prisoner, he looked at me suspiciously. I was wearing the only suit I owned, and we could both see that it had seen better days. The officer's eyes seemed to linger long and hard over my driver's license before he tilted his head toward me to speak.

"You're not local."

It was more of a statement than a question.

"No, sir. Well, I'm working in Atlanta." After calling the warden's office to confirm that my visit had been properly scheduled, he finally admitted me, brusquely directing me to the small room where the visit would take place. "Don't get lost in here; we don't promise to come and find you," he warned.

The visitation room was twenty feet square with a few stools bolted to the floor. Everything in the room was made of metal and secured. In front of the stools, wire mesh ran from a small ledge up to a ceiling twelve feet high. The room was an empty cage until I walked into it. For family visits, inmates and visitors had to be on opposite sides of the mesh interior wall; they spoke to one another through the wires of the mesh. Legal visits, on the other hand, were "contact visits"—the two of us would be on the same side of the room to permit more privacy. The room was small and, although I knew it couldn't be true, it felt like it was getting smaller by the second. I began worrying again about my lack of preparation. I'd scheduled to meet with the client for one hour, but I wasn't sure how I'd fill even fifteen minutes with what I knew. I sat down on one of the stools and waited. After fifteen minutes of growing anxiety, I finally heard the clanging of chains on the other side of the door.

The man who walked in seemed even more nervous than I was. He glanced at me, his face screwed up in a worried wince, and he quickly averted his gaze when I looked back. He didn't move far from the room's entrance, as if he didn't really want to enter the visitation room. He was a young, neatly groomed African American man with short hair—clean-shaven, medium frame and build—wearing bright, clean prison whites. He looked immediately familiar to me, like everyone I'd grown up with, friends from school, people I played sports or music with, someone I'd talk to on the street about the weather. The guard slowly unchained him, removing his handcuffs and the shackles around his ankles, and then locked eyes with me and told me I had one hour. The officer seemed to sense that both the prisoner and I were nervous and to take some pleasure in our discomfort, grinning at me before turning on his heel and leaving the room. The metal door banged loudly behind him and reverberated through the small space.

The condemned man didn't come any closer, and I didn't know what else to do, so I walked over and offered him my hand. He shook it cautiously. We sat down and he spoke first.

"I'm Henry," he said.

"I'm very sorry" were the first words I blurted out. Despite all my preparations and rehearsed remarks, I couldn't stop myself from apologizing repeatedly.

"I'm really sorry, I'm really sorry, uh, okay, I don't really know, uh, I'm just a law student, I'm not a real lawyer. . . . I'm so sorry I can't tell you very much, but I don't know very much."

The man looked at me worriedly. "Is everything all right with my case?"

"Oh, yes, sir. The lawyers at SPDC sent me down to tell you that they don't have a lawyer yet. . . . I mean, we don't have a lawyer for you yet, but you're not at risk of execution anytime in the next year. . . . We're working on finding you a lawyer, a real lawyer, and we hope the lawyer will be down to see you in the next few months. I'm just a law student. I'm really happy to help, I mean, if there's something I can do."

The man interrupted my chatter by quickly grabbing my hands.

"I'm not going to have an execution date anytime in the next year?"

"No, sir. They said it would be at least a year before you get an execution date." Those words didn't sound very comforting to me. But Henry just squeezed my hands tighter and tighter.

"Thank you, man. I mean, really, thank you! This is great news." His shoulders unhunched, and he looked at me with intense relief in his eyes.

"You are the first person I've met in over two years after coming to death row who is not another death row prisoner or a death row guard. I'm so glad you're here, and I'm so glad to get this news." He exhaled loudly and seemed to relax.

"I've been talking to my wife on the phone, but I haven't wanted her to come and visit me or bring the kids because I was afraid they'd show up and I'd have an execution date. I just don't want them here like that. Now I'm going to tell them they can come and visit. Thank you!"

I was astonished that he was so happy. I relaxed, too, and we began to talk. It turned out that we were exactly the same age. Henry asked me questions about myself, and I asked him about his life. Within an hour we were both lost in conversation. We talked about everything. He told me about his family, and he told me about his trial. He asked me about law school and my family. We talked about music, we talked about prison, we talked about what's important in life and what's not. I was completely absorbed in our conversation. We laughed at times, and there were moments when he was very emotional and sad. We kept talking and talking, and it was only when I heard a loud bang on the door that I realized I'd stayed way past my allotted time for the legal visit. I looked at my watch. I'd been there three hours.

The guard came in and he was angry. He snarled at me, "You should have been done a long time ago. You have to leave."

He began handcuffing Henry, pulling his hands together behind his back and locking them there. Then he roughly shackled Henry's ankles. The guard was so angry he put the cuffs on too tight. I could see Henry grimacing with pain.

I said, "I think those cuffs are on too tight. Can you loosen them, please?"

"I told you: You need to leave. You don't tell me how to do my job."

Henry gave me a smile and said, "It's okay, Bryan. Don't worry about this. Just come back and see me again, okay?" I could see him wince with each click of the chains being tightened around his waist.

I must have looked pretty distraught. Henry kept saying, "Don't worry, Bryan, don't worry. Come back, okay?"

As the officer pushed him toward the door, Henry turned back to look at me.

I started mumbling, "I'm really sorry. I'm really sor—"

"Don't worry about this, Bryan," he said, cutting me off. "Just come back."

I looked at him and struggled to say something appropriate, something reassuring, something that expressed my gratitude to him for being so patient with me. But I couldn't think of anything to say. Henry looked at me and smiled. The guard was shoving him toward the door roughly. I didn't like the way Henry was being treated, but he continued to smile until, just before the guard could push him fully out of the room, he planted his feet to resist the officer's shoving. He looked so calm. Then he did something completely unexpected. I watched him close his eyes and tilt his head back. I was confused by what he was doing, but then he opened his mouth and I understood. He began to sing. He had a tremendous baritone voice that was strong and clear. It startled both me and the guard, who stopped his pushing.

> I'm pressing on, the upward way
> New heights I'm gaining, every day
> Still praying as, I'm onward bound
> Lord, plant my feet on Higher Ground.

It was an old hymn they used to sing all the time in the church where I grew up. I hadn't heard it in years. Henry sang slowly and with great sincerity and conviction. It took a moment before the officer recovered and resumed pushing him out the door. Because his ankles were shackled and his hands were locked behind his back, Henry almost stumbled when the guard shoved him forward. He had to waddle to keep his balance, but he kept on singing. I could hear him as he went down the hall:

> Lord lift me up, and let me stand
> By faith on Heaven's tableland
> A higher plane, that I have found
> Lord, plant my feet on Higher Ground.

I sat down, completely stunned. Henry's voice was filled with desire. I experienced his song as a precious gift. I had come into the prison with such anxiety and fear about his willingness to tolerate my inadequacy. I didn't expect him to be compassionate or generous. I had no right to expect anything from a condemned man on death row. Yet he gave me an astonishing measure of his humanity. In that moment, Henry altered something in my understanding of human potential, redemption, and hopefulness.

I finished my internship committed to helping the death row prisoners I had met that month. Proximity to the condemned and incarcerated made the question of each person's humanity more urgent and meaningful, including my own. I went back to law school with an intense desire to understand the laws and doctrines that sanctioned the death penalty and extreme punishments. I piled up courses on constitutional law, litigation, appellate procedure, federal courts, and collateral remedies. I did extra work to broaden my understanding of how constitutional theory shapes criminal procedure. I plunged deeply into the law and the sociology of race, poverty, and power. Law school had seemed abstract and disconnected before, but after meeting the desperate and imprisoned, it all became relevant and critically important. Even my studies at the Kennedy School took on a new significance. Developing the skills to quantify and deconstruct the discrimination and inequality I saw became urgent and meaningful.

My short time on death row revealed that there was something missing in the way we treat people in our judicial system, that maybe we judge some people unfairly. The more I reflected on the experience, the more I recognized that I had been struggling my whole life with the question of how and why people are judged unfairly.

I grew up in a poor, rural, racially segregated settlement on the eastern shore of the Delmarva Peninsula, in Delaware, where the racial history of this country casts a long shadow. The coastal communities that stretched from Virginia and eastern Maryland to lower Delaware were unapologetically Southern. Many people in the region insisted on a racialized hierarchy that required symbols, markers, and constant reinforcement, in part because of the area's proximity to the North. Confederate flags were proudly displayed throughout the region, boldly and defiantly marking the cultural, social, and political landscape.

African Americans lived in racially segregated ghettos isolated by railroad tracks within small towns or in "colored sections" in the country. I grew up in a country settlement where some people lived in tiny shacks; families without indoor plumbing had to use outhouses. We shared our outdoor play space with chickens and pigs.

The black people around me were strong and determined but marginalized and excluded. The poultry plant bus came each day to pick up adults and take them to the factory where they would daily pluck, hack, and process thousands of chickens. My father left the area as a teenager because there was no local high school for black children. He returned with my mother and found work in a food factory; on weekends he did domestic work at beach cottages and rentals. My mother had a civilian job at an Air Force base. It seemed that we were all cloaked in an unwelcome garment of racial difference that constrained, confined, and restricted us.

My relatives worked hard all the time but never seemed to prosper. My grandfather was murdered when I was a teenager, but it didn't seem to matter much to the world outside our family.

My grandmother was the daughter of people who were enslaved in Caroline County, Virginia. She was born in the 1880s, her parents in the 1840s. Her father talked to her all the time about growing up in slavery and how he learned to read and write but kept it a secret. He hid the things he knew—until Emancipation. The legacy of slavery very much shaped my grandmother and the way she raised her nine children. It influenced the way she talked to me, the way she constantly told me to "Keep close."

When I visited her, she would hug me so tightly I could barely breathe. After a little while, she would ask me, "Bryan, do you still feel me hugging you?" If I said yes, she'd let me be; if I said no, she would assault me again. I said no a lot because it made me happy to be wrapped in her formidable arms. She never tired of pulling me to her.

"You can't understand most of the important things from a distance, Bryan. You have to get close," she told me all the time.

The distance I experienced in my first year of law school made me feel lost. Proximity to the condemned, to people unfairly judged; that was what guided me back to something that felt like home.

This book is about getting closer to mass incarceration and extreme punishment in America. It is about how easily we condemn people in this country and the injustice we create when we allow fear, anger, and distance to shape the way we treat the most vulnerable among us. It's also about a dramatic period in our recent history, a period that indelibly marked the lives of millions of Americans—of all races, ages, and sexes—and the American psyche as a whole.

When I first went to death row in December 1983, America was in the early stages of a radical transformation that would turn us into an unprecedentedly harsh and punitive nation and result in mass imprisonment that has no historical parallel. Today we have the highest rate of incarceration in the world. The prison population has increased from 300,000 people in the early 1970s to 2.3 million people today. There are nearly six million people on probation or on parole. One in every fifteen people born in the United States in 2001 is expected to go to jail or prison; one in every three black male babies born in this century is expected to be incarcerated.

We have shot, hanged, gassed, electrocuted, and lethally injected hundreds of people to carry out legally sanctioned executions. Thousands more await their execution on death row. Some states have no minimum age for prosecuting children as adults; we've sent a quarter million kids to adult jails and prisons to serve long prison terms, some under the age of twelve. For years, we've been the only country in the world that condemns children to life imprisonment without parole; nearly three thousand juveniles have been sentenced to die in prison.

Hundreds of thousands of nonviolent offenders have been forced to spend decades in prison. We've created laws that make writing a bad check or committing a petty theft or minor property crime an offense that can result in life imprisonment. We have declared a costly war on people with substance abuse problems. There are more than a half-million people in state or federal prisons for drug offenses today, up from just 41,000 in 1980.

We have abolished parole in many states. We have invented slogans like "Three strikes and you're out" to communicate our toughness. We've given up on rehabilitation, education, and services for the imprisoned because providing assistance to the incarcerated is apparently too kind and compassionate. We've institutionalized policies that reduce people to their worst acts and permanently label them "criminal," "murderer," "rapist," "thief," "drug dealer," "sex offender," "felon"—identities they cannot change regardless of the circumstances of their crimes or any improvements they might make in their lives.

The collateral consequences of mass incarceration have been equally profound. We ban poor women and, inevitably, their children from receiving food stamps and public housing if they have prior drug convictions. We have created a new caste system that forces thousands of people into homelessness, bans them from living with their families and in their communities, and renders them virtually unemployable. Some states permanently strip people with criminal convictions of the right to vote; as a result, in several Southern states disenfranchisement among African American men has reached levels unseen since before the Voting Rights Act of 1965.

We also make terrible mistakes. Scores of innocent people have been exonerated after being sentenced to death and nearly executed. Hundreds more have been released after being proved innocent of noncapital crimes through DNA testing. Presumptions of guilt, poverty, racial bias, and a host of other social, structural, and political dynamics have created a system that is defined by error, a system in which thousands of innocent people now suffer in prison.

Finally, we spend lots of money. Spending on jails and prisons by state and federal governments has risen from $6.9 billion in 1980 to nearly $80 billion today. Private prison builders and prison service companies have spent millions of dollars to persuade state and local governments to create new crimes, impose harsher sentences, and keep more people locked up so that they can earn more profits. Private profit has corrupted incentives to improve public safety, reduce the costs of mass incarceration, and most significantly, promote rehabilitation of the incarcerated. State governments have been forced to shift funds from public services, education, health, and welfare to pay for incarceration, and they now face unprecedented economic crises as a result. The privatization of prison health care, prison commerce, and a range of services has made mass incarceration a money-making windfall for a few and a costly nightmare for the rest of us.

After graduating from law school, I went back to the Deep South to represent the poor, the incarcerated, and the condemned. In the last thirty years, I've gotten close to people who have been wrongly convicted and sent to death row, people like Walter McMillian. In this book you will learn the story of Walter's case, which taught me about our system's disturbing indifference to inaccurate or unreliable verdicts, our comfort with bias, and our tolerance of unfair prosecutions and convictions. Walter's experience taught me how our system traumatizes and victimizes people when we exercise our power to convict and condemn irresponsibly—not just the accused but also their families, their communities, and even the victims of crime. But Walter's case also taught me something else: that there is light within this darkness.

Walter's story is one of many that I tell in the following chapters. I've represented abused and neglected children who were prosecuted as adults and suffered more abuse and mistreatment after being placed in adult facilities. I've represented women, whose numbers in prison have increased 640 percent in the last thirty years, and seen how our hysteria about drug addiction and our hostility to the poor have made us quick to criminalize and prosecute poor women when a pregnancy goes wrong. I've represented mentally disabled people whose illnesses have often landed them in prison for decades. I've gotten close to victims of violent crime and their families and witnessed how even many of the custodians of mass imprisonment—prison staff—have been made less healthy, more violent and angry, and less just and merciful.

I've also represented people who have committed terrible crimes but nonetheless struggle to recover and to find redemption. I have discovered, deep in the hearts of many condemned and incarcerated people, the scattered traces of hope and humanity—seeds of restoration that come to astonishing life when nurtured by very simple interventions.

Proximity has taught me some basic and humbling truths, including this vital lesson: *Each of us is more than the worst thing we've ever done*. My work with the poor and the incarcerated has persuaded me that the opposite of poverty is not wealth; the opposite of poverty is justice. Finally, I've come to believe that the true measure of our commitment to justice, the character of our society, our commitment to the rule of law, fairness, and equality cannot be measured by how we treat the rich, the powerful, the privileged, and the respected among us. The true measure of our character is how we treat the poor, the disfavored, the accused, the incarcerated, and the condemned.

We are all implicated when we allow other people to be mistreated. An absence of compassion can corrupt the decency of a community, a state, a nation. Fear and anger can make us vindictive and abusive, unjust and unfair, until we all suffer from the absence of mercy and we condemn ourselves as much as we victimize others. The closer we get to mass incarceration and extreme levels of punishment, the more I believe it's necessary to recognize that we all need mercy, we all need justice, and—perhaps—we all need some measure of unmerited grace.

Chapter One

Mockingbird Players

The temporary receptionist was an elegant African American woman wearing a dark, expensive business suit—a well-dressed exception to the usual crowd at the Southern Prisoners Defense Committee (SPDC) in Atlanta, where I had returned after graduation to work full time. On her first day, I'd rambled over to her in my regular uniform of jeans and sneakers and offered to answer any questions she might have to help her get acclimated. She looked at me coolly and waved me away after reminding me that she was, in fact, an experienced legal secretary. The next morning, when I arrived at work in another jeans and sneakers ensemble, she seemed startled, as if some strange vagrant had made a wrong turn into the office. She took a beat to compose herself, then summoned me over to confide that she was leaving in a week to work at a "real law office." I wished her luck. An hour later, she called my office to tell me that "Robert E. Lee" was on the phone. I smiled, pleased that I'd misjudged her; she clearly had a sense of humor.

"That's really funny."

"I'm not joking. That's what he said," she said, sounding bored, not playful. "Line two."

I picked up the line.

"Hello, this is Bryan Stevenson. May I help you?"

"Bryan, this is Robert E. Lee Key. Why in the hell would you want to represent someone like Walter McMillian? Do you know he's reputed to be one of the biggest drug dealers in all of South Alabama? I got your notice entering an appearance, but you don't want anything to do with this case."

"Sir?"

"This is Judge Key, and you don't want to have anything to do with this McMillian case. No one really understands how depraved this situation truly is, including me, but I know it's ugly. These men might even be Dixie Mafia."

The lecturing tone and bewildering phrases from a judge I'd never met left me completely confused. "Dixie Mafia"? I'd met Walter McMillian two weeks earlier, after spending a day on death row to begin work on five capital cases. I hadn't reviewed the trial transcript yet, but I did remember that the judge's last name was Key. No one had told me the Robert E. Lee part. I struggled for an image of "Dixie Mafia" that would fit Walter McMillian.

" 'Dixie Mafia'?"

"Yes, and there's no telling what else. Now, son, I'm just not going to appoint some out-of-state lawyer who's not a member of the Alabama bar to take on one of these death penalty cases, so you just go ahead and withdraw."

"I'm a member of the Alabama bar."

I lived in Atlanta, Georgia, but I had been admitted to the Alabama bar a year earlier after working on some cases in Alabama concerning jail and prison conditions.

"Well, I'm now sitting in Mobile. I'm not up in Monroeville anymore. If we have a hearing on your motion, you're going to have to come all the way from Atlanta to Mobile. I'm not going to accommodate you no kind of way."

"I understand, sir. I can come to Mobile, if necessary."

"Well, I'm also not going to appoint you because I don't think he's indigent. He's reported to have money buried all over Monroe County."

"Judge, I'm not seeking appointment. I've told Mr. McMillian that we would—" The dial tone interrupted my first affirmative statement of the phone call. I spent several minutes thinking we'd been accidentally disconnected before finally realizing that a judge had just hung up on me.

I was in my late twenties and about to start my fourth year at the SPDC when I met Walter McMillian. His case was one of the flood of cases I'd found myself frantically working on after learning of a growing crisis in Alabama. The state had nearly a hundred people on death row as well as the fastest-growing condemned population in the country, but it also had no public defender system, which meant that large numbers of death row prisoners had no legal representation of any kind. My friend Eva Ansley ran an Alabama prison project, which tracked cases and matched lawyers with the condemned men. In 1988, we discovered an opportunity to get federal funding to create a legal center that could represent people on death row. The plan was to use that funding to start a new nonprofit. We hoped to open it in Tuscaloosa and begin working on cases in the next year. I'd already worked on lots of death penalty cases in several Southern states, sometimes winning a stay of execution just minutes before an electrocution was scheduled. But I didn't think I was ready to take on the responsibilities of running a nonprofit law office. I planned to help get the organization off the ground, find a director, and then return to Atlanta.

When I'd visited death row a few weeks before that call from Robert E. Lee Key, I met with five desperate condemned men: Willie Tabb, Vernon Madison, Jesse Morrison, Harry Nicks, and Walter McMillian. It was an exhausting, emotionally taxing day, and the cases and clients had merged together in my mind on the long drive back to Atlanta.

But I remembered Walter. He was at least fifteen years older than me, not particularly well educated, and he hailed from a small rural community. The memorable thing about him was how insistent he was that he'd been wrongly convicted.

"Mr. Bryan, I know it may not matter to you, but it's important to me that you know that I'm innocent and didn't do what they said I did, not no kinda way," he told me in the meeting room. His voice was level but laced with emotion. I nodded to him. I had learned to accept what clients tell me until the facts suggest something else.

"Sure, of course I understand. When I review the record I'll have a better sense of what evidence they have, and we can talk about it."

"But . . . look, I'm sure I'm not the first person on death row to tell you that they're innocent, but I really need you to believe me. My life has been ruined! This lie they put on me is more than I can bear, and if I don't get help from someone who believes me—"

His lip began to quiver, and he clenched his fists to stop himself from crying. I sat quietly while he forced himself back into composure.

"I'm sorry, I know you'll do everything you can to help me," he said, his voice quieter. My instinct was to comfort him; his pain seemed so sincere. But there wasn't much I could do, and after several hours on the row talking to so many people, I could muster only enough energy to reassure him that I would look at everything carefully.

I had several transcripts piled up in my small Atlanta office ready to move to Tuscaloosa once the office opened. With Judge Robert E. Lee Key's peculiar comments still running through my head, I went through the mound of records until I found the transcripts from Walter McMillian's trial. There were only four volumes of trial proceedings, which meant that the trial had been short. The judge's dramatic warnings now made Mr. McMillian's emotional claim of innocence too intriguing to put off any longer. I started reading.

Even though he had lived in Monroe County his whole life, Walter McMillian had never heard of Harper Lee or *To Kill a Mockingbird*. Monroeville, Alabama, celebrated its native daughter Lee shamelessly after her award-winning book became a national bestseller in the 1960s. She returned to Monroe County but secluded herself and was rarely seen in public. Her reclusiveness proved no barrier to the county's continued efforts to market her literary classic—or to market itself by using the book's celebrity. Production of the film adaptation brought Gregory Peck to town for the infamous courtroom scenes; his performance won him an Academy Award. Local leaders later turned the old courthouse into a "Mockingbird" museum. A group of locals formed "The Mockingbird Players of Monroeville" to present a stage version of the story. The production was so popular that national and international tours were organized to provide an authentic presentation of the fictional story to audiences everywhere.

Sentimentality about Lee's story grew even as the harder truths of the book took no root. The story of an innocent black man bravely defended by a white lawyer in the 1930s fascinated millions of readers, despite its uncomfortable exploration of false accusations of rape involving a white woman. Lee's endearing characters, Atticus Finch and his precocious daughter, Scout, captivated readers while confronting them with some of the realities of race and justice in the South. A generation of future lawyers grew up hoping to become the courageous Atticus, who at one point arms himself to protect the defenseless black suspect from an angry mob of white men looking to lynch him.

Today, dozens of legal organizations hand out awards in the fictional lawyer's name to celebrate the model of advocacy described in Lee's novel. What is often overlooked is that the black man falsely accused in the story was not *successfully* defended by Atticus. Tom Robinson, the wrongly accused black defendant, is found guilty. Later he dies when, full of despair, he makes a desperate attempt to escape from prison. He is shot seventeen times in the back by his captors, dying ingloriously but not unlawfully.

Walter McMillian, like Tom Robinson, grew up in one of several poor black settlements outside of Monroeville, where he worked the fields with his family before he was old enough to attend school. The children of sharecroppers in southern Alabama were introduced to "plowin', plantin', and pickin'" as soon as they were old enough to be useful in the fields. Educational opportunities for black children in the 1950s were limited, but Walter's mother got him to the dilapidated "colored school" for a couple of years when he was young. By the time Walter was eight or nine, he became too valuable for picking cotton to justify the remote advantages of going to school. By the age of eleven, Walter could run a plow as well as any of his older siblings.

Times were changing—for better and for worse. Monroe County had been developed by plantation owners in the nineteenth century for the production of cotton. Situated in the coastal plain of southwest Alabama, the fertile, rich black soil of the area attracted white settlers from the Carolinas who amassed very successful plantations and a huge slave population. For decades after the Civil War, the large African American population toiled in the fields of the "Black Belt" as sharecroppers and tenant farmers, dependent on white landowners for survival. In the 1940s, thousands of African Americans left the region as part of the Great Migration and headed mostly to the Midwest and West Coast for jobs. Those who remained continued to work the land, but the out-migration of African Americans combined with other factors to make traditional agriculture less sustainable as the economic base of the region.

By the 1950s, small cotton farming was becoming increasingly less profitable, even with the low-wage labor provided by black sharecroppers and tenants. The State of Alabama agreed to help white landowners in the region transition to timber farming and forest products by providing extraordinary tax incentives for pulp and paper mills. Thirteen of the state's sixteen pulp and paper mills were opened during this period. Across the Black Belt, more and more acres were converted to growing pine trees for paper mills and industrial uses. African Americans, largely excluded from this new industry, found themselves confronting new economic challenges even as they won basic civil rights. The brutal era of sharecropping and Jim Crow was ending, but what followed was persistent unemployment and worsening poverty. The region's counties remained some of the poorest in America.

Walter was smart enough to see the trend. He started his own pulpwood business that evolved with the timber industry in the 1970s. He astutely—and bravely—borrowed money to buy his own power saw, tractor, and pulpwood truck. By the 1980s, he had developed a solid business that didn't generate a lot of extra money but afforded him a gratifying degree of independence. If he had worked at the mill or the factory or had had some other unskilled job—the kind that most poor black people in South Alabama worked—it would invariably mean working for white business owners and dealing with all the racial stress that that implied in Alabama in the 1970s and 1980s. Walter couldn't escape the reality of racism, but having his own business in a growing sector of the economy gave him a latitude that many African Americans did not enjoy.

That independence won Walter some measure of respect and admiration, but it also cultivated contempt and suspicion, especially outside of Monroeville's black community. Walter's freedom was, for some of the white people in town, well beyond what African Americans with limited education were able to achieve through legitimate means. Still, he was pleasant, respectful, generous, and accommodating, which made him well liked by the people with whom he did business, whether black or white.

Walter was not without his flaws. He had long been known as a ladies' man. Even though he had married young and had three children with his wife, Minnie, it was well known that he was romantically involved with other women. "Tree work" is notoriously demanding and dangerous. With few ordinary comforts in his life, the attention of women was something Walter did not easily resist. There was something about his rough exterior—his bushy long hair and uneven beard—combined with his generous and charming nature that attracted the attention of some women.

Walter grew up understanding how forbidden it was for a black man to be intimate with a white woman, but by the 1980s he had allowed himself to imagine that such matters might be changing. Perhaps if he hadn't been successful enough to live off his own business he would have more consistently kept in mind those racial lines that could never be crossed. As it was, Walter didn't initially think much of the flirtations of Karen Kelly, a young white woman he'd met at the Waffle House where he ate breakfast. She was attractive, but he didn't take her too seriously. When her flirtations became more explicit, Walter hesitated, and then persuaded himself that no one would ever know.

After a few weeks, it became clear that his relationship with Karen was trouble. At twenty-five, Karen was eighteen years younger than Walter, and she was married. As word got around that the two were "friends," she seemed to take a titillating pride in her intimacy with Walter. When her husband found out, things quickly turned ugly. Karen and her husband, Joe, had long been unhappy and were already planning to divorce, but her scandalous involvement with a black man outraged Karen's husband and his entire family. He initiated legal proceedings to gain custody of their children and became intent on publicly disgracing his wife by exposing her infidelity and revealing her relationship with a black man.

For his part, Walter had always stayed clear of the courts and far away from the law. Years earlier, he had been drawn into a bar fight that resulted in a misdemeanor conviction and a night in jail. It was the first and only time he had ever been in trouble. From that point on, he had no exposure to the criminal justice system.

When Walter received a subpoena from Karen Kelly's husband to testify at a hearing where the Kellys would be fighting over their children's custody, he knew it was going to cause him serious problems.

Unable to consult with his wife, Minnie, who had a better head for these kinds of crises, he nervously went to the courthouse. The lawyer for Kelly's husband called Walter to the stand. Walter had decided to acknowledge being a "friend" of Karen. Her lawyer objected to the crude questions posed to Walter by the husband's attorney about the nature of his friendship, sparing him from providing any details, but when he left the courtroom the anger and animosity toward him were palpable. Walter wanted to forget about the whole ordeal, but word spread quickly, and his reputation shifted. No longer the hard-working pulpwood man, known to white people almost exclusively for what he could do with a saw in the pine trees, Walter now represented something more worrisome.

Fears of interracial sex and marriage have deep roots in the United States. The confluence of race and sex was a powerful force in dismantling Reconstruction after the Civil War, sustaining Jim Crow laws for a century and fueling divisive racial politics throughout the twentieth century. In the aftermath of slavery, the creation of a system of racial hierarchy and segregation was largely designed to prevent intimate relationships like Walter and Karen's—relationships that were, in fact, legally prohibited by "anti-miscegenation statutes" (the word *miscegenation* came into use in the 1860s, when supporters of slavery coined the term to promote the fear of interracial sex and marriage and the race mixing that would result if slavery was abolished). For over a century, law enforcement officials in many Southern communities absolutely saw it as part of their duty to investigate and punish black men who had been intimate with white women.

Although the federal government had promised racial equality for freed former slaves during the short period of Reconstruction, the return of white supremacy and racial subordination came quickly after federal troops left Alabama in the 1870s. Voting rights were taken away from African Americans, and a series of racially restrictive laws enforced the racial hierarchy. "Racial integrity" laws were part of a plan to replicate slavery's racial hierarchy and reestablish the subordination of African Americans. Having criminalized interracial sex and marriage, states throughout the South would use the laws to justify the forced sterilization of poor and minority women. Forbidding sex between white women and black men became an intense preoccupation throughout the South.

In the 1880s, a few years before lynching became the standard response to interracial romance and a century before Walter and Karen Kelly began their affair, Tony Pace, an African American man, and Mary Cox, a white woman, fell in love in Alabama. They were arrested and convicted, and both were sentenced to two years in prison for violating Alabama's racial integrity laws. John Tompkins, a lawyer and part of a small minority of white professionals who considered the racial integrity laws to be unconstitutional, agreed to represent Tony and Mary to appeal their convictions. The Alabama Supreme Court reviewed the case in 1882. With rhetoric that would be quoted frequently over the next several decades, Alabama's highest court affirmed the convictions, using language that dripped with contempt for the idea of interracial romance:

> The evil tendency of the crime [of adultery or fornication] is greater when committed between persons of the two races. . . . Its result may be the amalgamation of the two races, producing a mongrel population and a degraded civilization, the prevention of which is dictated by a sound policy affecting the highest interests of society and government.

The U.S. Supreme Court reviewed the Alabama court's decision. Using "separate but equal" language that previewed the Court's infamous decision in *Plessy v. Ferguson* twenty years later, the Court unanimously upheld Alabama's restrictions on interracial sex and marriage and affirmed the prison terms imposed on Tony Pace and Mary Cox. Following the Court's decision, more states passed racial integrity laws that made it illegal for African Americans, and sometimes Native

Americans and Asian Americans, to marry or have sex with whites. While the restrictions were aggressively enforced in the South, they were also common in the Midwest and West. The State of Idaho banned interracial marriage and sex between white and black people in 1921 even though the state's population was 99.8 percent nonblack.

It wasn't until 1967 that the United States Supreme Court finally struck down anti-miscegenation statutes in *Loving v. Virginia,* but restrictions on interracial marriage persisted even after that landmark ruling. Alabama's state constitution still prohibited the practice in 1986 when Walter met Karen Kelly. Section 102 of the state constitution read:

> The legislature shall never pass any law to authorise or legalise any marriage between any white person and a Negro or descendant of a Negro.*

No one expected a relatively successful and independent man like Walter to follow every rule. Occasionally drinking too much, getting into a fight, or even having an extramarital affair—these weren't indiscretions significant enough to destroy the reputation and standing of an honest and industrious black man who could be trusted to do good work. But interracial dating, particularly with a married white woman, was for many whites, an unconscionable act. In the South, crimes like murder or assault might send you to prison, but interracial sex was a transgression in its own unique category of danger with correspondingly extreme punishments. Hundreds of black men have been lynched for even unsubstantiated suggestions of such intimacy.

Walter didn't know the legal history, but like every black man in

---

* Even though the restriction couldn't be enforced under federal law, the state ban on interracial marriage in Alabama continued into the twenty-first century. In 2000, reformers finally had enough votes to get the issue on the statewide ballot, where a majority of voters chose to eliminate the ban, although 41 percent voted to keep it. A 2011 poll of Mississippi Republicans found that 46 percent support a legal ban on interracial marriage, 40 percent oppose such a ban, and 14 percent are undecided.

Alabama he knew deep in his bones the perils of interracial romance. Nearly a dozen people had been lynched in Monroe County alone since its incorporation. Dozens of additional lynchings had taken place in neighboring counties—and the true power of those lynchings far exceeded their number. They were acts of terror more than anything else, inspiring fear that any encounter with a white person, any interracial social misstep, any unintended slight, any ill-advised look or comment could trigger a gruesome and lethal response.

Walter heard his parents and relatives talk about lynchings when he was a young child. When he was twelve, the body of Russell Charley, a black man from Monroe County, was found hanging from a tree in Vredenburgh, Alabama. The lynching of Charley, who was known by Walter's family, was believed to have been prompted by an interracial romance. Walter remembered well the terror that shot through the black community in Monroe County when Charley's lifeless, bullet-ridden body was found swinging in a tree.

And now it seemed to Walter that everyone in Monroe County was talking about his own relationship with Karen Kelly. It worried him in a way that few things ever had.

A few weeks later, an even more unthinkable act shocked Monroeville. In the late morning of November 1, 1986, Ronda Morrison, the beautiful young daughter of a respected local family, was found dead on the floor of Monroe Cleaners, the shop where the eighteen-year-old college student had worked. She had been shot in the back three times.

Murder was uncommon in Monroeville. An apparent robbery-murder in a popular downtown business was unprecedented. The death of young Ronda was a crime unlike anything the community had ever experienced. She was popular, an only child, and by all accounts without blemish. She was the kind of girl whom the entire white community embraced as a daughter. The police initially believed that no one from the community, black or white, would have done something so horrific.

Two Latino men had been spotted in Monroeville looking for work the day Ronda Morrison's body was found, and they became the first suspects. Police tracked them down in Florida and determined that the two men could not have committed the murder. The former owner of the cleaners, an older white man named Miles Jackson, fell under suspicion, but there was no evidence that pointed to him as a killer. The current owner of the cleaners, Rick Blair, was questioned but considered an unlikely suspect. Within a few weeks, the police had tapped out their leads.

People in Monroe County began to whisper about the incompetence of the police. When there were still no arrests several months later, the whispers became louder, and public criticisms of the police, sheriff, and local prosecutor were aired in the local newspaper and on local radio stations. Tom Tate was elected the new county sheriff days after the murder took place, and folks started to question whether he was up to the job. The Alabama Bureau of Investigation (ABI) was called in to investigate the murder but achieved no more success solving the crime than local officials had. People in Monroeville became anxious. Local businesses posted rewards offering thousands of dollars for information leading to an arrest. Gun sales, which were always robust, increased.

Meanwhile, Walter was wrestling with his own problems. He had been trying for weeks to end his relationship with Karen Kelly. The child custody proceedings and public scandal had taken a toll on her; she had started using drugs and seemed to fall apart. She began to associate with Ralph Myers, a white man with a badly disfigured face and lengthy criminal record who seemed to perfectly embody her fall from grace. Ralph was an unusual partner for Karen, but she was in such serious decline that nothing she did made any sense to her friends and family. The relationship brought Karen to rock bottom, beyond scandal and drug use into serious criminal behavior. Together they became involved in dealing drugs and were implicated in the murder of Vickie Lynn Pittman, a young woman from neighboring Escambia County.

Police had quick success in investigating the Pittman murder, rapidly concluding that Ralph Myers had been involved. When the police interrogated Ralph, they encountered a man as psychologically complicated as he was physically scarred. He was emotional and frail, and he craved attention—his only effective defense was his skill in manipulation and misdirection. Ralph believed that everything he said had to be epic, shocking, and elaborate. As a child living in foster care, he had been horribly burned in a fire. The burns so scarred and disfigured his face and neck that he needed multiple surgeries to regain basic functioning. He became quite used to strangers staring at his scars with pained expressions on their faces. He was a tragic outcast who lived on the margins, but he tried to compensate by pretending to have inside knowledge about all sorts of mysteries.

After initially denying any direct involvement in the Pittman murder, Myers conceded that he may have played some accidental role but quickly put the blame for the murder itself on more interesting local figures. He first accused a black man with a bad reputation named Isaac Dailey, but the police quickly discovered that Dailey had been in a jail cell on the night of the murder. Myers then confessed that he had made up the story because the true killer was none other than the elected sheriff of a nearby county.

As outrageous as the claim was, ABI agents appeared to take it seriously. They asked him more questions, but the more Myers talked, the less credible his story sounded. Officials began to suspect that Myers was the sole killer and was desperately trying to implicate others to minimize his culpability.

While the death of Vickie Pittman was news, it failed to compare with the continuing mystery surrounding the death of Ronda Morrison. Vickie came from a poor white family, several of whose members were incarcerated; she enjoyed none of the status of Ronda Morrison. The Morrison murder remained the focus of everyone's attention for months.

Ralph Myers was illiterate, but he knew that it was the Morrison crime that was preoccupying law enforcement investigators. When his allegations against the sheriff didn't seem to be going anywhere, he changed his story again and told investigators that he had been involved in the murder of Vickie Pittman along with Karen Kelly and her black boyfriend, Walter McMillian. But that wasn't all. He also told police that McMillian was responsible for the murder of Ronda Morrison. That assertion attracted the full attention of law enforcement officials.

It soon became apparent that Walter McMillian had never met Ralph Myers, let alone committed two murders with him. To prove that the two of them were in cahoots, an ABI agent asked Myers to meet Walter McMillian at a store while agents monitored the interaction. It had been several months since Ronda Morrison's murder.

Once Myers entered the store, he was not able to identify Walter McMillian among several black men present (he had to ask the owner of the store to point McMillian out). He then delivered a note to McMillian, purportedly written by Karen Kelly. According to witnesses, Walter seemed confused both by Myers, a man he had never seen before, and the note itself. Walter threw the note away and went back to what he was doing. He paid little attention to the whole odd encounter.

The monitoring ABI agents were left with nothing to suggest any relationship between Myers and McMillian and plenty of evidence indicating that the two men had never met. Still, they persisted with the McMillian theory. Time was passing—seven months, by this time— and the community was fearful and angry. Criticism was mounting. They desperately needed an arrest.

Monroe County Sheriff Tom Tate did not have much law enforcement experience. By his own description he was "very local" and took great pride in never having ventured too far from Monroeville. Now, four months into his term as sheriff, he faced a seemingly unsolvable murder and intense public pressure. When Myers told police about McMillian's relationship with Karen Kelly, it's likely that the infamous interracial affair was already well known to Tate as a result of the Kelly custody hearings that had generated so much gossip. But there was no evidence against McMillian—no evidence except that he was an African American man involved in an adulterous interracial affair, which meant he was reckless and possibly dangerous, even if he had no prior criminal history and a good reputation. Maybe that was evidence enough.

Chapter Two

Stand

After spending the first year and a half of my legal career sleeping on Steve Bright's living room couch in Atlanta, it was time to find an apartment of my own. When I'd started working in Atlanta, staff were scrambling to handle one crisis after another. I was immediately thrown into litigation with pressing deadlines and didn't have time to find a place to live—and my $14,000 annual salary didn't leave me with much money for rent—so Steve kindly took me in. Living in Steve's small Grant Park duplex allowed me to question him nonstop about the complex issues and challenges our cases and clients presented. Each day we dissected big and small issues from morning until midnight. I loved it. But when a law school classmate, Charles Bliss, moved to Atlanta for a job with the Atlanta Legal Aid Society, we realized that if we pooled our meager salaries, we could afford a low-rent apartment. Charlie and I had started at Harvard Law School together and had lived in the same dorm as first-year students. He was a white kid from North Carolina who seemed to share my confusion about what we were experiencing during law school. We frequently retreated to the school gym to play basketball and to try to make sense of things.

Charlie and I found a place near Atlanta's Inman Park. After a year, a rent increase forced us to move to the Virginia Highlands section of the city, where we stayed for a year before another rent increase sent us to Midtown Atlanta. The two-bedroom apartment we shared in Midtown was the nicest place in the nicest neighborhood we'd yet found. Because of my growing caseload in Alabama, I didn't get to spend much time there.

My plan for a new law project to represent people on death row in Alabama was starting to take shape. My hope was to get the project off the ground in Alabama and eventually return to Atlanta to live. My docket of new death penalty cases in Alabama meant I was working insane hours driving back and forth from Atlanta and simultaneously trying to resolve several prison condition cases I had filed in various Southern states.

Conditions of confinement for prisoners were getting worse everywhere. In the 1970s, the Attica Prison riots drew national attention to horrible prison abuses. The takeover of Attica by inmates allowed the country to learn about cruel practices within prisons such as solitary confinement, where inmates are isolated in a small confined space for weeks or months. Prisoners in some facilities would be placed in a "sweatbox," a casket-sized hole or a box situated where the inmate would be forced to endure extreme heat for days or weeks. Some prisoners were tortured with electric cattle prods as punishment for violations of the prison's rule. Inmates at some facilities would be chained to "hitching posts," their arms fastened above their heads in a painful position where they'd be forced to stand for hours. The practice, which wasn't declared unconstitutional until 2002, was one of many degrading and dangerous punishments imposed on incarcerated people. Terrible food and living conditions were widespread.

The death of forty-two people at the end of the Attica standoff exposed the danger of prison abuse and inhumane conditions. The increased attention also led to several Supreme Court rulings that provided basic due process protections for imprisoned people. Wary of potential violence, several states implemented reforms to eliminate the most abusive practices. But a decade later, the rapidly growing prison population inevitably led to a deterioration in the conditions of confinement.

We were getting scores of letters from prisoners who continued to complain about horrible conditions. Prisoners reported that they were still being beaten by correctional staff and subjected to humiliation in stockades and other degrading punishments. An alarming number of cases came to our office involving prisoners who had been found dead in their cells.

I was working on several of these cases, including one in Gadsden, Alabama, where jail officials claimed that a thirty-nine-year-old black man had died of natural causes after being arrested for traffic violations. His family maintained that he was beaten by police and jail officials who then denied him his asthma inhaler and medication despite his begging for it. I'd spent a lot of time with the grief-stricken family of Lourida Ruffin and heard what an affectionate father he had been, how kind he had been, and how people had assumed things about him that weren't true. At six feet five inches tall and over 250 pounds, he could seem a little intimidating, but his wife and mother insisted that he was sweet and gentle.

Gadsden police had stopped Mr. Ruffin one night because they said his car was swerving. Police discovered that his license had expired a few weeks earlier, so he was taken into custody. When he arrived at the city jail badly bruised and bleeding, Mr. Ruffin told the other inmates that he had been beaten terribly and was desperately in need of his inhaler and asthma medication. When I started investigating the case, inmates at the jail told me they saw officers beating Mr. Ruffin before taking him to an isolation cell. Several hours later they saw medical personnel remove his body from the cell on a gurney.

Despite the reforms of the 1970s and early 1980s, inmate death in jails and prisons was still a serious problem. Suicide, prisoner-on-prisoner violence, inadequate medical care, staff abuse, and guard violence claimed the lives of hundreds of prisoners every year.

I soon received other complaints from people in the Gadsden community. The parents of a black teenager who had been shot and killed by police told me that their son had been stopped for a minor traffic violation after running a red light. Their young son had just started driving and became very nervous when the police officer approached him. His family maintained that he reached down to the floor where he kept his gym bag to retrieve his newly issued driver's license. The police claimed he was reaching for a weapon—no weapon was ever found—and the teen was shot dead while he sat in his car. The officer who shot the boy said that the teen had been menacing and had moved quickly, in a threatening manner. The child's parents told me their son *was* generally nervous and easily frightened but was also obedient and would never have hurt anyone. He was very religious and a good student, and he had the kind of reputation that allowed the family to persuade civil rights leaders to push for an investigation into his death. Their pleas reached our office, and I was looking into the case along with the jail and prison cases.

Figuring out Alabama civil and criminal law while managing death penalty cases in several other states kept me very busy. The additional prison conditions litigation meant a lot of long-distance driving and extremely long hours. My weathered 1975 Honda Civic was struggling to keep up. The radio had stopped working consistently a year earlier; it would come to life only if I hit a pothole or stopped suddenly enough to violently shake the car and spark a connection.

After making the three-hour drive back from Gadsden earlier in the day and heading straight to the office, it was once again approaching midnight as I left the office for home. I got in my car, and to my delight the radio came on as soon as I turned the ignition. In just over three years of law practice I had become one of those people for whom such small events could make a big difference in my joy quotient. On this late night, not only was my radio working but the station was also hosting a retrospective on the music of Sly and the Family Stone. I'd grown up listening to Sly and found myself rolling joyfully through the streets of Atlanta to tunes like "Dance to the Music," "Everybody Is a Star," and "Family Affair."

Our Midtown Atlanta apartment was on a dense residential street. Some nights I had to park halfway down the block or even around the corner to find a space. But tonight I was lucky: I parked my rattling Civic just steps from our new front door just as Sly was starting "Hot Fun in the Summertime." It was late, and I needed to get to bed, but the moment was too good to let pass, so I remained in the car listening to the music. Each time a tune ended I told myself to go inside, but then another irresistible song would begin, and I would find myself unable to leave. I was singing along to "Stand!" the soaring Sly anthem with the great gospel-themed ending, when I saw a flashing police light approaching. I was parked a few doors up from our apartment, so I assumed that the officers would drive by in pursuit of some urgent mission. When they came to a stop twenty feet in front of me, I wondered what was going on.

Our section of the street only ran one way. My parked car was facing in the proper direction; the police car had come down the street in the wrong direction. I noticed for the first time that it wasn't an ordinary police cruiser but one of the special Atlanta SWAT cars. The officers had a spotlight attached to their vehicle, and they directed it at me sitting in my car. Only then did it occur to me that they might be there for me, but I couldn't imagine why. I had been parked on the street for about fifteen minutes listening to Sly. Only one of my car speakers worked and not very well. I knew the music couldn't be heard outside the car.

The officers sat there with their light pointed at me for a minute or so. I turned off the radio before "Stand!" was over. I had case files on my car seat about Lourida Ruffin and the young man who had been shot in Gadsden. Eventually two police officers got out of their vehicle. I noticed immediately that they weren't wearing the standard Atlanta police uniform. Instead they were ominously dressed in military style, black boots with black pants and vests.

I decided to get out of my car and go home. Even though they were intensely staring at me in my car, I was still hoping that they were in the area for something unrelated to me. Or if they were concerned that something was wrong with me, I figured I would let them know that everything was okay. It certainly never occurred to me that getting out of my car was wrong or dangerous.

As soon as I opened my car door and got out, the police officer who had started walking toward my vehicle drew his weapon and pointed it at me. I must have looked completely bewildered.

My first instinct was to run. I quickly decided that wouldn't be smart. Then I thought for an instant that maybe these weren't real police officers.

"Move and I'll blow your head off!" The officer shouted the words, but I couldn't make any sense of what he meant. I tried to stay calm; it was the first time in my life anyone had ever pointed a gun at me.

"Put your hands up!" The officer was a white man about my height. In the darkness I could only make out his black uniform and his pointed weapon.

I put my hands up and noticed that he seemed nervous. I don't remember deciding to speak, I just remember the words coming out: "It's all right. It's okay."

I'm sure I sounded afraid because I was terrified.

I kept saying the words over and over again. "It's okay, it's okay." Finally I said, "I live here, this is my apartment."

I looked at the officer who was pointing the gun at my head less than fifteen feet away. I thought I saw his hands shaking.

I kept saying as calmly as I could: "It's okay, it's okay."

The second officer, who had not drawn his weapon, inched cautiously toward me. He stepped on the sidewalk, circled behind my parked car, and came up behind me while the other officer continued to point the gun at me. He grabbed me by the arms and pushed me up against the back of my car. The other officer then lowered his weapon.

"What are you doing out here?" said the second officer, who seemed older than the one who had drawn his weapon. He sounded angry.

"I live here. I moved into that house down the street just a few months ago. My roommate is inside. You can go ask him." I hated how afraid I sounded and the way my voice was shaking.

"What are you doing out in the street?"

"I was just listening to the radio." He placed my hands on the car and bent me over the back of the vehicle. The SWAT car's bright spotlight was still focused on me. I noticed people up the block turning on their lights and peering out of their front doors. The house next to ours came to life, and a middle-aged white man and woman walked outside and stared at me as I was leaned over the vehicle.

The officer holding me asked me for my driver's license but wouldn't let me move my arms to retrieve it. I told him that it was in my back pocket, and he fished my wallet out from my pants. The other officer was now leaning inside my car and going through my papers. I knew that he had no probable cause to enter my vehicle and that he was conducting an illegal search. I was about to say something when I saw him open the glove compartment. Opening objects in a parked vehicle was so incredibly illegal that I realized he wasn't paying any attention to the rules, so saying something about it would be pointless.

There was nothing interesting in my car. There were no drugs, no alcohol, not even tobacco. I kept a giant-size bag of peanut M&Ms and Bazooka bubble gum in the glove compartment to help stave off hunger when I didn't have time for a meal. There were just a few M&Ms left in the bag, which the officer inspected carefully. He put his nose into the bag before tossing it back. I wouldn't be eating those M&Ms.

I had not lived at our new address long enough to get a new driver's license, so the address on my license didn't match the new location. There was no legal requirement to update the driver's license, but it prompted the officer to hold me there for another ten minutes while he went back to his car to run a search on me. My neighbors grew bolder as the encounter dragged on. Even though it was late, people were coming out of their homes to watch. I could hear them talking about all the burglaries in the neighborhood. There was a particularly vocal older white woman who loudly demanded that I be questioned about items she was missing.

"Ask him about my radio and my vacuum cleaner!" Another lady asked about her cat who had been absent for three days. I kept waiting for my apartment light to come on and for Charlie to walk outside and help me out. He had been dating a woman who also worked at Legal Aid and had been spending a lot of time at her house. It occurred to me that he might not be home.

Finally, the officer returned and spoke to his partner: "They don't have anything on him." He sounded disappointed.

I found my nerve and took my hands off the car. "This is so messed up. I live here. You shouldn't have done this. Why did you do this?"

The older officer frowned at me. "Someone called about a suspected burglar. There have been a lot of burglaries in this neighborhood." Then he grinned. "We're going to let you go. You should be happy," he said.

With that, they walked away, got in their SWAT car, and drove off. The neighbors looked me over one last time before retreating back into their homes. I couldn't decide whether I should race to my door so that they could see that I lived in the neighborhood or wait until they were all gone so that no one would know where the "suspected criminal" lived. I decided to wait.

I gathered up my papers, which the cop had scattered all over the car and onto the sidewalk. I unhappily threw my M&Ms into a trash can on the street and then walked into my apartment. To my great relief, Charlie was there. I woke him to tell the story.

"They never even apologized," I kept saying. Charlie shared my outrage but soon fell back asleep. I couldn't sleep at all.

The next morning I told Steve about the incident. He was furious and urged me to file a complaint with the Atlanta Police Department. Some folks in the office said I should explain in my complaint that I was a civil rights attorney working on police misconduct cases. It seemed to me that no one should need those kinds of credentials to complain about misconduct by police officers.

I started writing my complaint determined not to reveal that I was an attorney. When I replayed the whole incident in my mind, what bothered me most was the moment when the officer drew his weapon and I thought about running. I was a twenty-eight-year-old lawyer who had worked on police misconduct cases. I had the judgment to speak calmly to the officer when he threatened to shoot me. When I thought about what I would have done when I was sixteen years old or nineteen or even twenty-four, I was scared to realize that *I* might have run. The more I thought about it, the more concerned I became about all the young black boys and men in that neighborhood. Did they know not to run? Did they know to stay calm and say, "It's okay"?

I detailed all of my concerns. I found Bureau of Justice statistics reporting that black men were eight times more likely to be killed by the police than whites. By the end of the twentieth century the rate of police shootings would improve so that men of color were "only" four times more likely to be killed by law enforcement, but the problem would get worse as some states passed "Stand Your Ground" laws empowering armed citizens to use lethal force as well.

I kept writing my memo to the Atlanta Police Department and before I knew it I had typed close to nine pages outlining all the things I thought had gone wrong. For two pages I detailed the completely illegal search of the vehicle and the absence of probable cause. I even cited about a half-dozen cases. I read over the complaint and realized that I had done everything but say, "I'm a lawyer."

I filed my complaint with the police department and tried to forget about the incident, but I couldn't. I kept thinking about what had happened. I began to feel embarrassed that I hadn't asserted more control during the encounter. I hadn't told the officers I was a lawyer or informed them that what they were doing was illegal. Should I have said more to them? Despite the work I'd done assisting people on death row, I questioned how prepared I was to do really difficult things. I even started having second thoughts about going to Alabama to start a law office. I couldn't stop thinking about how at risk young kids are when they get stopped by the police.

My complaint made it through the review process at the Atlanta Police Department. Every few weeks I'd get a letter explaining that the police officers had done nothing wrong and that police work is very difficult. I appealed these dismissals unsuccessfully up the chain of command. Finally, I requested a meeting with the chief of police and the police officers who had stopped me. This request was denied, but the deputy chief met with me. I had asked for an apology and suggested training to prevent similar incidents. The deputy chief nodded politely as I explained what had happened. When I finished, he apologized to me, but I suspected that he just wanted me to leave. He promised that the officers would be required to do some "extra homework on community relations." I didn't feel vindicated.

My caseload was getting crazy. The lawyers defending the Gadsden City Jail finally acknowledged that Mr. Ruffin's rights had been violated and that he had been illegally denied his asthma medicine. We won a decent settlement for Mr. Ruffin's family, so they would at least receive some financial help. I turned the other police misconduct cases over to other lawyers because my death penalty docket was so full.

I had no time to make war with the Atlanta Police when I had clients facing execution. Still, I couldn't stop thinking about how dangerous and unfair the situation was and how I'd done nothing wrong. And what if I had had drugs in my car? I would have been arrested and then would have needed to convince my attorney to believe me when I explained that the police had entered the car illegally. Would I get an attorney who would take such a claim seriously? Would a judge believe that I'd done nothing wrong? Would they believe someone who was just like me but happened not to be a lawyer? Someone like me who was unemployed or had a prior criminal record?

I decided to talk to youth groups, churches, and community organizations about the challenges posed by the presumption of guilt assigned to the poor and people of color. I spoke at local meetings and tried to sensitize people to the need to insist on accountability from law enforcement. I argued that police could improve public safety without abusing people. Even when I was in Alabama, I made time for talks at community events whenever anyone asked.

I was in a poor rural county in Alabama after another trip to pull records in a death penalty case when I was invited to speak at a small African American church. Only about two dozen people showed up.

One of the community leaders introduced me, and I went to the front of the church and began my talk about the death penalty, increasing incarceration rates, abuse of power within prisons, discriminatory law enforcement, and the need for reform. At one point, I decided to talk about my encounter with the police in Atlanta, and I realized that I was getting a bit emotional. My voice got shaky, and I had to rein myself in to finish my remarks.

During the talk, I noticed an older black man in a wheelchair who had come in just before the program started. He was in his seventies and was wearing an old brown suit. His gray hair was cut short with unruly tufts here and there. He looked at me intensely throughout my presentation but showed no emotion or reaction during most of the talk. His focused stare was unnerving. A young boy who was about twelve had wheeled him into the church, probably his grandson or a relative. I noticed that the man occasionally directed the boy to fetch things for him. He would wordlessly nod his head, and the boy seemed to know that the man wanted a fan or a hymnal.

After I finished speaking, the group sang a hymn to end the session. The older man didn't sing but simply closed his eyes and sat back in his chair. After the program, people came up to me; most folks were very kind and expressed appreciation for my having taken the time to come and talk to them. Several young black boys walked up to shake my hand. I was pleased that people seemed to value the information I shared. The man in the wheelchair was waiting in the back of the church. He was still staring at me. When everyone else had left, he nodded to the young boy, who quickly wheeled him up to me.

The man's expression never changed as he approached me. He stopped in front of me, leaned forward in his wheelchair, and said forcefully, "Do you know what you're doing?" He looked very serious, and he wasn't smiling.

His question threw me. I couldn't tell what he was really asking or whether he was being hostile. I didn't know what to say. He then wagged his finger at me, and asked again. "Do you know what you're doing?"

I tried to smile to defuse the situation but I was completely baffled. "I think so. . . ."

He cut me off and said loudly, "I'll tell you what you're doing. You're beating the drum for justice!" He had an impassioned look on his face. He said it again emphatically, "You've got to beat the drum for justice."

He leaned back in his chair, and I stopped smiling. Something about what he said had sobered me. I answered him softly, "Yes, sir."

He leaned forward again and said hoarsely, "You've got to keep beating the drum for justice." He gestured and after a long while said again, "Beat the drum for justice."

He leaned back, and in an instant he seemed tired and out of breath. He looked at me sympathetically and waved me closer. I did so, and he pulled me by the arm and leaned forward. He spoke very quietly, almost a whisper, but with a fierceness that was unforgettable.

"You see this scar on the top of my head?" He tilted his head to show me. "I got that scar in Greene County, Alabama, trying to register to vote in 1964. You see this scar on the side of my head?" He turned his head to the left and I saw a four-inch scar just above his right ear. "I got that scar in Mississippi demanding civil rights."

His voice grew stronger. He tightened his grip on my arm and lowered his head some more. "You see that mark?" There was a dark circle at the base of his skull. "I got that bruise in Birmingham after the Children's Crusade."

He leaned back and looked at me intensely. "People think these are my scars, cuts, and bruises."

For the first time I noticed that his eyes were wet with tears. He placed his hands on his head. "These aren't my scars, cuts, and bruises. These are my medals of honor."

He stared at me for a long moment, wiped his eyes, and nodded to the boy, who wheeled him away.

I stood there with a lump in my throat, staring after him.

After a moment, I realized that the time to open the Alabama office had come.

Chapter Three

Trials and Tribulation

After months of frustration, failure, and growing public scorn, Sheriff Thomas Tate, ABI lead investigator Simon Benson, and the district attorney's investigator, Larry Ikner, decided to arrest Walter McMillian based primarily on Ralph Myers's allegation. They hadn't yet done much investigation into McMillian, so they decided to arrest him on a pretextual charge while they built their case. Myers claimed to be terrified of McMillian; one of the officers suggested to Myers that McMillian might have sexually assaulted him; the idea was so provocative and inflammatory that Myers immediately recognized its usefulness and somberly acknowledged that it was true. Alabama law had outlawed nonprocreative sex, so officials planned to arrest McMillian on sodomy charges.

On June 7, 1987, Sheriff Tate led an army of more than a dozen officers to a back-country road that they knew Walter would use on his return home from work. Officers stopped Walter's truck and drew their weapons, then forced Walter from his vehicle and surrounded him. Tate told him he was under arrest. When Walter frantically asked the sheriff what he had done, the sheriff told him that he was being charged with sodomy. Confused by the term, Walter told the sheriff that he did not understand the meaning of the word. When the sheriff explained the charge in crude terms, Walter was incredulous and couldn't help but laugh at the notion. This provoked Tate, who unleashed a torrent of racial slurs and threats. Walter would report for years that all he heard throughout his arrest, over and over again, was the word *nigger.* "Nigger this," "nigger that," followed by insults and threats of lynching.

"We're going to keep all you niggers from running around with these white girls. I ought to take you off and hang you like we done that nigger in Mobile," Tate reportedly told Walter.

The sheriff was referring to the lynching of a young African American man named Michael Donald in Mobile, about sixty miles south. Donald was walking home from the store one evening, hours after a mistrial was declared in the prosecution of a black man accused of shooting a white police officer. Many white people were shocked by the verdict and blamed the mistrial on the African Americans who had been permitted to serve on the jury. After burning a cross on the courthouse lawn, a group of enraged white men who were members of the Ku Klux Klan went out searching for someone to victimize. They found Donald as he was walking home and descended on him. After severely beating the young black man, they hanged him from a nearby tree, where his lifeless body was discovered several hours later.

Local police ignored the obvious evidence that the death was a hate crime and hypothesized that Donald must have been involved in drug dealing, which his mother adamantly denied. Outraged by the lack of local law enforcement interest in the case, the black community and civil rights activists persuaded the United States Department of Justice to get involved. Three white men were arrested two years later and details of the lynching were finally made public.

It had been more than three years since the arrests, but when Tate and the other officers started making threats of lynching, Walter was terrified. He was also confused. They said he was being arrested for raping another man, but they were throwing questions at him about the murder of Ronda Morrison. Walter vehemently denied both allegations. When it became clear that the officers would get no help from Walter in making a case against him, they locked him up and proceeded with their investigation.

When Monroe County District Attorney Ted Pearson first heard his investigators' evidence against Walter McMillian, he must have been disappointed. Ralph Myers's story of the crime was pretty far-fetched; his knack for dramatic embellishment made even the most basic allegations unnecessarily complicated.

Here's Myers's account of the murder of Ronda Morrison: On the day of the murder, Myers was getting gas when Walter McMillian saw him at the gas station and forced him at gunpoint to get in Walter's truck and drive to Monroeville. Myers didn't really know Walter before that day. Once in the truck, Walter told Myers he needed him to drive because Walter's arm was hurt. Myers protested but had no choice. Walter directed Myers to drive him to Jackson Cleaners in downtown Monroeville and instructed him to wait in the truck while McMillian went inside alone. After waiting a long time, Myers drove down the street to a grocery store to buy cigarettes. He returned ten minutes later. After another long wait, Myers finally saw McMillian emerge from the store and return to the truck. Upon entering the truck, he admitted that he had killed the store clerk. Myers then drove McMillian back to the gas station so that Myers could retrieve his vehicle. Before Myers left, Walter threatened to kill him if he ever told anyone what he had seen or done.

In summary, an African American man planning a robbery-murder in the heart of Monroeville in the middle of the day stops at a gas station and randomly selects a white man to become his accomplice by asking him to drive him to and from the crime scene because his arm is injured, even though he had been able to drive himself to the gas station where he encountered Myers and to drive his truck home after returning Myers to the gas station.

Law enforcement officers knew that Myers's story would be very difficult to prove, so they arrested Walter for sodomy, which served to shock the community and further demonize McMillian; it also gave police an opportunity to bring Walter's truck to the jail for Bill Hooks, a jailhouse informant, to see.

Bill Hooks was a young black man with a reputation as a jailhouse snitch. He had been in the county jail for several days on burglary charges when McMillian was arrested. Hooks was promised release from jail and reward money if he could connect McMillian's truck to the Morrison murder. Hooks eagerly told investigators that he had driven by Jackson Cleaners near the time of the crime and had seen a truck tear away from the cleaners with two men inside. At the jail, Hooks positively identified Walter's truck as the one he'd seen at the cleaners nearly six months earlier.

This second witness gave law enforcement officials what they needed to charge Walter McMillian with capital murder in the shooting death of Ronda Morrison.

When the indictment was announced, there was joy and relief in the community that someone had been charged. Sheriff Tate, the district attorney, and other law enforcement officers who had become targets of criticism were cheered. The absence of an arrest had disrupted life in Monroeville, and now things could settle down.

People who knew Walter found it difficult to believe he could be responsible for a sensational murder. He had no history of crime or violence, and for most folks who knew him, robbery just didn't make sense for a man who worked as hard as Walter.

Black residents told Sheriff Tate that he had arrested the wrong man. Tate still had not investigated McMillian himself, his life or background, or even his whereabouts on the day of the murder. He knew about the affair with Karen Kelly and had heard the suspicion and rumors that Walter's independence must mean he was dealing drugs. Given his eagerness to make an arrest, this seemed to be enough for

Tate to accept Myers's accusations. As it turned out, on the day of the murder, a fish fry was held at Walter's house. Members of Walter's family spent the day out in front of the house, selling food to pass-ersby. Evelyn Smith, Walter's sister, was a local minister, and she and her family occasionally raised money for the church by selling food on the roadside. Because Walter's house was closer to the main road, they often sold from his front yard. There were at least a dozen church parishioners at the house all morning with Walter and his family on the day Ronda Morrison was murdered.

Walter didn't have a tree job that day. He had decided to replace the transmission in his truck and called over his mechanic friend, Jimmy Hunter, to help. By 9:30 in the morning, the two men had dismantled Walter's truck, completely removing the transmission. By 11 o'clock, relatives had arrived and had started frying fish and other food to sell. Some church members didn't get there until later.

"Sister, we would have been here long ago, but the traffic in Monroe-ville was completely backed up. Cop cars and fire trucks, looked like something bad happened up at that cleaners," Evelyn Smith recalled one of the members saying.

Police reported that the Morrison murder took place around 10:15 A.M., eleven miles or so from McMillian's home, at the same time that a dozen church members were at Walter's home selling food while Walter and Jimmy worked on his truck. In the early afternoon, Ernest Welch, a white man whom black residents called "the furniture man" because he worked for a local furniture store, arrived to collect money from Walter's mother for a purchase she had made on credit. Welch told the folks gathered at the house that his niece had been murdered at Jackson Cleaners that morning. They discussed the shocking news with Welch for some time.

Taking into account the church members, Walter's family, and the people who were constantly stopping at the house to buy sandwiches, dozens of people were able to confirm that Walter could not have committed the murder. That group included a police officer who stopped by the house to buy a sandwich and noted in his police log that he had bought food at McMillian's house with Walter and a crowd of church folks present.

Based on their personal knowledge of Walter's whereabouts at the time of the Morrison murder, family members, church members, black pastors, and others all pleaded with Sheriff Tate to release McMillian. Tate wouldn't do it. The arrest had been too long in the making to admit yet another failure. After some discussion, the district attorney, the sheriff, and the ABI investigator agreed to stick with the McMillian accusation.

Walter's alibi wasn't the only problem for law enforcement. Ralph Myers began to have second thoughts about his allegations against McMillian. He was also facing indictment in the Morrison murder. He'd been promised that he wouldn't get the death penalty and would get favorable treatment in exchange for his testimony, but it was starting to dawn on him that admitting to involvement in a high-profile murder that he actually had nothing to do with was probably not smart.

A few days before the capital murder charges against McMillian were made public, Myers summoned police investigators and told them his allegations against McMillian weren't true. At this point, Tate and his investigators had little interest in Myers's recantation. Instead, they decided to pressure Myers to produce more incriminating details. When Myers protested that he didn't have more incriminating details because, well, the story wasn't true, the investigators weren't having it. It's not clear who decided to put both Myers and McMillian on death row before trial to create additional pressure, but it was a nearly unprecedented maneuver that proved very effective.

It is illegal to subject pretrial detainees like Walter and Myers to confinement that constitutes punishment. Pretrial detainees are generally housed in local jails, where they enjoy more privileges and more latitude than convicted criminals who are sent to prison. Putting someone who has not yet been tried in a prison reserved for convicted felons is almost never done. As is putting someone not yet convicted of a crime on death row. Even the other death row prisoners were shocked. Death row is the most restrictive punitive confinement permitted. Prisoners are locked in a small cell by themselves for twenty-three hours a day. Condemned inmates have limited opportunity for exercise or visitation and are held in disturbingly close proximity to the electric chair.

Sheriff Tate drove Walter to Holman Correctional Facility, a short ride away in Atmore, Alabama. Before the trip, the sheriff again threatened Walter with racial slurs and terrifying plans. It's unclear how Tate was able to persuade Holman's warden to house two pretrial detainees on death row, although Tate knew people at the prison from his days as a probation officer. The transfer of Myers and McMillian from the county jail to death row took place on August 1, 1987, less than a month before the scheduled execution of Wayne Ritter.

When Walter McMillian arrived on Alabama's death row—just ten years after the modern death penalty was reinstituted—an entire community of condemned men awaited him. Most of the hundred or so death row prisoners who had been sentenced to execution in Alabama since capital punishment was restored in 1975 were black, although to Walter's surprise nearly 40 percent of them were white. Everyone was poor, and everyone asked him why he was there.

Condemned prisoners on Alabama's death row unit are housed in windowless concrete buildings that are notoriously hot and uncomfortable. Each death row inmate was placed in a five-by-eight-foot cell with a metal door, a commode, and a steel bunk. The temperatures in August consistently reached over 100 degrees for days and sometimes weeks at a time. Incarcerated men would trap rats, poisonous spiders, and snakes they found inside the prison to pass the time and to keep safe. Isolated and remote, most prisoners got few visits and even fewer privileges.

Existence at Holman centered on Alabama's electric chair. The large wooden chair was built in the 1930s, and inmates had painted it yellow before attaching its leather straps and electrodes. They called it "Yellow Mama." The executions at Holman resumed just a few years before Walter arrived. John Evans and Arthur Jones had recently been electrocuted in Holman's execution chamber. Russ Canan, an attorney with the Southern Prisoners Defense Committee in Atlanta, had volunteered to represent Evans. Evans filmed what became an after-school special for kids where he shared the story of his life with school-children and urged them to avoid the mistakes he had made.

After courts refused to block the Evans execution following multiple appeals, Canan went to the prison to witness the execution at Evans's request. It was worse than Russ could have ever imagined. He later filed a much-reviewed affidavit describing the entire horrific process:

At 8:30 P.M. the first jolt of 1,900 volts of electricity passed through Mr. Evans's body. It lasted thirty seconds. Sparks and flames erupted from the electrode tied to Mr. Evans's left leg. His body slammed against the straps holding him in the electric chair and his fist clenched permanently. The electrode apparently burst from the strap holding it in place. A large puff of greyish smoke and sparks poured out from under the hood that covered Mr. Evans's face. An overpowering stench of burnt flesh and clothing began pervading the witness room. Two doctors examined Mr. Evans and declared that he was not dead.

The electrode on the left leg was refastened. At 8:30 P.M. [sic] Mr. Evans was administered a second thirty-second jolt of electricity. The stench of burning flesh was nauseating. More smoke emanated from his leg and head. Again, the doctors examined Mr. Evans. The doctors reported that his heart was still beating, and that he was still alive.

At that time, I asked the prison commissioner, who was communicating on an open telephone line to Governor George Wallace to grant clemency on the grounds that Mr. Evans was being subjected to cruel and unusual punishment. The request for clemency was denied.

At 8:40 P.M., a third charge of electricity, thirty seconds in duration, was passed through Mr. Evans's body. At 8:44, the doctors pronounced him dead. The execution of John Evans took fourteen minutes.

Walter McMillian knew nothing about any of this before he arrived at Holman. But with another scheduled execution fast approaching, condemned prisoners were talking about the electric chair constantly when Walter arrived. For his first three weeks on Alabama's death row, the horrific execution of John Evans was pretty much all he heard about.

The surreal whirlwind of the preceding weeks had left Walter devastated. After living his whole life free and unrestrained by anyone or anything, he found himself confined and threatened in a way he could never have imagined. The intense rage of the arresting officers and the racist taunts and threats from uniformed police officers who did not know him were shocking. He saw in the people who arrested him and processed him at the courthouse, even in other inmates at the jail, a contempt that he'd never experienced before. He had always been well liked and gotten along with just about everybody. He genuinely believed the accusations against him had been a serious misunderstanding and that once officials talked to his family to confirm his alibi, he'd be released in a couple of days. When the days turned into weeks, Walter began to sink into deep despair. His family assured him that the police would soon let him go, but nothing happened.

His body reacted to the shock of his situation. A lifelong smoker, Walter tried to smoke to calm his nerves, but at Holman he found the experience of smoking nauseating and quit immediately. For days he couldn't taste anything he ate. He couldn't orient or calm himself. When he woke each morning, he would feel normal for a few minutes and then sink into terror upon remembering where he was. Prison officials had shaved his head and all the hair from his face. Looking in a mirror, he didn't recognize himself.

The county jails where Walter had been housed before his transfer were awful. But the small, hot prison cell on Holman's death row was far worse. He was used to working outside among the trees with the scent of fresh pine on the cool breeze. Now he found himself staring at the bleak walls of death row. Fear and anguish unlike anything he'd ever experienced settled on Walter.

Death row prisoners were constantly advising him, but he had no way of knowing whom to believe. The judge had earlier appointed an attorney to represent him, a white man Walter didn't trust. His family raised money to hire the only black criminal lawyers in the region, J. L. Chestnut and Bruce Boynton from Selma. Chestnut was fiery and had done a lot of work in the black community to enforce civil rights. Boynton's mother, Amelia Boynton Robinson, was a legendary activist; Boynton himself had strong civil rights credentials as well.

Despite their collective experience, Chestnut and Boynton failed to persuade local officials to release Walter and couldn't prevent his transfer to Holman. If anything, hiring outside lawyers seemed to provoke Monroe County officials even more. On the trip to Holman, Tate was furious that McMillian had involved outside counsel; he mocked Walter for thinking it would make any difference. Although the money to hire Chestnut and Boynton was raised by family members through church donations and by financing their meager possessions, local law enforcement interpreted it as evidence of Walter's secret money hoard and double life—confirmation that he wasn't the innocent black man he pretended to be.

Walter tried to adjust to Holman, but things only got worse. With a scheduled execution approaching, people on the row were agitated and angry. Other prisoners had advised him to take action and file a federal complaint, since he couldn't legally be held on death row.

When Walter, who could barely read or write, failed to file the various pleadings, writs, motions, and lawsuits the other prisoners had advised him to file, they blamed him for his predicament.

"Fight for yourself. Don't trust your lawyer. They can't put you on death row without being convicted." Walter heard this constantly, but he couldn't imagine how to file a pleading in court himself.

"There were days when I couldn't breathe," Walter recalled later. "I hadn't ever experienced anything like this before in my life. I was around all these murderers, and yet it felt like sometimes they were the only ones trying to help me. I prayed, I read the Bible, and I'd be lying if I didn't tell you that I was scared, terrified just about every day."

Ralph Myers was faring no better. He had also been charged with capital murder in the death of Ronda Morrison, and his refusal to continue cooperating with law enforcement meant that he was sent to death row, too. He was placed on a different tier to prevent contact with McMillian. Whatever advantage Myers thought he could gain by saying he knew something about the Morrison murder was clearly gone now. He was depressed and sinking deeper into an emotional crisis. From the time he was burned as a child, he had always feared fire, heat, and small spaces. As the prisoners talked more and more about the details of the Evans's execution and Wayne Ritter's impending execution, Myers became more and more distraught.

On the night of the Ritter execution, Myers was in full crisis, sobbing in his cell. There is a tradition on death row in Alabama that, at the time scheduled for the execution, the condemned prisoners bang on their cell doors with cups in protest. At midnight, while all the other prisoners banged away, Myers curled up on the floor in the corner of his cell, hyperventilating and flinching with each clang he heard. When the stench of burned flesh that many on the row claimed they could smell during the execution wafted into his cell, Myers dissolved. He called Tate the next morning and told him that he would say whatever he wanted if he would get him off death row.

Tate initially justified keeping Myers and McMillian on death row for safety reasons. But Tate immediately picked Myers up and brought him back to the county jail the day after the Ritter execution. Tate didn't appear to discuss with anyone the decision to move Myers off death row. Ordinarily, the Alabama Department of Corrections couldn't just put people on death row or let them off without court orders or legal filings—and certainly no prison warden could do so on his own. But nothing about the prosecution of Walter McMillian was turning out to be ordinary.

Once removed from death row and back in Monroe County, Myers affirmed his initial accusations against McMillian. With Myers back as the primary witness and Bill Hooks ready to say that he saw Walter's truck at the crime scene, the district attorney believed that he could proceed against McMillian. The case was scheduled for trial in February 1988.

Ted Pearson had been the district attorney for nearly twenty years. He and his family had lived in South Alabama for generations. He knew the local customs, values, and traditions well and had put them to good use in the courtroom. He was getting older and had plans to retire soon, but he hated that his office had been criticized for failing to solve the Morrison murder more quickly. Pearson was determined to leave office with a victory and likely saw the prosecution of Walter McMillian as one of the most important cases of his career.

In 1987, all forty elected district attorneys in Alabama were white, even though there are sixteen majority-black counties in the state. When African Americans began to exercise their right to vote in the 1970s, there was deep concern among some prosecutors and judges about how the racial demographics in some counties would compli- cate their reelections. Legislators had aligned counties to maintain white majorities for judicial circuits that included a majority-black county. Still, Pearson had to be more mindful of the concerns of black residents than at the beginning of his career—even if that mindfulness didn't translate into any substantive changes during his tenure.

Like Tate, Pearson had heard from many black residents that they believed Walter McMillian was innocent. But Pearson was confident he could win a guilty verdict despite the suspect testimony of Ralph Myers and Bill Hooks and the strong doubts in the black community. His one lingering concern may have been a recent United States Supreme Court case that threatened a longstanding feature of high-profile criminal trials in the South: the all-white jury.

When a serious felony case went to trial in a county like Monroe County, which was 40 percent black, it was not uncommon for prosecutors to exclude all African Americans from jury service. In fact, twenty years after the civil rights revolution, the jury remained an institution largely unchanged by the legal requirements of racial integration and diversity. As far back as the 1880s, the Supreme Court ruled in *Strauder v. West Virginia* that excluding black people from jury service was unconstitutional, but juries remained all-white for decades afterward. In 1945, the Supreme Court upheld a Texas statute that limited the number of black jurors to exactly one per case. In Deep South states, jury rolls were pulled from voting rolls, which excluded African Americans. After the Voting Rights Act passed, court clerks and judges still kept the jury rolls mostly white through various tactics designed to undermine the law. Local jury commissions used statutory requirements that jurors be "intelligent and upright" to exclude African Americans and women.

In the 1970s, the Supreme Court ruled that underrepresentation of racial minorities and women in jury pools was unconstitutional, which in some communities at least led to black people being summoned to the courthouse for possible selection as jurors (if not selected). The Court had repeatedly made clear, though, that the Constitution does not require that racial minorities and women actually *serve* on juries—it only forbids excluding jurors on the basis of race or gender.

For many African Americans, the use of wholly discretionary peremptory strikes to select a jury of twelve remained a serious barrier to serving on a jury. In the mid-1960s, the Court held that using peremptory strikes in a racially discriminatory manner was unconstitutional, but the justices created an evidentiary standard for proving racial bias that was so high that no one had successfully challenged peremptory strikes in twenty years. The practice of striking all or almost all African American potential jurors continued virtually unchanged after the Court's ruling.

So defendants like Walter McMillian, even in counties that were 40 or 50 percent black, frequently found themselves staring at all-white juries, especially in death penalty cases. Then, in 1986, the Supreme Court ruled in *Batson v. Kentucky* that prosecutors could be challenged more directly about using peremptory strikes in a racially discriminatory manner, giving hope to black defendants—and forcing prosecutors to find more creative ways to exclude black jurors.

Walter was learning some of this history as the months passed. Everyone on death row wanted to advise him, and everyone had a story to tell. The novelty of a pretrial capital defendant on death row seemed to motivate other prisoners to get in Walter's ear every day. Walter tried to listen politely, but he'd already decided to leave the lawyering to his lawyers. That didn't mean that he wasn't very concerned about what he was hearing from folks on the row, especially about race and the kind of jury he would get.

Nearly everyone on death row had been tried by an all-white or nearly all-white jury. Death row prisoner Jesse Morrison told Walter that his prosecutor in Barbour County had used twenty-one out of twenty-two peremptory strikes to exclude all the black people in the jury pool. Vernon Madison from Mobile said that the prosecutor struck all ten black people qualified for jury service in his case. Willie Tabb from Lamar County, Willie Williams from Houston County, Claude Raines from Jefferson County, Gregory Acres from Montgomery County, and Neil Owens from Russell County were among the many black men on death row who had been tried by all-white juries after prosecutors struck all of the African American prospective jurors. Earl McGahee was tried by an all-white jury in Dallas County, even though the county is 60 percent African American. In Albert Jefferson's case, the prosecutor had organized the list of prospective jurors summoned to court into four groups of roughly twenty-five people each, identified as "strong," "medium," "weak," and "black." All twenty-six black people in the jury pool could be found on the "black" list, and the prosecutors excluded them all. Joe Duncan, Grady Bankhead, and Colon Guthrie were among some of the white condemned prisoners who told a similar story.

District attorney Ted Pearson had to be concerned about the new *Batson* decision; he knew veteran civil rights lawyers like Chestnut and Boynton would not hesitate to object to racially discriminatory jury selection, even though he wasn't too worried about Judge Robert E. Lee Key taking those objections seriously. But the extraordinary publicity surrounding the Morrison murder gave Pearson another idea.

In high-profile cases, it's fairly standard for defense lawyers to file a motion to change venue—to move the case from the county where the crime took place to a different county where there is less pretrial publicity and sentiment to convict. The motions are almost never granted, but every now and then an appellate court finds that the atmosphere in a county had been so prejudicial that the trial should have been moved. In Alabama, asking to change venue was an essentially futile act. Alabama courts had almost never reversed a conviction because the trial judge had refused to change venue.

When the court scheduled a hearing in October 1987 on pretrial motions in Walter's case, Chestnut and Boynton showed up with no expectation that any of their motions would be granted. They were more focused on preparing for trial, which was scheduled to begin in February 1988. The pretrial motion hearing was a formality.

Chestnut and Boynton presented their change-of-venue motion. Pearson stood up and said that due to the extraordinary pretrial coverage of the Morrison murder, he agreed that the trial should be moved. Judge Key nodded sympathetically; Chestnut, who knew his way around the Alabama courts, was sure something bad was about to happen. He was also certain the judge and the DA had already conspired.

"The defendant's motion to change venue is granted," the judge ruled.

When the judge suggested that it be moved to a neighboring county so that witnesses wouldn't have far to travel, Chestnut remained hopeful. Almost all of the bordering counties had fairly large African American populations: Wilcox County was 72 percent black; Conecuh was 46 percent black; Clarke County was 45 percent black; Butler 42 percent; Escambia was 32 percent black. Only affluent Baldwin County to the south, with its beautiful Gulf of Mexico beaches, was atypical, with an African American population of just 9 percent.

The judge took very little time deciding where the trial should be moved.

"We'll go to Baldwin County."

Chestnut and Boynton immediately complained, but the judge reminded them it was their motion. When they sought to withdraw the motion, the judge said he couldn't authorize a trial in a community where so many people had formed opinions about the accused. The case would be tried in Bay Minette, the seat of Baldwin County.

The change of venue was disastrous for Walter. Chestnut and Boynton knew there would be very few, if any, black jurors. They also understood that while jurors from Baldwin County might be less personally connected to Ronda Morrison and her family, it was an extremely conservative county that had made even less progress leaving behind the racial politics of Jim Crow than its neighbors.

Given what he'd heard from other death row prisoners about all-white juries, Walter worried about the venue change as well. But he still put his faith in this fact: No one could hear the evidence and believe that he committed this crime. He just didn't believe that a jury, black or white, could convict him on the nonsensical story told by Ralph Myers—not when he had an unquestionable alibi with close to a dozen witnesses.

The February trial was postponed. Once again, Ralph Myers was having second thoughts. After months in the county jail, away from death row, Myers again realized he didn't want to implicate himself in a murder he had not committed. He waited until the morning that the trial was set to begin before he told investigators that he could not testify because what they wanted him to say was not true. He tried to wrangle for more favorable treatment but decided that there was no punishment he was willing to accept for a murder he hadn't committed.

Myers's refusal to cooperate got him sent back to death row. Back at Holman, it wasn't long before he again showed serious emotional and psychological distress. After a couple of weeks, prison officials were so concerned that they sent him to the state hospital for the mentally ill. The Taylor Hardin Secure Medical Facility in Tuscaloosa did all of the diagnostic and assessment work for courts managing people accused of crimes who might be incompetent to stand trial due to mental illness. It had frequently been criticized by defense lawyers for almost never finding serious mental disabilities that would prevent defendants from going to trial.

Myers's time at Taylor Hardin did very little to change his predicament. He hoped that he might be returned to the county jail after his thirty-day stint at the hospital, but instead he was returned to death row. Realizing he could not escape the situation he'd created for himself, Myers told investigators he was ready to testify against McMillian.

A new trial date was scheduled for August 1988. Walter had been on death row for over a year. As hard as he had tried to adjust, he couldn't accept the nightmare his life had become. Although he was nervous, he had been convinced that he was going home back in February, when the first trial was scheduled. His lawyers seemed happy that Myers was struggling and told Walter it was a good sign when the trial was continued because Myers refused to testify. But it meant another six months on death row for Walter, and he couldn't see anything encouraging about that. When they finally moved him to the Baldwin County Jail in Bay Minette for the August trial, Walter left death row confident he'd never return. He had become friends with several men on the row and was surprised by how conflicted he felt about leaving them, knowing what they would soon face. Yet when they called his name to the transfer office, he lost no time gathering his things and getting in the van to leave.

A week later, Walter sat in the van with shackles pinching his ankles and chains tightly wound around his waist. He could feel his feet beginning to swell because the circulation was cut off by the metal digging into his skin. The handcuffs were too tight, and he was becoming uncharacteristically angry.

"Why you got these chains on me this tight?"

The two Baldwin County deputies who had picked him up a week earlier had not been friendly on the trip from death row to the courthouse. Now that he had been convicted of capital murder, they were downright hostile. One seemed to laugh in response to Walter's question.

"Them chains is the same as they were when we picked you up. They just feel tighter because we got you now."

"You need to loosen this, man, I can't ride like this."

"It ain't going to happen, so you should get your mind off it."

Walter suddenly recognized the man. At the end of the trial when the jury had found Walter guilty, his family and several of the black people who had attended the trial were in shocked disbelief. Sheriff Tate claimed that Walter's twenty-four-year-old son, Johnny, said, "Somebody's going to pay for what they've done to my father." Tate asked deputies to arrest Johnny, and there was a scuffle. Walter saw the officers wrestle his child to the ground and place him in handcuffs. The more he looked at the two deputies driving him back to death row, the more convinced he became that one of them had tackled his son.

The van began to move. They wouldn't tell Walter where he was going, but as soon as they got on the road it was clear that they were taking him back to death row. He had been upset and distraught on the day of his arrest, but he was so sure he'd be released soon. He got frustrated when the days turned into weeks at the county jail. He was depressed and terrified when they took him to death row before trial before being convicted of any crime, and the weeks became months. But when the nearly all-white jury pronounced him guilty, after fifteen months of waiting for vindication, he was shocked, paralyzed. Now he felt himself coming back to life—but all he could feel was seething anger. The deputies were driving him back to death row and talking about a gun show they were planning to attend. Walter realized that he had been foolish to give everyone the benefit of the doubt. He knew Tate was vicious and no good, but he assumed that the others were just doing what they had been told. Now he was feeling something that could only be described as rage.

"Hey, I'm going to sue all of y'all!"

He knew he was screaming and that it wasn't going to make any difference. "I'm going to sue all of y'all!" he repeated. The officers paid him no attention.

"Loose these chains. Loose these chains."

He couldn't remember when he'd last lost control, but he felt himself falling apart. With some struggle he became silent. Thoughts of the trial flew back into his mind. It had been short, methodical, and clinical. Jury selection lasted just a few hours. Pearson used his peremptory strikes to exclude all but one of the handful of African Americans who had been summoned to serve on the jury. His lawyers objected, but the judge summarily dismissed their complaints. The State put Myers on the stand to tell his absurd story about Walter forcing him to drive to Jackson Cleaners because his arm hurt. This version had Myers going into the cleaners where he saw Walter standing over the dead body of Ronda Morrison. Bizarrely, he also claimed that a third person was present and involved in the murder, a mysterious white man with salt and pepper hair who was clearly in charge of the crime and who directed Walter to kill Myers too, but Walter couldn't because he was out of bullets. Walter thought the testimony was so nonsensical he couldn't believe that people were taking it seriously. Why wasn't everyone laughing?

Chestnut's cross-examination of Myers made it clear that the witness was lying. When Chestnut finished, Walter was sure that the State would simply announce that they had made a mistake. Instead, the prosecutor brought Myers back up to repeat his accusations as if the logic and contradictions in the testimony were completely irrelevant, as if repeating his lies enough times in this quiet room would make them true.

Bill Hooks testified that he'd seen Walter's truck pull out of the cleaners at the time of the murder and that he recognized the truck because it had been modified as a "low-rider." Walter instantly whispered to his lawyers that he hadn't turned his truck into a "low-rider" until several months after Morrison was murdered. His lawyers didn't do much with that information, which frustrated Walter. Then another white man Walter had never heard of, Joe Hightower, took the stand and said that he had seen the truck at the cleaners, too.

There were a dozen people who could talk about the fish fry and insist that Walter was at home when Ronda Morrison was killed. His lawyers called only three of them. Everybody seemed to be rushing to get the trial over with, and Walter couldn't understand it. The State then called a white man, Ernest Welch, who said he was the "furniture man" who collected money at the McMillian house on the day they were having a fish fry—but it wasn't the same day that Ronda Morrison was murdered. He said he remembered better than anyone when she was murdered because he was her uncle. He said that he had been so devastated that he went to the McMillian residence to collect money on a different day.

The lawyers made their arguments, the jury retired, and less than three hours later they filed back into the courtroom. Stone-faced, one by one, they pronounced Walter McMillian guilty.

Chapter Four

The Old Rugged Cross

In February 1989, Eva Ansley and I opened our new nonprofit law center in Tuscaloosa, dedicated to providing free, quality legal services to condemned men and women on death row in Alabama. We never thought it would be easy, but it turned out to be even harder than we had expected.

In the first few months of operation our first director resigned, the University of Alabama School of Law where we had set up the office withdrew their support and promise of office space, and we discovered just how hard it was to find lawyers to come to Alabama and do full-time death penalty work for less than $25,000 a year.

Obstacles were multiplying rapidly. We were denied funding from the state legislature, which we needed to get federal matching dollars. After several disheartening meetings with our board, it had become clear that we had no support in the state for the project. State bar leaders were committed to seeing our operation succeed—some because they felt it was unacceptable that condemned prisoners could not obtain legal assistance, others because they wanted more executions at a faster pace and felt that the absence of counsel was slowing them down—but we now realized that we would have to do it on our own and raise the money ourselves. Eva and I regrouped and decided to start again in Montgomery, the state capital. The project would eventually be named the Equal Justice Initiative (EJI).

I found a small building near downtown Montgomery, and in the summer of 1989 we signed a lease. The building was a good start: a rented two-story Greek Revival house built in 1882, near the historic district called "Old Alabama Town." It was painted yellow and had a charming porch that made it feel open and welcoming—a nice contrast from the daunting courtrooms, institutional waiting rooms, and prison walls that defined so much of the lives of our clients' family members. The office was cold in the winter, it was almost impossible to keep squirrels out of the attic, and there wasn't enough electricity to run the copier and a coffeepot at the same time without blowing a fuse. But from the start it felt like a home and a place to work—and given the hours we would spend there, it was always a little of both.

Eva took on administrative duties for our new project, which were pretty challenging given that federal dollars came with all kinds of complex reporting and accounting requirements. Eva was fearless and smart, and she sorted everything out so that a few dollars could trickle in. We hired a receptionist and tried to figure out how to survive. I had worked on fund-raising for the Southern Prisoners Defense Committee almost as soon as I started there, so I had some experience asking for money to support our work. I was sure there would be a way to raise enough for the new Alabama office to meet the minimum federal matching requirements. We just needed some time—something, as it turned out, we wouldn't get at all.

A flood of execution dates awaited us. Between the passage of Alabama's new death penalty statute in 1975 and the end of 1988, there had been only three executions in Alabama. But in 1989, driven by a change in the Supreme Court's treatment of death penalty appeals and shifts in the political winds, the attorney general's office began vigorously seeking executions of condemned prisoners. By the end of 1989, the number of people executed by the State of Alabama would double.

Months before our center opened, I started visiting Alabama's death row every month, traveling from Atlanta to see a handful of new clients, including Walter McMillian. They were all grateful for the help, but as the spring of 1989 approached they all made the same request at the end of our meetings: Help Michael Lindsey. Lindsey's execution was scheduled for May 1989. Later, they would ask me to help Horace Dunkins, whose execution date was scheduled for July 1989. I painfully explained the constraints on resources and time, telling them how frantic we were just trying to get the new office up and running. Although they said they understood, they were clearly anguished about getting legal assistance while other men faced looming executions.

Both Lindsey and Dunkins had volunteer lawyers who had reached out to me for help because they were overwhelmed. Lindsey's lawyer, David Bagwell, was a respected civil attorney from Mobile; he had worked on the case of Wayne Ritter, who'd been executed a year earlier. That experience left Bagwell disillusioned and angry. He wrote a scathing letter published in the state bar association's journal in which he vowed "never to take another death penalty case, even if they disbar me for my refusal" and urged other civil lawyers not to take death penalty cases. Bagwell's public complaints made it hard for courts to appoint other civil lawyers for last-stage appeals in a death penalty case, not that they were particularly inclined to do so. But it had another effect as well. Prisoners got word of the letter and talked about it among themselves, especially about a chilling comment buried in Bagwell's jeremiad: "I generally favor the death penalty because mad dogs ought to die." The prisoners became even more distrustful of lawyers, even the ones who claimed they would help.

After further pleading by our other clients, we decided to do what we could for Michael Lindsey, whose execution date was fast approaching. We tried to make arguments about an interesting twist in that case: His jury had never decided that Michael Lindsey should be executed at all.

Lindsey received a sentence of life imprisonment without parole from his jury, but the judge had "overridden" it and imposed a death sentence on his own. Death sentences resulting from "judge override" were an anomaly, even back in 1989. In almost every state, juries made the decision to impose the death penalty or life in prison without parole. If the jury imposed or rejected death, that was the final judgment. Only Florida and Alabama allowed the jury's decision to be overridden by a judge—and Florida later put restrictions on the practice that severely curtailed it. It remains the law in Alabama, where judges almost exclusively use this power to turn life sentences into death sentences, although they're also authorized to reduce death verdicts to life if they so choose. Since 1976, judges in Alabama have overridden jury sentencing verdicts in capital cases 111 times. In 91 percent of these cases, judges replaced life verdicts from juries with death sentences.

The practice has been further complicated by the increasingly competitive nature of judicial elections in the state. Alabama elects all of its judges in highly competitive partisan elections, one of only six states to do so (thirty-two states have some form of nonpartisan judicial election process). The elections attract campaign contributions from business interests seeking tort reform or from trial lawyers who want to protect large civil verdicts, but since most voters are unschooled in these areas, the campaigns invariably focus on crime and punishment. Each judge competes to be the toughest on crime. The people financing these elections are largely unconcerned with whatever modest differences exist between candidates on crime, but punishment gets the votes. Judge overrides are an incredibly potent political tool. No judge wants to deal with attack ads that highlight the grisly details of a murder case in which the judge failed to impose the most severe punishment. Seen in that light, it's not surprising that judge overrides tend to increase in election years.

We wrote a letter to the governor of Alabama, Guy Hunt, asking him to stop the Lindsey execution on the grounds that the jury, empowered to pass judgment on him, had decided against putting him to death. Governor Hunt quickly denied our request for clemency, declaring that he would not "go against the wishes of the community expressed by the jury that Mr. Lindsey be put to death," even though we stressed that the community's representatives—the jury—had done the opposite; it clearly elected to spare Lindsey's life. It didn't matter. As peculiar as the practice is, the U.S. Supreme Court upheld judicial override in an earlier Florida case, which left us with no constitutional basis to block Michael Lindsey's execution. He was electrocuted on May 26, 1989.

Immediately after Lindsey, we were faced with Horace Dunkins's execution date. Once again, we tried to help in whatever ways we could, even though time was quickly running out and there was little hope. Mr. Dunkins suffered from intellectual disabilities, and the trial judge found he had "mental retardation" based on his school records and earlier testing. Just a few months before his execution was scheduled, the Supreme Court upheld the practice of executing the "mentally retarded." Thirteen years later, in *Atkins v. Virginia*, the Court recognized that executing people with intellectual disabilities is cruel and unusual punishment and banned the practice as unconstitutional. For many condemned and disabled people like Horace Dunkins, the ban came too late.

The Dunkins family called frequently, trying to figure out what could be done with only days to go before his execution, but there were very few options. When it became clear there was no way to stop the execution, the family turned their attention to what would happen to Mr. Dunkins's body after his death. They seemed particularly concerned, for religious reasons, with preventing the state from performing an autopsy on their son's body. The date of the execution arrived, and Horace Dunkins was killed in a botched execution that made national news. Correctional officials had plugged the electrodes into the chair incorrectly, so only a partial electrical charge was delivered to Mr. Dunkins's body when the electric chair was activated. After several agonizing minutes, the chair was turned off but Mr. Dunkins was still alive, unconscious but breathing. Officials waited several more minutes "for the body to cool" before realizing that the electrodes had not been connected properly. They made alterations and electrocuted Mr. Dunkins again, and this time it worked. They killed him. Following this cruelly mishandled execution, the state performed an autopsy—against the family's repeated requests.

I received a call from Mr. Dunkins's distraught father after the execution. He said, "They could take his life, even though he didn't get a fair trial and he didn't deserve that, but they had no right to mess with his body and soul, too. We want to sue them." We provided some aid to the volunteer lawyer on the case and a suit was filed, although there wasn't much hope. There were a few depositions but no judgment of relief. The civil suit failed to slow down the State of Alabama, which moved ahead aggressively with more execution dates.

We relocated to our new office in Montgomery in the shadow of these two executions. The men on death row were more agitated and unnerved than ever. When Herbert Richardson received word in July that his execution was scheduled for August 18, he called me collect from death row: "Mr. Stevenson, this is Herbert Richardson, and I've just received notice that the state plans to execute me on August 18. I need your help. You can't say no. I know you're helping some of the guys and y'all are opening an office, so please help me."

I replied, "I'm really sorry to hear about your execution date. It's been a very tough summer. What does your volunteer lawyer say?" I was still working on the best way to talk to condemned people about how to respond to news of an execution date. I wanted to say something reassuring like, "Don't worry," but of course that would be a remarkable request to make of anyone—news of a scheduled execution was nothing if not unimaginably worrisome. "Sorry" didn't seem quite right either, but it tended to be the best I could think of.

"I don't have a volunteer lawyer, Mr. Stevenson. I don't have anyone. My volunteer lawyer said he couldn't do any more to help me over a year ago. I need *your* help."

We still didn't have computers or law books, and I didn't have other lawyers on staff. I had hired a classmate of mine from Harvard Law

School who agreed to join our staff and moved to Alabama from his home in Boston. I was thrilled to finally have some help. He had been in Montgomery for a few days when I had to leave town for a fund-raising trip. When I returned, he was gone. He left a note explaining that he didn't realize how challenging it would be for him to live in Alabama. He hadn't been there a week.

Trying to stop an execution would mean nonstop work eighteen hours a day for a month, desperately trying to get a stay order from a court. Only an all-out effort would get it done, and it was still wildly improbable that we'd succeed in blocking the execution. When I could think of nothing to fill the silence, Richardson continued: "Mr. Stevenson, I have thirty days. Please say you'll help me."

I didn't know what else to do but be truthful. "Mr. Richardson, I'm so sorry, but I don't have books, staff, computers, or anything we need to take on new cases yet. I haven't even hired lawyers. I'm trying to get things set up—"

"But I have an execution date. You have to represent me. What's the point of all that other stuff if you're not going to help people like me?" I could hear his breath growing ragged.

"They're going to kill me," he said.

"I know what you're saying, and I'm trying to figure out how to help. We're just so overextended—" I didn't know what to say, and a long silence fell between us. I could hear him breathing heavily on the phone, and I could imagine how frustrated he must be. I was bracing myself for him to say something angry or bitter, steeling myself to absorb his understandable rage. But then the phone suddenly went silent. He'd hung up.

I was unnerved by the call for the rest of the day and couldn't find sleep that night. I was haunted by my helpless bureaucratic demurrals in the face of his desperation and the silence of his response.

The next day he called again, to my relief.

"Mr. Stevenson, I'm sorry, but you have to represent me. I don't need you to tell me that you can stop this execution; I don't need you to say you can get a stay. But I have twenty-nine days left, and I don't think I can make it if there is no hope at all. Just say you'll do something and let me have some hope."

It was impossible for me to say no, so I said yes.

"I'm not sure there is anything that we can do to block this, given where things are," I told him somberly. "But we'll try."

"If you could do something, anything . . . well, I'd be very grateful."

Herbert Richardson was a Vietnam War veteran whose nightmarish experiences in brutal conditions left him traumatized and scarred. He enlisted in the Army in 1964 at the age of eighteen, at a time when America was heavily involved in combat. He was assigned to the 11th Aviation Group, 1st Cavalry Division, and was sent to Camp Radcliff in An Khe, Vietnam. The camp was near Pleiku, an area known for extremely heavy fighting in the mid-1960s. Herbert endured perilous missions in which he saw friends get killed or seriously injured. On one mission, his entire platoon was killed in an ambush, and he was severely injured. He regained consciousness coated in the blood of his fellow soldiers; he was disoriented and unable to move. It didn't take long before he experienced a complete mental breakdown. He attempted suicide after suffering severe headaches. Despite multiple referrals from commanding officers for psychiatric evaluation, he remained in combat for seven months before his "crying outbursts" and "uncommunicative withdrawal" resulted in an honorable discharge in December 1966. Not surprisingly, his trauma followed him home to Brooklyn, New York, where he had nightmares, suffered disabling headaches, and sometimes ran out of his house screaming "Incoming!" He married and had children, but his post-traumatic stress disorder continued to undermine his ability to manage his behavior. He ended up in a veterans hospital in New York City, where he had a slow, difficult recovery from severe head pain associated with his war injuries.

Herbert became one of thousands of combat veterans who end up in jail or prison after completing their military service. One of the country's least-discussed postwar problems is how frequently combat veterans bring the traumas of war back with them and are incarcerated after returning to their communities. By the mid-1980s, nearly 20 percent of the people in jails and prisons in the United States had served in the military. While the rate declined in the 1990s as the shadows cast by the Vietnam War began to recede, it has picked up again as a result of the military conflicts in Iraq and Afghanistan.

Herbert's care at the veterans hospital in New York City slowly allowed him to recover. He eventually met a nurse there, a woman from Dothan, Alabama, whose compassionate care made him feel comfortable and hopeful for the first time, perhaps, in his entire life. When she was around, he felt alive and believed things would be all right. She had saved his life. When she moved back home to Alabama, Herbert followed.

He tried to date her and even told her he wanted to marry her. At first she resisted because she knew that Herbert was still suffering the effects of his time in combat, but ultimately she gave in. They had a brief intimate relationship, and Herbert had never been happier. He became intensely protective of his girlfriend. But she began to see his desperate and relentless focus on her as something closer to obsessive need than love. She tried to end the relationship. After months of unsuccessfully trying to create distance from Herbert, she finally insisted that he stay away.

Instead, Herbert moved even closer to her home in Dothan, which elevated her anxieties. It got to the point where she refused to allow him to see her, talk to her, or get anywhere near her. Herbert was convinced that she was just confused and would eventually come back to him. He was deluded by obsession; his logic and reasoning became corrupted, irrational, and increasingly dangerous.

Herbert was not unintelligent—in fact, he was quite smart, with a particular aptitude for electronics and mechanics. And he had a big heart. But he was still recovering from the trauma of the war as well as some serious traumas that preceded his military experience. His mother had died when he was just three years old, and he had struggled with drugs and alcohol before he decided to enlist. The horrors of war had added a new level of distress to an already damaged psyche.

He came up with an idea to win back his girlfriend. He decided that if she felt threatened, she would come to him for protection. He concocted a tragically misguided plan: He would construct a small bomb and place it on her front porch. He would detonate the bomb and then run to her aid to save her and then they would live happily ever after. It was the kind of reckless use of explosives that wouldn't have been sensible in a combat zone, much less in a poor black neighborhood in Dothan, Alabama. One morning, Herbert completed his assembly of the bomb and placed it on his former girlfriend's porch. The woman's niece and another little girl came out instead and saw the peculiar package.

The ten-year-old niece was drawn to the odd bag with a clock on it and picked up the device. She shook the clock to see if it would tick, which triggered a violent explosion. The child was killed instantly, and her twelve-year-old friend, who was standing next to her, was traumatized. Herbert knew both children. In this community, children were always roaming the streets looking for something to do. Herbert loved kids and would invite them into his yard, pay them to do errands, and talk to them. He started making cereal and cooking for the kids who would wander by. The two girls had come by his house for breakfast.

Herbert, watching the house from across the street, was devastated. He had planned to run to his girlfriend's aid when the bomb exploded to reinforce his readiness to protect her and to keep her safe. When the child picked up the bomb and it detonated, Herbert ran across the street and found himself in a circle of grieving neighbors.

It didn't take long for police to make an arrest. They found pipes and other bomb-making materials in Herbert's car and front yard. Because the victims were black and poor, this wasn't the kind of case that would usually be prosecuted as a capital crime, but Herbert wasn't local. His identity as an outsider, a Northerner, and the nature of the crime seemed to generate heightened contempt from law enforcement officials. Placing a bomb anywhere in Dothan, even in a poor section of town, posed a different kind of threat than "typical" domestic violence. The prosecutor argued that Herbert was not just tragically misguided and reckless; he was evil. The State sought the death penalty. After striking all of the black prospective jurors in a county that is 28 percent black, the prosecutor told the all-white jury in his closing argument that a conviction was appropriate because Herbert was "associated with Black Muslims from New York City" and deserved no mercy.

Alabama's capital statute requires that any murder eligible for the death penalty be intentional, but it was clear that Herbert had no intent to kill the child. The State decided to invoke an unprecedented theory of "transferred intent" to make the crime eligible for the death penalty. But Herbert had no intention to kill *anyone*. Herbert was advised to deny any culpability but ultimately argued that this was reckless murder, not capital murder, which could be punished with life imprisonment but not the death penalty.

During the trial, the appointed defense lawyer presented no evidence about Herbert's background, his military service, his trauma from the war, his relationship with the victim, his obsession with the girlfriend—nothing. Alabama's statute at the time limited what court-appointed lawyers could be paid for their out-of-court preparation time to $1,000, so the lawyer spent almost no time on the case. The trial lasted just over a day, and the judge quickly condemned Herbert to death.

Following the imposition of the death sentence, Herbert's appointed lawyer, who was later disbarred for poor performance in other cases, told Herbert that he didn't see any reason to appeal the conviction or sentence because the trial had been as fair as he could expect. Herbert reminded him that he'd been sentenced to death. He wanted to appeal no matter how unlikely the prospects, but his lawyer filed no brief.

Herbert was confined on death row for eleven years, until it was his time to face "Yellow Mama." A volunteer lawyer had challenged the intent questions in a desperate appeal but was unsuccessful. Herbert's execution was now set for August 18, just three weeks away.

After my call with Herbert, I filed a flurry of stay motions in various courts. I knew the odds were low that we would block the execution. By the late 1980s, the U.S. Supreme Court had grown impatient with challenges to capital punishment. The Court had justified reauthorization of the death penalty in the mid-1970s on the promise that proceedings would be subject to heightened scrutiny and meticulous compliance with the law but then began to retreat from the existing review procedures. The Court's rulings had become increasingly hostile to death row prisoners and less committed to the notion that "death is different," requiring more careful review.

The Court decided to bar claims from federal *habeas corpus* review if they weren't initially presented to state courts. Federal courts were then forbidden to consider new evidence unless it was first presented to state courts. The Court began insisting that federal judges defer more to state court rulings, which tended to be more indulgent of errors and defects in capital proceedings.

In the 1980s, the Court rejected a constitutional challenge to imposing the death penalty on juveniles; upheld the death penalty for disabled people suffering from "mental retardation"; and, in a widely condemned opinion, found no constitutional violation in the extreme racial disparities that could be seen throughout most death penalty jurisdictions.

By the end of the decade, some justices had become openly critical of the review that death penalty cases received. Chief Justice William Rehnquist urged restrictions on death penalty appeals and the endless efforts of lawyers to stop executions. "Let's get on with it," he famously declared at a bar association event in 1988. Finality, not fairness, had become the new priority in death penalty jurisprudence.

Two weeks after my first conversation with Herbert Richardson, I was frantically trying to get a stay of execution. Even though it was very late in the process, I was hoping that we might win a stay when I saw some of the compelling issues in Herbert's case. While his guilt wasn't really in question, there were persuasive reasons why this case should not have been a capital murder case, above and beyond the absence of a specific intent to kill. And even if you disregard that part of it, there was strong evidence that the death penalty should not be imposed because of Herbert's trauma, military service, and childhood difficulties. None of this compelling mitigating evidence was presented at trial, and it should have been. The death penalty can be imposed fairly only after carefully considering all the reasons why death might not be the appropriate sentence, and that didn't happen in Herbert's case. I was increasingly becoming convinced that Herbert was facing execution because he had been an easy target. He was unaided and easily condemned by a system that was inattentive to the precise legal requirements of capital punishment. I was deeply distressed that, had he gotten the right help at the right time, Herbert would not be on death row with an execution date in less than two weeks.

I asked several courts to stay Herbert's execution because of his ineffective lawyer, racial bias during the trial, the inflammatory comments made by the prosecutor, and the lack of mitigation evidence presented. Each court said, "Too late." We got a hastily scheduled hearing in the trial court in Dothan, where I tried to present evidence that the bomb Herbert had constructed was designed to go off at a certain time. I found an expert to testify that the bomb was a timed device and not intended to kill on contact. I knew that the court would probably conclude that this evidence should have been presented at trial or in prior proceedings, but I hoped that the judge could be persuaded.

Herbert was in court with me, and we both immediately recognized the lack of interest on the judge's face. This heightened Herbert's anxiety. He began a whispered dialogue with me, imploring me to get the testifying expert to say things about his intent that were really outside the expert's knowledge. He became contentious and started making comments that were audible to the judge. Meanwhile, the judge kept stressing that the evidence wasn't newly discovered and should have been presented at trial, so it couldn't create a basis for a stay of execution. I asked for a brief recess to try and calm Herbert down.

"He's not saying what I need him to say!"

His breathing was panicked. He held his head and told me he had a severe headache. "I didn't intend to kill anybody and he has to explain that!" he cried.

I tried to comfort him. "Mr. Richardson, we've covered this. The expert isn't allowed to speak to your mental state. He's testified that the bomb was designed to be detonated, but he can't really explain your motivations—the Court won't permit that, and he really can't speak to that."

"They're not even paying attention to what he's saying," he said sadly, rubbing his temples.

"I know, but remember, this is just the first step. We didn't expect much from this judge, but this will help us on appeal. I know this is frustrating for you." He looked at me worriedly before sighing in resignation. He sat glumly through the rest of the hearing, holding his head, which I found even more disheartening than when he was argumentative and distraught.

Because I hadn't hired any lawyers yet, I didn't have co-counsel to sit with me and help manage documents or help with the defendant during the hearing. At the end of the proceeding, Herbert was shackled and sent back to death row, vexed, disappointed, and unhappy. I wasn't feeling much better as I packed up my things and headed out of the courtroom. It would have been nice to debrief with someone, to evaluate whether what was presented might provide a basis for a stay. I had no expectation that the local judge would grant a stay, but I was hopeful that maybe a reviewing court would recognize that this wasn't an intentional killing and that a stay should be granted. So much was going on that I couldn't objectively evaluate if we had presented enough evidence to change the picture of the case. I mostly felt bad that I'd left Herbert in such a distraught state.

On my way out, I saw a group of black women and children huddled together in the back of the courtroom. Seven or eight of them were watching me intensely. The hearing had been set in the late afternoon when there were no other proceedings scheduled. I was curious about who these people might be, but honestly, I was too tired to really care. I smiled and nodded a weary greeting to the three women who seemed most focused on me, which they took as a cue to approach me as I was about to walk out the door.

The woman who spoke seemed nervous and somewhat fearful. She spoke hesitantly: "I'm Rena Mae's mother—the victim's mother. They said they would help us, but they never did. MaryLynn can't hear right, her hearing ain't never been right since that bomb, and her sister has nerve problems. I got 'em, too. We were hoping you would help us."

The stunned look on my face prompted her to say more. "I know you're busy. It's just that we could use the help." I realized that she'd cautiously offered her hand to me as she spoke, and I held it in mine.

"I'm so very sorry you haven't received the help you've been promised. But I actually represent Herbert Richardson in this case," I said as gently as I could.

"We know that. I know you might not be able to do anything right now, but when this is over, can you help us? They said we'd get some money for medical help and help for my daughter's hearing."

A young woman had quietly approached the woman as she spoke to me and embraced her. While she was probably in her early twenties, she acted in every other respect like a very small child. She leaned her head into her mother's side like a much younger child would and looked at me sadly. Another woman approached and spoke somewhat defiantly. "I'm her auntie," she said. "We don't believe in killin' people."

I wasn't exactly sure what she was trying to say, but I looked at her and replied, "Yes, I don't believe in killing people, either."

The aunt seemed to relax a little. "All this grievin' is hard. We can't cheer for that man you trying to help but don't want to have to grieve for him, too. There shouldn't be no more killing behind this."

"I don't know what I can do to help you all but I do want to help. Please contact me after August 18, and I'll see what I can find out."

The aunt then asked me if she could have her son write to me because he was in prison and needed a lawyer. She sighed with relief when I gave her my card. As we all left the courthouse, we offered each other solemn goodbyes.

"We'll pray for you," the aunt said as they departed.

On the way to my car, I considered asking them to say something to the prosecutor and state lawyers about not wanting Mr. Richardson to be executed, although it was clear that the State wasn't acting on behalf of these victims. The courtroom had been filled with state lawyers and other officials watching the hearing, but they had long since fled the courthouse without so much as a word to any of the battered souls standing in the back of the room. I was haunted by the tragic irony that they felt I was their best hope for help.

The trial judge had denied our request for a stay of execution by the time I got back to Montgomery. He ruled our evidence was "untimely," meaning that he could not consider it. With less than a week before the execution, the next few days involved one frantic filing after the next. Finally, on the day before the execution, I filed a petition for review and a motion for a stay of execution in the U.S. Supreme Court. Even in death penalty cases, the Court grants review only in a small percentage of the cases filed. A petition for *certiorari*, a request to review a lower court's ruling, is very rarely granted, but I'd known all along that the Supreme Court was our best chance for a stay of execution. Even when lower courts granted a stay, the State would appeal, so the Supreme Court would almost always make the final decision to permit an execution to proceed or not.

The execution was scheduled for 12:01 A.M. on August 18. I had finally finished the petition and faxed it to the Court late on the night of August 16 and had spent the next morning in my Montgomery office, waiting anxiously for the Court's decision. I tried to busy myself by reading files in other cases, including Walter McMillian's. I didn't expect we'd hear from the Court until the afternoon, but that didn't keep me from staring at the phone all morning. Whenever the phone rang, my pulse quickened. Eva and Doris, our receptionist, knew that I was anxiously awaiting the call. We had submitted an extensive clemency petition to the governor with affidavits from family members and color photographs, but I didn't expect anything in response. The petition detailed Herbert's military service and explained why military veterans suffering from post-traumatic stress disorder are worthy of compassion.

I wasn't very hopeful. Michael Lindsey had received a life verdict from the jury and was executed instead; Horace Dunkins was intellectually disabled, and the governor had not spared him, either. Herbert would likely be seen as even less sympathetic.

I spoke with Herbert regularly during the day by phone to let him know there was no news. I couldn't rely on the prison to get a message to him if the Court ruled, so I asked him to call me every two hours. Whatever the news, I wanted him to hear it from someone who cared about him.

Herbert had met a woman from Mobile with whom he had corresponded over the years. They had decided to get married a week before the execution. Herbert had no money, nothing to offer her if he was executed. But he was a military veteran, so his survivors were entitled to receive an American flag upon his death. He designated his new wife as the person to whom the flag should be presented. In the days leading up to the execution, it seemed that Herbert was more concerned about his flag than his impending execution. He kept asking me to check with the government about how his flag would be delivered and urging me to get a commitment in writing.

His new wife's family had agreed to spend the last few hours with Herbert before the execution. The prison allowed family members to stay until about 10:00 P.M., when they would begin to prepare the condemned for execution. I was still in my office waiting to receive word from the Supreme Court. When the clock passed 5:00 P.M. without any news, I allowed myself to become cautiously hopeful. If the Court wasn't troubled by anything we'd presented, I expected an earlier ruling on our motion for a stay. So the later it got, the more encouraged I became. At 6:00 P.M. I was pacing in my small office, nervously running through the possibilities of what the Court might be debating so close to the execution hour. Eva and our new investigator, Brenda Lewis, waited with me. Finally, a little before 7:00 P.M., the phone rang. The clerk of the Court was on the line.

"Mr. Stevenson, I'm calling to let you know that the Court has just entered an order in Case No. 89-5395; the motion for a stay of execution and petition for writ of *certiorari* have been denied. We'll fax copies of the order to your office shortly."

And with that, the conversation ended. When I hung up, all I could think was, why would I need a copy of the order? To whom did the clerk think I would show it? In a matter of hours, Herbert would be dead. There would be no more appeals, no more records to keep. I'm not sure why I was struck by these peculiar details. Maybe thinking about the procedural absurdities of the Court's order was less overwhelming than thinking about its meaning. I had promised Herbert I would be with him during the execution, and it took me a few minutes to realize I needed to move quickly to get to the prison two hours away.

I jumped in my car and raced to Atmore. As I drove down the interstate to reach the prison, I noticed the long rays of sunlight retreating even as the heat of the Alabama summer persisted. When I arrived at the prison, it was completely dark. Outside the prison entrance were dozens of men with guns sitting on the backs of trucks that lined the long road to the prison parking area. They were state troopers, local police officers, deputy sheriffs, and what appeared to be part of a National Guard unit. I don't know why the State felt they needed a militia to guard the entrance to the prison on the night of an execution. It was surreal to see all of these armed men gathered near midnight to make sure a life would be taken without incident. It fascinated me that someone thought there might be some violent, armed resistance to the scheduled execution of an indigent black man.

I entered the prison and saw an older white woman—the correctional officer who managed the visitation yard. I had become a regular at death row visiting my new clients at least once a month, so she saw me frequently but had never been particularly friendly. Tonight she approached me with unusual warmth and familiarity when I arrived. I thought she was going to hug me.

Men in suits and ties hovered in the lobby, eyeing me suspiciously as I walked into the visitation room at a little past nine. The visitation area at Holman is a large circular room surrounded by glass so that officers can look in from any vantage point. There are a dozen small tables with chairs inside for visiting family who come on visitation days, typically scheduled two or three times a month. During the week of a scheduled execution, only the condemned prisoner facing a scheduled death is permitted to have family visits.

When I got inside the visiting room, the family had less than an hour left with Herbert. He was calmer than I had ever seen him. He smiled at me when I walked in and gave me a hug.

"Hey y'all, this is my lawyer."

He said it with a pride that was surprising and moving to me.

"Hello everyone," I said. Herbert still had his arm around my shoulder, and I wanted to say something comforting but couldn't think of anything before Herbert jumped in again.

"I told the prison people that I want all my possessions distributed just as I've said or my lawyer will sue you till you all have to work for him." He chuckled, and people laughed.

I met Herbert's bride and her family and spent the next forty-five minutes with one eye on the clock, knowing that at 10:00 P.M. the guards would take Herbert to the back, and we would never see him alive again. Herbert tried to keep things light. He told his family how he had persuaded me to take his case and bragged that I only represented people who were smart and charming.

"He's too young to have represented me at trial, but if he had been there I wouldn't be on death row now." He said it with a smile, but I was starting to feel shaken. I was really struck at how hard he was working to make everyone around him feel better in the face of his own death. I had never seen him so energetic and gracious. His family and I smiled and laughed, but all of us felt the strain of the moment. His wife became more and more tearful as the minutes ticked away. Shortly before 10 P.M., the commissioner of the Alabama Department of Corrections, the warden, and several other men wearing suits gestured to the visitation officer. She came into the room meekly and regretfully said, "It's time, folks. We've got to end the visit. Say your goodbyes."

I watched the men in the hallway; they had clearly been expecting the officer to do something more decisive and effective. They wanted things to proceed on schedule and were clearly ready to move to the next stage to prepare for the execution. One of the state officials walked over to the guard when she left the room and pointed at his watch. Inside the room, Herbert's wife began to sob. She put her arms around his neck and refused to let him go. After a couple of minutes, her crying turned into groaning, distressed and desperate.

The officials in the lobby were growing more impatient and gestured at the visitation officer, who came back into the room. "I'm sorry," she said as firmly as she could muster, "but you have to leave now." She looked at me, and I looked away. Herbert's wife began sobbing again. Her sister and other family members began to cry, too. Herbert's wife grabbed him even more tightly. I hadn't thought about how difficult this moment would be. It was surreal in a way I hadn't anticipated. In an instant a flood of sadness and tragedy had overtaken everyone, and I began to worry that it would be impossible for this family to leave Herbert.

By now the officials were angry. I looked through the window and saw the warden radio for more officers to come into the area. Someone else gestured for the officer to go back into the room and bring the family members out. I heard them tell her not to come out without the family. The officer looked frantic. Despite her uniform, she'd always seemed a little out of place at the prison, and she looked especially uncomfortable now. She had once volunteered to me that her grandson wanted to be a lawyer and that she was hoping he would. She looked around the room nervously and then came up to me. She had tears in her eyes and looked at me desperately.

"Please, please, help me get these people out of here, please." I began to worry that things were going to get ugly, but I couldn't sort out what to do. It seemed impossibly hard for them to expect people to just calmly abandon someone they loved so that he could be executed. I wanted to prevent things from getting out of control but felt powerless to do anything.

By this time, Herbert's wife had started saying loudly, "I'm not going to leave you."

Herbert had made a peculiar request the week before the execution. He said that if he was executed as scheduled, he wanted me to get the prison to play a recording of a hymn, "The Old Rugged Cross," as he walked to the electric chair. I had been slightly embarrassed to raise the request when I spoke with prison officials, but to my utter amazement they had agreed to do it.

I remembered as a child that they always sang this hymn at somber moments during church services, on Communion Sundays, and Good Friday. It was sad like few other hymns I'd heard. I don't know why exactly, but I started to hum it as I saw more uniformed officers enter the vestibule outside the visitation room. It seemed like something that might help. But help what?

After a few minutes, the family joined me. I went over to Herbert's wife as she held him tightly, sobbing softly. I whispered to her, "We have to let him go." Herbert saw the officers lining up outside, and he pulled away from her slowly and told me to take her out of the room.

Herbert's wife clung to me and sobbed hysterically as I led her out of the visitation room with her family tearfully following. The experience was heartbreaking, and I wanted to cry. But I just kept humming instead.

The prison had made arrangements for me to go back to the death chamber in about an hour to be with Herbert before the execution. Although I had worked on several death penalty cases with clients who had execution dates, I'd never before been present at an execution. In the cases where I had actually been counsel for the condemned while I was in Georgia, we'd always won stays of execution. I grew anxious thinking about witnessing the spectacle of a man being electrocuted, burned to death in front of me. I'd been so focused on obtaining the stay and then on what to say to Herbert when I got to the prison that I hadn't actually thought about witnessing the execution. I no longer wanted to be there for that, but I didn't want to abandon Herbert. To leave him in a room alone with people who wanted him dead made me realize that I couldn't back out. All of a sudden the room felt incredibly hot, like there was no air anywhere. The visitation officer came up to me after I had escorted the family out and whispered in my ear, "Thank you." I was vexed by her thinking of me as an accomplice and didn't know what to say.

When there were less than thirty minutes before the execution, they took me back to the cell next to the execution chamber deep inside the prison where they were holding Herbert until it was time to put him in the electric chair. They had shaved the hair off his body to facilitate a "clean" execution. The state had done nothing to modify the electric chair since the disastrous Evans execution. I thought about the botched execution of Horace Dunkins a month earlier and became even more distraught. I had tried to read up on what should happen at an execution; I had some misguided thought that I could intervene if they did something incorrectly.

Herbert was much more emotional when he saw me than he'd been in the visitation room. He looked shaken, and it was clear that he was upset. It must have been humiliating to be shaved in preparation for an execution. He looked worried, and when I walked into the chamber he grabbed my hands and asked if we could pray, and we did. When we were done, his face took on a distant look and then he turned to me.

"Hey, man, thank you. I know this ain't easy for you either, but I'm grateful to you for standing with me."

I smiled and gave him a hug. His face sagged with an unbearable sadness.

"It's been a very strange day, Bryan, really strange. Most people who feel fine don't get to think all day about this being their last day alive with certainty that they will be killed. It's different than being in Vietnam . . . much stranger."

He nodded at all the officers who were milling about nervously. "It's been strange for them, too.

"All day long people have been asking me, 'What can I do to help you?' When I woke up this morning, they kept coming to me, 'Can we get you some breakfast?' At midday they came to me, 'Can we get you some lunch?' All day long, 'What can we do to help you?' This evening, 'What do you want for your meal, how can we help you?' 'Do you need stamps for your letters?' 'Do you want water?' 'Do you want coffee?' 'Can we get you the phone?' 'How can we help you?' "

Herbert sighed and looked away.

"It's been so strange, Bryan. More people have asked me what they can do to help me in the last fourteen hours of my life than ever asked me in the years when I was coming up." He looked at me, and his face twisted in confusion.

I gave Herbert one last long hug, but I was thinking about what he'd said. I thought of all the evidence that the court had never reviewed about his childhood. I was thinking about all of the trauma and difficulty that had followed him home from Vietnam. I couldn't help but ask myself, Where were these people when he really needed them? Where were all of these helpful people when Herbert was three and his mother died? Where were they when he was seven and trying to recover from physical abuse? Where were they when he was a young teen struggling with drugs and alcohol? Where were they when he returned from Vietnam traumatized and disabled?

I saw the cassette tape recorder that had been set up in the hallway and watched an officer bring over a tape. The sad strains of "The Old Rugged Cross" began to play as they pulled Herbert away from me.

There was a shamefulness about the experience of Herbert's execution I couldn't shake. Everyone I saw at the prison seemed surrounded by a cloud of regret and remorse. The prison officials had pumped themselves up to carry out the execution with determination and resolve, but even they revealed extreme discomfort and some measure of shame. Maybe I was imagining it but it seemed that everyone recognized what was taking place was wrong. Abstractions about capital punishment were one thing, but the details of systematically killing someone who is not a threat are completely different.

I couldn't stop thinking about it on the trip home. I thought about Herbert, about how desperately he wanted the American flag he earned through his military service in Vietnam. I thought about his family and about the victim's family and the tragedy the crime created for them. I thought about the visitation officer, the Department of Corrections officials, the men who were paid to shave Herbert's body so that he could be killed more efficiently. I thought about the officers who had strapped him into the chair. I kept thinking that no one could actually believe this was a good thing to do or even a necessary thing to do.

The next day there were articles in the press about the execution. Some state officials expressed happiness and excitement that an execution had taken place, but I knew that none of them had actually dealt with the details of killing Herbert. In debates about the death penalty, I had started arguing that we would never think it was humane to pay someone to rape people convicted of rape or assault and abuse someone guilty of assault or abuse. Yet we were comfortable killing people who kill, in part because we think we can do it in a manner that doesn't implicate our own humanity, the way that raping or abusing someone would. I couldn't stop thinking that we don't spend much time contemplating the details of what killing someone actually involves.

I went back to my office the next day with renewed energy. I picked up my other case files and made updated plans for how to assist each client to maximize the chance of avoiding an execution. Eventually, I recognized that all my fresh resolve didn't change much—I was really only trying to reconcile myself to the realities of Herbert's death. I was comforted by the exercise just the same. I felt more determined to recruit staff and obtain resources to meet the growing challenges of providing legal assistance to condemned people. Eva and I talked about a few people who had expressed interest in joining our staff. There was some new financial support possible from a foundation, and that afternoon we finally received the office equipment we had ordered. By the end of the day, I was persuaded things would improve, even while I felt newly burdened by the weight of it all.

Chapter Five

Of the Coming of John

"It would have been so much easier if he had been out in the woods hunting by himself when that girl was killed." Armelia Hand, Walter McMillian's older sister, paused while the crowd in the small trailer called out in affirmation. I sat on a couch and looked out at the nearly two dozen family members who were staring at me as Armelia spoke.

"At least then we could understand how it might be possible for him to have done this." She paused and looked down at the floor of the room where we had gathered.

"But because we were standing next to him that whole morning . . . We *know* where he was. . . . We know what he was doing!" People hummed in agreement as her voice grew louder and more distraught. It was the kind of wordless testimony of struggle and anguish I heard all the time growing up in a small rural black church.

"Just about everybody in here was standing next to him, talking to him, laughing with him, eating with him. Then the police come along months later, say he killed somebody miles away at the same time we were standing next to him. Then they take him away when you know it's a lie."

She was now struggling to speak. Her hands were trembling and the emotion in her voice was making it hard to get her words out.

"We were with him all day! What are we supposed to do, Mr. Stevenson? Tell us, what are we supposed to do with that?"

Her face twisted in pain. "I feel like I've been convicted, too."

The small crowd responded to each statement with shouts of "Yes!" and "That's right!"

"I feel like they done put me on death row, too. What do we tell these children about how to stay out of harm's way when you can be at your own house, minding your own business, surrounded by your entire family, and they still put some murder on you that you ain't do and send you to death row?"

I sat on the crowded sofa in my suit, staring into the face of a lot of pain. I hadn't expected to have such an intense meeting when I arrived. Folks were desperate for answers and trying to reconcile themselves to a situation that made no sense. I was struggling to think of something appropriate to say when a younger woman spoke up.

"Johnny D could have never done this no kind of way, whether we was with him or not," she said, using the nickname Walter's family and friends had given him. "He's just not like that."

The younger woman was Walter's niece. She continued with her rebuttal to the very idea that Walter would need an alibi, which seemed to generate support among the crowd.

I was relieved to have the pressure off me for a moment, as Walter's large family seemed to be moving toward some sort of debate over whether Walter's character rendered an alibi unnecessary—or even insulting. It had been a long day. I was no longer sure what time it was, but I knew it was very late, and I was wearing down. I'd spent several intense hours on death row earlier in the day with Walter going over his trial transcript. Before my meeting with Walter, I spent time with other new clients on the row. Their cases weren't active, and there were no deadlines on the horizon, but I hadn't seen them since the Richardson execution and they had been anxious to talk.

Now that Walter's case record was complete, appeal pleadings would be due soon, and time was critical. I should have returned to Montgomery directly from the prison, but Walter's family wanted to meet, and since they were less than an hour from the prison I had promised to come to Monroeville.

Walter's wife, Minnie Belle McMillian, and his daughter Jackie were waiting patiently when I pulled up to the McMillians' dilapidated house in Repton, which was off the main road leading into Monroeville. Walter had told me I would know I was close when I passed a cluster of liquor stores on the county line between Conecuh and Monroe counties. Monroe County is a "dry county" where no alcoholic beverages can be sold; for the convenience of its thirsty citizens, several package stores marked the boundary with Conecuh County. Walter's house was just a few miles from the county line.

I pulled into the driveway and was surprised at the profound disrepair; this was a poor family's home. The front porch was propped on three cinder blocks piled precariously beneath wood flooring that showed signs of rot. The blue window panes were in desperate need of paint, and a makeshift set of stairs that didn't connect to the structure was the only access to the home. The yard was littered with abandoned car parts, tires, broken pieces of furniture, and other detritus. Before getting out of my car, I decided to put on my well-worn suit jacket, even though I had noticed earlier that it was missing buttons on both jacket sleeves.

Minnie walked out the front door and apologized for the appearance of the yard as I carefully stepped onto the porch. She kindly invited me inside while a woman in her early twenties lingered behind her.

"Let me fix something for you to eat. You been at the prison all day," she said. Minnie looked tired but otherwise appeared as I had imagined—patient and strong—based on Walter's descriptions and my own guesses from our phone conversations. Because the State had made Walter's affair with Karen Kelly part of its case in court, the trial had been especially difficult for Minnie. But she looked like she was still standing strong.

"Oh, no, thank you. I appreciate it, but it's fine. Walter and I ate some things on the visitation yard."

"They don't have nothing on that prison yard but chips and sodas. Let me cook you something good."

"That's very kind, I appreciate it, but I'm really okay. I know you've been working all day, too."

"Well, yes, I'm on twelve-hour shifts at the plant. Them people don't want to hear nothing about your business, your sickness, your nerves, your out-of-town guests, and definitely nothing about your family problems." She didn't sound angry or bitter, just sad. She walked over to me, gently looped her arm with mine, and slowly led me into the house. We sat down on a sofa in the crowded living room. Chairs that didn't match were piled with papers and clothes; her grandchildren's toys were scattered on the floor. Minnie sat close to me, almost leaning on me as she continued speaking softly.

"Work people tell you to be there, and so you got to go. I'm trying to get her through school and it ain't easy." She nodded to her daughter, Jackie, who looked back at her mother sympathetically. Jackie walked across the room and sat near us. Walter and Minnie had mentioned their children—Jackie, Johnny, and "Boot"—to me several times. Jackie's name was always followed by "She's in college." I had begun to think of her as Jackie "She's in College" McMillian. All of the kids were in their twenties but still very close and protective of their mother.

I told them about my visit with Walter. Minnie hadn't been to the prison in several months and seemed grateful that I had spent some time there. I went over the appeals process with them and talked about the next steps in the case. They confirmed Walter's alibi and updated me on all the rumors in town currently circulating about the case.

"I believe it was that old man Miles Jackson who done it," Minnie said emphatically.

"I think it's the new owner, Rick Blair," Jackie said. "Everybody knows they found a white man's skin under that girl's fingernails where she had fought whoever killed her."

"Well, we're going to get to the truth," I said. I tried to sound confident, but given what I'd read in the trial transcript, I thought it very unlikely that the police would turn over their evidence to me or let me see the files and the materials collected from the crime scene. Even in the transcript, the law enforcement officers who had investigated Walter seemed lawless. These police put Walter on death row while he was a pretrial detainee; I feared that they would not scrupulously follow the legal requirement to turn over all exculpatory evidence that could help him prove his innocence.

We talked for well over an hour—or they talked while I listened. You could tell how traumatizing the last eighteen months since Walter's arrest had been.

"The trial was the worst," Minnie said. "They just ignored what we told them about Johnny D being home. Nobody has explained to me why they did that. Why did they do that?" She looked at me as if she honestly hoped I could provide an answer.

"This trial was constructed with lies," I said. I was wary about expressing such strong opinions to Walter's family because I hadn't investigated the case enough to be sure there was more evidence to convict Walter. But reading the record of his trial had outraged me, and I felt that anger returning—not just about the injustice done to Walter but also about the way it had burdened the entire community. Everyone in the poor, black community who talked to me about the case had expressed hopelessness. This one massive miscarriage of justice had afflicted the whole community with despair and made it hard for me to be dispassionate.

"One lie after the other," I continued. "People were fed so many lies that by the time y'all started telling the truth, it was just easier to believe *you* were the ones who were lying. It frustrates me to even read it in the trial record, so I can only imagine how you all feel."

The phone rang, and Jackie jumped up to answer it. She came back a few minutes later. "Eddie said that people are getting restless. They want to know when he's going to be there."

Minnie stood up and straightened her dress. "Well, we should probably get going down there. They been waiting most of the day for you."

When I looked confused, Minnie smiled. "Oh, I told the rest of the family we would bring you down there, since it's so hard to find where they live if you've never been there before. His sisters, nephews, nieces, and other folks all want to meet you." I tried not to show my alarm, but I was getting worried about the time.

We piled into my two-door Corolla, which was stacked with papers, trial transcripts, and court records. "You must spend your money on other things," Jackie joked as we pulled away.

"Yes, expensive suits are my spending priority these days," I replied.

"There's nothing wrong with your suit or your car," Minnie said protectively.

I followed their directions down a long, winding dirt road full of impossible turns through a heavily wooded area. As darkness fell around us, the road twisted through dense forest for several miles until it came to a short, narrow bridge with room for only one car to pass. It looked shaky and unstable, so I slowed the car to a stop.

"It's okay. It hasn't rained that much, and that's the only time when it's really a problem," Minnie said.

"What kind of problem?" I didn't want to sound scared, but we were in the middle of nowhere and in the pitch-black night I couldn't tell whether it was a swamp, a creek, or a small river under the bridge.

"It will be all right. People drive through here every day," Jackie chimed in.

It would have been too embarrassing to turn around, so I drove slowly across the bridge and was relieved when we had made it to the other side. I continued for another mile until the forest began to give way to trailers, a few small homes, and finally, an entire community hidden away in the woods.

We pulled up a hill until we reached a trailer that was glowing in the darkness, lit by a fire burning in a barrel out front. Six or seven small children were playing outside; they dashed into the trailer when they saw our car pull up. As we got out of the car, a tall man emerged from the trailer. He walked up to us and hugged Minnie and Jackie before shaking my hand.

"They been waiting for you," he told me. "I know you probably got a lot of work to do, but we appreciate you coming to meet with us. I'm Giles, Walter's nephew."

Giles led me to the trailer and opened the door for me to step inside. The small home was packed with more than thirty people, whose chattering fell silent when I walked in. I was startled by the size of the group, which stared at me appraisingly and then, one by one, started to smile at me. Then, to my amazement, the room broke into loud applause. I was stunned by the gesture. No one had ever applauded me just for showing up. There were older women, younger women, men Walter's age, and several men much older. Their faces were creased with a by-now familiar look of anxiety. When the applause had died down, I began to speak.

"Thank you, that's very kind," I started. "I'm so glad to meet you all. Mr. McMillian told me he had a large family, but I didn't expect so many of you to be here. I saw him today, and he wants me to pass along his thanks and his gratitude to all of you for sticking by him. I hope you know how much your support means. He has to wake up on death row every morning, and that's not easy. But he knows he's not alone. He talks about you all the time."

"Sit down, Mr. Stevenson," someone shouted. I took a seat on an empty couch that seemed to have been reserved for me and Minnie sat down beside me. Everyone else stood, facing me.

"We don't have any money. We gave it all to the first lawyer," called out one of the men.

"I understand that, and I won't take a penny. I work for a nonprofit law office, and we provide legal assistance at no cost to the people we represent," I replied.

"Well, how do you pay the bills?" asked one young woman. People laughed at the question.

"We get donations from foundations and people who support our work."

"Well, you get Johnny D home, and I'll make all kinds of donations," said another woman slyly. People laughed and I smiled.

An older woman spoke up. It was Armelia Hand. "We don't have much, Mr. Stevenson, but you have someone we love in your care. Anything we have, you have. These people have broken our hearts," she said.

I began answering questions and listening to comments and testimonials about Walter, the town, race, the police, the trial, and the way the whole family was now being treated by people in the community. The hours passed, and I knew that I had probably exhausted whatever helpful information could be obtained from Walter's family, but folks still wanted to talk. There seemed to be therapeutic relief in voicing their concerns to me. Before long I heard some hopefulness in their questions and comments. I explained the appeals process and talked about the kind of issues that were already apparent from the record. I began to feel encouraged that some of the information I provided maybe eased their anxiety. We started to joke some, and before I knew it I felt embraced in a way that energized me.

An older woman had given me a tall glass of sweet iced tea as I sat there listening and responding to questions. I drank the first glass thirstily because I was a little nervous (the tea was very good). The woman watched me drain the glass and smiled at me with a look of great satisfaction. She quickly filled the glass, and no matter how much or how little I drank, she minded my glass religiously the entire evening. After over three hours, Minnie grabbed my hand and announced that they should let me go. It was close to midnight, and it would take me at least two hours to get to Montgomery. I said my farewells and exchanged hugs with practically everyone in the room before stepping out into the dark night.

December is rarely bitter cold in South Alabama during the day, but at night the temperatures can drop, a dramatic reminder that it's winter, even in the South. Without an overcoat, I cranked up the heat for the long drive home after dropping Minnie and Jackie back at their house. The meeting with the family had been inspiring. There were clearly a lot of people who cared deeply about Walter and consequently cared about what I did and how I could help. But it was also clear that people had been traumatized by what had happened. Several of the people I met weren't actually related but had been at the fish fry on the day of the crime. They were so deeply disturbed by Walter's conviction that they, too, had come over when they heard that I was coming. They needed a place to share their hurt and confusion.

In 1903, W.E.B. Du Bois included in his seminal work, *The Souls of Black Folk,* a brilliant but haunting short story. I thought about "Of the Coming of John" on the drive home. In Du Bois's story, a young black man in coastal Georgia is sent off hundreds of miles to a school that trains black teachers. The entire black community where he was born had raised the money for his tuition. The community invests in John so that he can one day return and teach African American children who are barred from attending the public school. Casual and fun-loving, John almost flunks out of his new school until he considers the trust he's been given and the shame he would face if he returned without graduating. Newly focused, sober, and intensely committed to succeed, he graduates with honors and returns to his community intent on changing things.

John convinces the white judge who controls the town to allow him to open a school for black children. His education has empowered him, and he has strong opinions about racial freedom and equality that land him and the black community in trouble. The judge shuts down the school when he hears what John's been teaching. John walks home after the school's closing frustrated and distraught. On the trip home he sees his sister being groped by the judge's adult son and he reacts violently, striking the man in the head with a piece of wood. John continues home to say goodbye to his mother. Du Bois ends the tragic story when the furious judge catches up to John with the lynch mob he has assembled.

I read the story several times in college because I identified with John as the hope of an entire community. None of my aunts or uncles had graduated from college; many hadn't graduated from high school. The people in my church always encouraged me and never asked me for anything back, but I felt a debt accumulating. Du Bois understood this dynamic deeply and brought it to life in a way that absolutely fascinated me. (I just hoped that my parallel with John wouldn't extend to the getting lynched part.)

Driving home that night from meeting Walter's family, I thought of the story in a whole new way. I had never before considered how devastated John's community must have felt after his lynching. Things would become so much harder for the people who had given everything to help make John a teacher. For the surviving black community, there would be more obstacles to opportunity and progress and much heartache. John's education had led not to liberation and progress but to violence and tragedy. There would be more distrust, more animosity, and more injustice.

Walter's family and most poor black people in his community were similarly burdened by Walter's conviction. Even if they hadn't been at his house the day of the crime, most black people in Monroeville knew someone who had been with Walter that day. The pain in that trailer was tangible—I could feel it. The community seemed desperate for some hope of justice. The realization left me anxious but determined.

I'd gotten used to taking calls from lots of people concerning Walter's case. Most were poor and black, and they offered encouragement and support, and my visit with the family generated even more of those calls. And occasionally, a white person for whom Walter had worked would call to offer support, like Sam Crook. When Sam called, he insisted that I come and see him the next time I was back in town.

"I'm a rebel," he said toward the end of our call. "Part of the 117th division of the Confederate Army."

"Sir?"

"My people were heroes of the Confederacy. I've inherited their land, their title, and their pride. I love this county, but I know what happened to Walter McMillian ain't right."

"Well, I appreciate your call."

"You're going to need some backup, someone who knows some of these people you're going against, and I'm going to help you."

"I'd be very grateful for your help."

"I'll tell you something else." He lowered his voice. "Do you think your phone is being tapped?"

"No, sir, I think my phone is clear."

Sam's voice rose in volume again.

"Well, I've decided I ain't going to let them string him up. I'll get some boys, and we'll go cut him down before we let them take him. I'm just not going to stand for them putting a good man down for something I know he didn't do."

Sam Crook spoke in grand proclamations. I hesitated over how to respond.

"Well . . . thank you," was all I could manage.

When I later asked Walter about Sam Crook, he just smiled. "I've done a lot of work for him. He's been good to me. He's a very interesting guy."

I saw Walter just about every other week for those first few months, and I learned some of his habits. "Interesting" was Walter's euphemism for odd people, and having worked for hundreds of people throughout the county over the years, he'd encountered no shortage of "interesting" people. The more unusual or bizarre the person was, the more "interesting" they would become in Walter's parlance. "Very interesting" and "real interesting" and finally "Now, he's reeeeaaaalll interesting" were the markers for strange and stranger characters. Walter seemed reluctant to say anything bad about anyone. He'd just chuckle if he thought someone was odd.

Walter grew much more relaxed during our visits. As we became more comfortable with each other, he would sometimes veer into topics that had nothing to do with the case. We talked about the guards at the prison and his experiences dealing with other prisoners. He talked about people back home he thought would visit but hadn't. In these conversations, Walter showed remarkable empathy. He spent a lot of time imagining what other people were thinking and feeling that might mitigate their behavior. He guessed what frustrations guards must be experiencing to excuse the rude things they said to him. He gave voice to how hard it must be to visit someone on death row.

We talked about food he liked, jobs he'd worked when he was younger. We talked about race and power, the things we saw that were funny, and the things we saw that were sad. It made him feel better to have a normal conversation with someone who wasn't on the row or a guard, and I always spent extra time with him to talk about things unrelated to the case. Not just for him but for myself as well.

I was trying so hard to get the project off the ground that my work had quickly become my life. I found something refreshing in the moments I spent with clients when we didn't relate to one another as attorney and client but as friends. Walter's case was becoming the most complicated and time-consuming I'd ever worked on, and spending time with him was comforting even though it made me feel the pressure of his mistreatment in ways that became increasingly personal.

"Man, all these guys talk about how you're working on their case. You must not ever get any peace," he told me once.

"Well, everybody needs help, so we're trying."

He gave me an odd look that I hadn't seen before. I think he wasn't sure whether he could give me advice—he hadn't done that yet. Finally, he seemed to say what he was thinking.

"Well, you know you can't help everybody," he looked at me earnestly. "You'll kill yourself if you try to do that." He continued looking at me with concern.

I smiled. "I know."

"I mean, you gotta help *me*. You shouldn't hold nothing back on my case," he said with a smile. "I expect you to fight all comers to get me out of here. Take 'em all down, if necessary."

"Stand up to giants, slay wild beasts, wrestle alligators . . . ," I joked.

"Yeah, and get somebody ready to take over the battle in case they chop your head off, 'cause I'm still going to need help if they take you out."

The more time I spent with Walter, the more I was persuaded that he was a kind, decent man with a generous nature. He freely acknowledged that he'd made poor decisions, particularly where women were concerned. By all accounts—from friends, family, and associates like Sam Crook—Walter generally tried to do the right thing. I never regarded our time together as wasted or unproductive.

In all death penalty cases, spending time with clients is important. Developing the trust of clients is not only necessary to manage the complexities of the litigation and deal with the stress of a potential execution; it's also key to effective advocacy. A client's life often depends on his lawyer's ability to create a mitigation narrative that contextualizes his poor decisions or violent behavior. Uncovering things about someone's background that no one has previously discovered—things that might be hard to discuss but are critically important—requires trust. Getting someone to acknowledge he has been the victim of child sexual abuse, neglect, or abandonment won't happen without the kind of comfort that takes hours and multiple visits to develop. Talking about sports, TV, popular culture, or anything else the client wants to discuss is absolutely appropriate to building a relationship that makes effective work possible. But it also creates genuine connections with clients. And that's certainly what happened with Walter.

Shortly after my first trip to see Walter's family, I received a call from a young man named Darnell Houston who told me that he could prove that Walter was innocent. His voice shook with nerves but he was determined to speak to me. He didn't want to talk on the phone, so I drove down to meet with him one afternoon. He lived in a rural part of Monroe County on farmland that his family had worked since the time of slavery. Darnell was a sincere young man, and I could tell he'd been debating for a while whether to contact me.

When I arrived at his home, he walked out to greet me. He was a young black man in his twenties who had joined the "Jheri curl" craze. I had already noticed that the popular process of chemically treating black hair to make it looser and easier to style had come to Monroeville; I'd seen several black men, young and old, sporting the look with pride. The cheerful bounce of Darnell's hair contrasted with his worried demeanor. As soon as we sat down, he got right to business.

"Mr. Stevenson," he began. "I can prove that Walter McMillian is innocent."

"Really?"

"Bill Hooks is lying. I didn't know he was even involved in that case until they told me he was part of how they put Walter McMillian on death row. First, I didn't believe Bill could have been part of this, but then I found out that he testified that he drove by that cleaners on the day that girl was killed, and that's a lie."

"How do you know?"

"We were working together all that day. We both worked at the NAPA auto parts store last November. I remember that Saturday when that girl was killed because ambulances and police started racing up the street. It went on for like thirty minutes. I'd been working in town for a couple of years and had never seen anything like it."

"You were working on the Saturday morning that Ronda Morrison was killed?"

"Yes, sir, with Bill Hooks from about eight in the morning till we closed after lunch, *after* all them ambulances went by our shop. It was probably close to eleven when the sirens started. Bill was working on a car in the shop with me. There ain't but one way out the store; he never left the entire morning. If he said he drove by the cleaners when that girl was killed, he's lying."

One of the most frustrating things about reading Walter's trial record had been that the State's witnesses—Ralph Myers, Bill Hooks, and Joe Hightower—were so obviously not believable. Their testimony was laughably inconsistent and completely lacking in credibility. Myers's account of his role in the crime—Walter kidnapping him to drive him to the crime scene and then dropping him off afterward—never made any sense. Hooks, a critical witness against McMillian, wasn't persuasive or reliable in the transcript—he just repeated the same story he'd given the police about driving by the cleaners at the time of the crime. His response to every line of questioning was to repeat over and over again that he saw Walter McMillian walk out of the store with a bag, get into his "low-rider" truck, and get driven away by a white man. He could not answer any of Chestnut's questions about what else he saw that day or what he was doing in the area. He just kept repeating that he saw McMillian at the cleaners. But the state needed Hooks's testimony.

My plan had been to immediately appeal Walter's conviction to the Alabama Court of Criminal Appeals. The State had done so little to prove Walter's guilt that there weren't a lot of legal issues to appeal, but the evidence against him was so unpersuasive that I was hopeful the court might overturn the conviction simply because it was so unreliable. Once the case was on direct appeal, no new evidence would be considered. The time for filing a motion for a new trial in the trial court—the last chance to introduce new facts before an appeal begins—had already expired. Chestnut and Boynton, Walter's lawyers for the initial trial, had filed a motion before withdrawing, and Judge Key had quickly denied it. Darnell said he told Walter's former lawyers what he told me and they had raised it in the motion for a new trial, but no one took it seriously.

In capital cases, a motion for a new trial is routinely filed but rarely granted. But if the defendant alleges new evidence that could lead to a different outcome in the case—or that undermines the reliability of the trial—there is typically a hearing. After speaking with Darnell, I thought about refiling his assertions before the case went up on appeal and maybe, just maybe, we could persuade local officials to retreat from the case against Walter. I made a motion to reconsider the denial of a new trial for Mr. McMillian. I immediately got an affidavit from Darnell stating that Hooks's testimony was a lie. I took the risk of talking to a few local lawyers about whether the new prosecutor might acknowledge that the conviction was unreliable and support a new trial if there was compelling new evidence.

Several people had suggested that Tom Chapman, the new Monroe County district attorney and a former criminal defense attorney, would be fairer and more sympathetic to someone wrongly convicted than lifelong prosecutor Ted Pearson. After Pearson's long tenure as D.A., Chapman's election represented something of a new era. He was in his forties and had talked about modernizing law enforcement in the region. Some said that he was ambitious and might want to run for statewide office someday. I also discovered that he had represented Karen Kelly in a prior proceeding, which told me that he was already familiar with the case. I was hopeful.

I was still sorting out how to proceed when Darnell called me at my office.

"Mr. Stevenson, you have to help. They arrested me this morning and took me to the jail. I just got out on bond."

"What?"

"I asked them what I had done. They told me I was being charged with perjury." He sounded terrified.

"Perjury? Based on what you told Mr. McMillian's lawyers a year ago? Have they come to interview you or talk to you since we got your statement? You were supposed to let me know if you heard from them."

"No, sir. I haven't heard from any of them. They just came and arrested me and told me I had been indicted for perjury."

I hung up with Darnell, shocked and furious. It was unheard of to indict someone for perjury without any investigation or compelling evidence to establish that a false statement had been made. Police and prosecutors had found out that Darnell was talking to us and they decided to punish him for it.

A few days later, I called the new D.A. to set up a meeting.

On my way to his office, I decided to give him a chance to explain what was going on, instead of angrily complaining about the insanity of indicting someone for perjury because he had contradicted a State's witness. I decided to wait until after my meeting before filing my stack of motions. This was my first meeting with anyone associated with Walter's prosecution, and I didn't want to begin with an angry accusation. I had allowed myself to believe that the people who had prosecuted Walter were just misguided, possibly incompetent. I knew some of them were bigoted and abusive, but I guess I held out the hope that they could be reoriented. Indicting Darnell was a worrisome signal that they were willing to threaten and intimidate people.

The Monroe County courthouse is situated in the heart of downtown Monroeville. I drove into town, parked, and entered the courthouse looking for the district attorney's office. On my only other trip to the courthouse a month earlier, I had gone to the clerk's office to pick up files and the staff had asked me where I was from. When I said Montgomery, they launched into a lecture about Monroeville's prominence as a result of Harper Lee and her famous novel. I remember how the clerk had chatted me up.

"Have you read the book? It's a wonderful story. This is a famous place. They made the old courthouse a museum, and when they made the movie Gregory Peck came here. You should go over there and stand where Mr. Peck stood—I mean, where Atticus Finch stood."

She giggled with excitement, although I imagine she said the same thing to every out-of-town attorney who wandered in. She continued talking enthusiastically about the story until I promised to visit the museum as soon as I could. I refrained from explaining that I was too busy working on the case of an innocent black man the community was trying to execute after a racially biased prosecution.

During this trip I was in a different frame of mind. The last thing I was interested in was a fictional story about justice. I walked through the courthouse until I found the district attorney's office. I announced myself to the secretary, who eyed me suspiciously before directing me into Chapman's office. He walked over to shake my hand.

Chapman started off by saying, "Mr. Stevenson, lots of people want to meet you. I told them you were coming down but decided that just you and I should talk." It didn't surprise me that word had gotten around and that people were talking about Walter's new attorney. I had talked to enough people in the community to know that people would be discussing my efforts on Walter's behalf. My guess is that Judge Key had already characterized me as misguided and uncooperative simply because I didn't get off the case, as he had directed.

Chapman had a medium build, curly hair, and glasses that suggested he didn't mind looking like someone who spent time reading and studying. I'd met prosecutors who dressed and presented like they would rather be out hunting ducks than running a law office, but Chapman was professional and courteous and approached me with a pleasant demeanor. I was intrigued that he would immediately give voice to the concerns of other people in law enforcement and was initially encouraged that he meant for us to have a candid conversation free of distractions and posturing.

"Well, I appreciate that," I said. "I'm very concerned about this McMillian case. I've read the record, and to be honest I have serious doubts about his guilt and the reliability of this conviction."

"Well, this was a big case, there's no doubt about that. You do understand that I didn't have anything to do with the prosecution, don't you?"

"Yes, I do."

"This was one of the most outrageous crimes in Monroe County history, and your client made a lot of people here extremely angry. People are still angry, Mr. Stevenson. There's not enough bad that can happen to Walter McMillian for some of them."

This was a disappointing beginning—he seemed completely convinced of Walter's guilt. But I pressed on.

"Well, it was an outrageous, tragic crime, so anger is understandable," I replied. "But it doesn't accomplish anything to convict the wrong person. Whether Mr. McMillian has done anything wrong is what the trial should resolve. If the trial is unfair, or if witnesses have given false testimony, then we can't really know whether he's guilty or not."

"Well, you may be the only person right now who thinks the trial was unfair. Like I said, I wasn't involved in the prosecution."

I was becoming frustrated, and Chapman probably saw me shift in my seat. I thought about the dozens of black people I'd met who had complained bitterly about Walter's prosecution, and I was starting to see Chapman as either naive or willfully indifferent—or worse. I tried unsuccessfully not to let my disappointment show.

"I'm not the only person with questions about this case, Mr. Chapman. There's a whole community of people, some of whom claim to have been with Walter McMillian miles away when the crime was committed, who believe in his innocence. There are people for whom he's worked who are absolutely convinced that he did not commit this crime."

"I've talked to some of those people," Chapman responded, "and they can only have uninformed opinions. They don't have facts. Look, I can tell you right now that nobody cares who slept with Karen Kelly. There is evidence that implicates Walter McMillian for this murder, and my job is to defend this conviction." He was becoming more argumentative, and his voice was rising. The calm and curious look he had initially given me was shifting into anger and disgust.

"Well, you've indicted someone for perjury for contradicting the state's case. Do you intend to prosecute everyone who challenges the evidence in this case?"

My voice was now rising in exactly the way I wanted to avoid, but I was provoked by his attitude. "Alabama case law is clear that a perjury charge can't be filed in the absence of clear and convincing evidence that a false statement has been made," I went on. "A perjury indictment seems like a tactic designed to intimidate and discourage people from coming forward with evidence that contradicts the State's case. The charge against Mr. Houston seems really inappropriate, Mr. Chapman, and legally indefensible."

I knew I was lecturing him and knew he didn't like it, but I wanted him to know that we were going to defend Walter in a serious way.

"Are you representing Darnell Houston now, too?"

"Yes, I am."

"Well, I'm not sure you can do that, Mr. Stevenson. I think you might have a conflict there," he said, and then his voice shifted from argumentative to blandly matter-of-fact. "But don't worry, I may drop the perjury charges against Houston. Now that the judge has denied your motion to reopen the case, I don't have any interest in pursuing charges against Darnell Houston. But I do want people to know that if they make false statements concerning this case, they are going to be held accountable."

I was confused and a little stunned.

"What are you talking about? The motion to reconsider has been denied?"

"Yes, the judge has already denied your motion. You must not have gotten your copy of his order. He's down in Mobile now, so sometimes there are mail issues."

I tried to conceal my surprise about the court's ruling on the motion without even permitting a hearing. I asked, "So you have no interest in investigating what Darnell Houston is saying about the possibility that the State's main witness may be lying?"

"Ralph Myers is the State's main witness."

It was clear that Chapman had looked more deeply into the case than he had initially claimed.

"Without Hooks's testimony, the conviction wouldn't be valid," I said, leveling my voice. "Under the State's theory, Myers is an accomplice, and state law requires confirmation of accomplice testimony, which can only come from Hooks. Mr. Houston says that Hooks is lying, which makes his testimony a critical issue that should be heard in court."

I knew I was right. The law was as clear as it possibly could be on this question. But I also knew that I was talking to someone who didn't care what the law said. I knew that what I was saying wouldn't persuade Chapman, but I felt the need to say it anyway.

Chapman stood up. I could tell he was annoyed by my lecturing and legal arguments, and I was pretty sure he thought I was being pushy. "That sounds like an issue you'll need to raise on appeal, Mr. Stevenson. You can tell Mr. Houston that the charges against him are being dropped. I can do that for y'all, but that's about it."

His tone was dismissive, and when he turned his back to me I knew he'd ended the meeting and was now eager to get me out of his office.

I left his office extremely frustrated. Chapman had not been unfriendly or hostile. Yet his indifference to McMillian's innocence claim was hard for me to accept. Reading the record had shown me that there were people who were willing to ignore evidence, logic, and common sense to convict someone and reassure the community that the crime had been solved and the murderer punished. But talking face-to-face with someone about the case made the irrational thinking swirling around Walter's conviction much, much harder to accept.

Chapman hadn't prosecuted the case, and I had hoped that he might not want to defend something so unreliable, but it was clear that he was locked into this narrative just like everyone else who had been involved. I'd seen the abuse of power in many cases before, but there was something especially upsetting about it here, where not only a single defendant was being victimized but an entire community as well. I filed my stack of motions just to make sure that if they didn't dismiss the charges they knew we would fight them. Walking down the hallway to my car I saw yet another flyer about the next production of *To Kill a Mockingbird*, which just added to my outrage.

Darnell had remained home after he posted bond. I stopped by his house to discuss my meeting with the D.A. He was thrilled to hear that the charges against him would be dropped, but he was still shaken by the whole experience. I explained that what the State had done to him was illegal and that we could pursue a civil action against them, but he had no interest in that. I didn't actually think a civil suit was a good idea since it would just leave him vulnerable to more harassment, but I didn't want him to think I was unwilling to fight on his behalf.

"Mr. Stevenson, all I wanted to do is tell the truth. I can't go to jail, and I'll be honest—these folks have scared me."

"I understand," I said, "but what they did is illegal and I want you to know you have done nothing wrong. They're the ones who have acted very, very inappropriately. They're trying to intimidate you."

"Well, it's working. What I told you is true, and I stand by it. But I can't have these folks coming after me."

"Well, the judge has denied our motion, so you don't have to testify or come to court at this point. Let me know if you have any more problems with them or if they come to speak with you about this. You can tell people that I'm your lawyer and refer them to me, okay?"

"Yes, okay. But does that mean you are my lawyer?"

"Yes, I'll represent you if anyone creates any issues behind what you've disclosed." He looked a little relieved but was still pretty rattled when I left.

I got in my car with the sinking realization that if everyone who tried to help us on this case was going to be threatened, it would be very difficult to prove Walter's innocence. If his case wasn't overturned on direct appeal, we'd have a chance to file a postconviction petition later, and we would need new evidence, new witnesses, and new facts to prove Walter's innocence. Based on the experience with Darnell, this would be extremely challenging. I decided not to worry about it now and turned my attention to the appeal. With the reconsideration denied, the appeal brief was due in twenty-eight days. I wasn't even sure how much time had elapsed since the judge's ruling, as I had never received the order.

I left for home frustrated and worried. On my drives between Monroeville and Montgomery, I had gotten used to looking at the rural farmland, the cotton fields, and the hilly countryside; I would think about what life here must have been like decades ago. This time I didn't have to imagine it. Darnell's despair, his sadness in recognizing that they could do whatever they wanted to him with impunity, was utterly disheartening. From what I could see, there simply was no commitment to the rule of law, no accountability, and little shame. Arresting someone for coming forward with credible evidence that challenged the reliability of a capital murder conviction? The more I thought about it, the more disoriented and provoked I became. It was also sobering. If they arrested people who said things that were inconvenient, how would they react if I challenged them even harder?

As I left town, I watched the sun set and darkness descend across the county landscape as it had for centuries. People would be heading home now, some to very comfortable houses where they could relax easily, secure and proud of their community. Others, people like Darnell and Walter's family, would be returning to less comfortable homes. They would not rest as easily, nor would there be much thought of community pride. For them the darkness brought a familiar unease, an uncertainty weighted with a wary, lingering fear as old as the settlement of the county itself; discomfort too longstanding and constant to merit discussion but too burdensome to ever forget. I drove away as quickly as I could.

Chapter Six

Surely Doomed

"He's just a little boy."

It was late, and I had picked up the phone after hours because no one else was in the building; it was becoming a bad habit. The older woman on the other end of the line was pleading with me after offering a heartfelt description of her grandson, who had just been jailed for murder.

"He's already been in the jail for two nights, and I can't get to him. I'm in Virginia, and my health is not good. Please tell me you'll do something."

I hesitated before answering her. Only a handful of countries permitted the death penalty for children—and the United States was one of them. Many of my Alabama clients were on death row for crimes they were accused of committing when they were sixteen- or seventeen-year-old children. Many states had changed their laws to make it easier to prosecute children as adults, and my clients were getting younger and younger. Alabama had more juveniles sentenced to death per capita than any other state—or any other country in the world. I was determined to manage the growing demand for our services by taking on new cases only if the client was facing execution or formally condemned to death row.

This woman had told me that her grandson was only fourteen. While the Supreme Court had upheld the death penalty for juveniles in a 1989 ruling, a year earlier the Court had barred the death penalty for children under the age of fifteen. Whatever perils this child faced, he was not going to be sent to death row. This lady's grandson might be facing life imprisonment without parole, but given the overwhelming number of death penalty cases on our docket, I couldn't rationalize taking on his case.

As I considered how to answer this woman's plea, she started speaking quickly, at a whisper: "Lord, please help us. Lead this man and protect us from any choice that is not yours. Help me find the words, Lord. Tell me what to say, Lord—"

I didn't want to interrupt her prayer, so I waited until she finished.

"Ma'am, I can't take the case, but I will drive down to the jail and see your grandson tomorrow. I'll see what I can do. We likely won't be able to represent him, but let me find out what's going on, and perhaps we can help you find a lawyer who can assist you."

"Mr. Stevenson, I'm so grateful."

I was tired and already feeling overwhelmed with the cases I had. And cases with juveniles took an especially severe emotional toll on everyone who touched them. But I needed to go to a courthouse near the county where this boy was being held, so it wouldn't be that big a deal to stop by and see the child.

The next morning I drove for over an hour to the county. When I got to the courthouse, I checked the clerk's file on the case and found a lengthy incident report. Because I was an attorney investigating the case on behalf of the family, the clerk let me read the file, although she wouldn't make a copy or let me take it out of the office because it involved a minor. The clerk's office was small, but it wasn't especially busy, so I sat down on an uncomfortable metal chair in a cramped corner of the room to read the statement, which mostly confirmed everything the grandmother had told me.

Charlie was fourteen years old. He weighed less than 100 pounds and was just five feet tall. He didn't have any juvenile criminal history—no prior arrests, no misconduct in school, no delinquencies or prior court appearances. He was a good student who had earned several certificates for perfect attendance at his school. His mother described him as a "great kid" who always did what she asked. But Charlie had, by his own account, shot and killed a man named George.

George was Charlie's mother's boyfriend. She referred to their relationship as a "mistake." George would often come home drunk and begin acting violently. There were three occasions in the year and a half leading up to the night of the shooting when George beat Charlie's mother so mercilessly that she required medical treatment. She never left George or made him leave, even though she told several people that she knew she should.

On the night of the shooting, George had come home very drunk. Charlie and his mother were playing cards when he arrived. He entered the house shouting, "Hey, where are you?" Charlie's mother followed his voice to the kitchen, where she let him know that she and Charlie were home playing cards. The two adults had argued earlier in the evening because she had begged him not to go out, fearing that he would come home drunk. Now she looked at him angrily when she saw him standing there, reeking of alcohol. He looked back at her, mirroring her contempt and disgust, and in a flash, he punched her hard in the face. She didn't expect him to hit her so quickly or violently—he hadn't done it like that before. She collapsed to the floor with the crush of his blow.

Charlie was standing behind his mother and saw her head slam against their metal kitchen counter as she fell. George saw Charlie standing there and glared at him coldly before brushing past him toward the bedroom, where Charlie heard him fall noisily onto the bed. Charlie's mother was lying on the floor, unconscious and bleeding badly. He knelt by his mother's side and tried to stop the bleeding.

There was some blood on her face, but it poured from an ugly cut on the back of her head. Charlie tried feverishly to revive her. He started crying, futilely asking his mother what to do. He got up and put paper towels behind her head but couldn't stop the bleeding. He frantically searched for the cloth kitchen towel because he thought that would work better and found it wrapped around a pot on the stove. His mother had cooked black-eyed peas for dinner; he loved black-eyed peas. They'd eaten together before they'd started playing pinochle, his favorite card game.

Charlie replaced the paper towels with the cloth towel and panicked all over again when he saw how much blood there was. He was quietly begging his mother to wake up when it appeared to him that she wasn't breathing. He thought he should call an ambulance, but the phone was in the bedroom with George. George had never hit Charlie, but he terrified him just the same. As a younger child, whenever Charlie got very scared or anxious, he would sometimes start trembling and shaking. The shaking would almost always be followed by a nosebleed.

Sitting on the kitchen floor with his mother's blood all around him, Charlie could feel himself starting to tremble, and within seconds the blood slowly began to trickle out of his nose. His mother would always run to get something to help with his nosebleeds, but now she just lay on the floor. He wiped the blood from his nose and focused on the fact that he had to do something. His trembling stopped. His mother hadn't moved in nearly fifteen minutes. The house was quiet. The only sound he heard was George breathing heavily in the other room; soon he could hear him snoring.

Charlie had been slowly stroking his mother's hair, desperately hoping that she would open her eyes. The blood from her head had saturated the towel and was spreading onto Charlie's pants. Charlie thought his mother might be dying or was maybe even already dead. He had to call an ambulance. He stood up, flooded with anxiety, and cautiously made his way to the bedroom. Charlie saw George on the bed asleep and felt a surge of hatred for this man. He had never liked him, never understood why his mother had let him live with them. George didn't like Charlie, either; he was rarely friendly to the boy. Even when he wasn't drunk, George seemed angry all the time. His mother had told Charlie that George could be sweet, but Charlie never saw any of that. Charlie knew that George's first wife and child had been killed in a car accident and that was why Charlie's mom said he drank so much. In the eighteen months that George lived with them, it seemed to Charlie that there had been nothing but violence, loud arguments, pushing and shoving, threats, and turmoil. His mother had stopped smiling the way she used to; she'd become nervous and jumpy, and now, he thought, she's on the kitchen floor, dead.

Charlie walked to the dresser against the back wall of the bedroom to reach the phone. He had called 911 a year earlier, after George had hit his mom, but she had directed him to do so and told him what to say. When he reached the phone, he wasn't sure why he didn't just pick up the receiver. He could never really explain why he opened the dresser drawer instead, put his hand under the folded white T-shirts his mom had laundered, and felt for the handgun he knew George kept hidden there. He'd found it there when George had said Charlie could wear an Auburn University T-shirt someone had given him. It was way too small for George and way too big for Charlie, but he'd been grateful to have it; it had been one of George's few kind gestures. This time he didn't pull his hand back in fear as he had before. He picked up the gun. He'd never fired a gun before, but he knew he could do it.

George was now snoring rhythmically.

Charlie walked over to the bed, his arms stretched out, pointing the gun at George's head. As Charlie hovered over him, the snoring stopped. The room grew very, very quiet. And that's when Charlie pulled the trigger.

The sound of the bullet firing was much louder than Charlie had expected. The gun jerked and pushed Charlie a step back; he almost lost his balance and fell. He looked at George and squeezed his eyes closed; it was horrible. He could feel himself starting to tremble again, and that's when he heard his mother moaning in the kitchen. He couldn't believe she was alive. He ran back to the phone and called 911, then sat next to his mother until the police arrived.

After learning all of this, I was positive they would not prosecute Charlie as an adult. I continued to read the file and the notes from the initial court appearance. The prosecutor did not dispute the account that Charlie and his mother had given. It was only when I continued reading that I discovered that George was a local police officer. The prosecutor made a long argument about what a great man George had been and how upsetting his death had been for everyone in the community. "George was a law enforcement officer who served with honor," the prosecutor argued. "It is a great loss for the county and a tragedy that a good person could be so heartlessly killed by this young man." The prosecutor insisted that Charlie be tried as an adult, and he announced that he intended to seek the maximum punishment permitted by law. The judge agreed that this was capital murder and that the boy should be tried as an adult. Charlie was immediately taken to the county jail for adults.

The small county jail was across the street from the courthouse. Like many Southern communities, the courthouse anchored the square that marked the town center. I stepped outside and walked across the street to the jail to see this young man. The jailers clearly didn't receive a lot of out-of-town lawyers for legal visits. The deputy on duty looked at me suspiciously before taking me into the jail, where I sat in the small attorney meeting room waiting for Charlie. From the time I finished reading the file, I couldn't stop thinking about how tragic this case was—and my somber thoughts weren't interrupted until a small child was pushed into the visiting room. This boy seemed way too short, way too thin, and way too scared to be fourteen. I looked at the jailer, who seemed to share my surprise at how small and terrified the child appeared. I asked them to remove the handcuffs. Sometimes in jails like this, the guards resist uncuffing clients, arguing that it's not safe or permitted to take the handcuffs off a suspect during a legal visit. They worry that if a person gets upset or becomes violent, being uncuffed will make him or her harder to subdue.

This guard didn't hesitate to take the handcuffs off this child before leaving the room.

We were sitting at a wooden table that was probably four by six feet. Charlie was on one side of the table, and I was on the other. It had been three days since his arrest.

"Charlie, my name is Bryan. Your grandmother called me and asked me if I would come and see you. I'm a lawyer, and I help people who get in trouble or who are accused of crimes, and I'd like to help you."

The boy wouldn't make eye contact with me. He was tiny, but he had big, beautiful eyes. He had a close haircut that was common for little boys because it required no maintenance. It made him look even younger than he was. I thought I saw tattoos or symbols on his neck, but when I looked more closely, I realized that they were bruises.

"Charlie, are you okay?"

He was staring intensely to my left, looking at the wall as if he saw something there. His distant look was so alarming that I actually turned to see if there was something of interest behind me, but it was just a blank wall. The disconnected look, the sadness in his face, and his complete lack of engagement—qualities he shared with a lot of the other teenagers I'd worked with—were the only things that made me believe he was fourteen. I sat and waited for a very long time in the hope that he would give me some kind of response, but the room remained silent. He stared at the wall and then looked down at his own wrists. He wrapped his right hand around his left wrist where the handcuffs had been and rubbed the spot where the metal had pinched him.

"Charlie, I want to make sure you're doing okay, so I just need you to answer a few questions for me, okay?" I knew he could hear me; whenever I spoke, he would lift his head and return his gaze to the spot on the wall.

"Charlie, if I were you, I'd be pretty scared and really worried right now, but I'd also want someone to help me. I'd like to help, okay?" I waited for a response, but none was forthcoming.

"Charlie, can you speak? Are you okay?" He stared at the wall when I spoke and then back at his wrists when I was finished, but he didn't say a word.

"We don't have to talk about George. We don't have to talk about what happened; we can talk about whatever you want. Is there something you want to talk about?" I was waiting for longer and longer stretches after each question, desperately hoping that he would say something, but he didn't.

"Do you want to talk about your mom? She's going to be fine. I've checked, and even though she can't visit you, she's going to be fine. She's worried about you."

I thought talking about his mother would spark something in Charlie's eyes. When it didn't, I became even more concerned about the child.

I noticed that there was a second chair on Charlie's side of the table, and I realized that lawyers were apparently supposed to sit on that side and the clients on the side I chose, where there was only one chair. I'd sat in the wrong place.

I lowered my voice and spoke more softly, "Charlie, you've got to talk to me. I can't help you if you don't. Would you just say your name—say something, please?" He continued to stare at the wall. I waited and then stood up and walked around the table. He didn't look at me as I moved but returned his gaze to his wrist. I sat in the chair next to him, leaned close, and said quietly, "Charlie, I'm really sorry if you're upset, but please talk to me. I can't help you if you don't talk to me." He leaned back in his chair for the first time, nearly placing his head on the wall behind us. I pulled my chair closer to him and leaned back in mine. We sat silently for a long time and then I started saying silly things, because I didn't know what else to do.

"Well, you won't tell me what you're thinking, so I guess I'm going to just have to tell you what I'm thinking. I bet you think you know what I'm thinking," I said playfully, "but in fact you really couldn't possibly imagine. You probably think I'm thinking about the law, or the judge, or the po-lice, or why won't this young man speak with me. But what I'm actually thinking about is food. Yes, that's right, Charlie," I continued teasingly, "I'm thinking about fried chicken and collard greens cooked with turkey meat and sweet potato biscuits. . . . You ever had a sweet potato biscuit?"

Nothing.

"You've probably never had a sweet potato biscuit, and that's a shame."

Still nothing. I kept going.

"I'm thinking about getting a new car because my car is so old." I waited. Nothing. "Charlie, you're supposed to say, 'How old is it, Bryan?' and then I say my car is so old—"

He never smiled or responded; he just continued looking at the spot on the wall, his face frozen in sadness.

"What kind of car do you think I should get?" I went through a range of ridiculous musings that yielded nothing from Charlie. He continued to lean back, and his body seemed a little less tense. I noticed that our shoulders were now touching.

After a while I tried again. "Come on, Charlie, what's going on? You've got to talk to me, son." I started leaning on him somewhat playfully, until he sat forward a bit, and then I finally felt him lean back into me. I took a chance and put my arm around him, and he immediately began to shake. His trembling intensified before he finally leaned completely into me and started crying. I put my head to his and said, "It's okay, it's all right." He was sobbing when he finally spoke. It didn't take me long to realize that he wasn't talking about what had happened with George or with his mom but about what had happened at the jail.

"There were three men who hurt me on the first night. They touched me and made me do things." Tears were streaming down his face. His voice was high-pitched and strained with anguish.

"They came back the next night and hurt me a lot," he said, becoming more hysterical with each word. Then he looked in my face for the first time.

"There were so many last night. I don't know how many there were, but they hurt me . . . ."

He was crying too hard to finish his sentence. He gripped my jacket with a force I wouldn't have imagined he was capable of exerting.

I held him and told him as gently as I could, "It's going to be okay. It's going to be okay." I'd never held anyone who gripped me as tightly as that child or who cried as hard or as long. It seemed like his tears would never end. He would tire and then start again. I just decided to hold him until he stopped. It was almost an hour before he calmed down and the crying stopped. I promised him that I would try to get him out of there right away. He begged me not to leave, but I assured him that I would be back that day. We never talked about the crime.

When I left the jail, I was more angry than sad. I kept asking myself, "Who is responsible for this? How could we ever allow this?" I went directly to the sheriff's office inside the jail and explained to the overweight, middle-aged sheriff what the child had told me, and I insisted that they immediately place him in a protected single cell. The sheriff listened with a distracted look on his face, but when I said I was going to see the judge, he agreed to move the child into a protected area immediately. I then went back across the street to the courthouse and found the judge, who called the prosecutor. When the prosecutor arrived in the judge's chambers, I told them that the child had been sexually abused and raped. They agreed to move him to a nearby juvenile facility within the next several hours.

I decided to take on the case. We ultimately got Charlie's case transferred to juvenile court, where the shooting was adjudicated as a juvenile offense. That meant Charlie wouldn't be sent to an adult prison, and he would likely be released before he turned eighteen, in just a few years. I visited Charlie regularly, and in time he recovered. He was a smart, sensitive child who was tormented by what he'd done and what he'd been through.

At a talk I gave at a church months later, I spoke about Charlie and the plight of incarcerated children. Afterward, an older married couple approached me and insisted that they had to help Charlie. I tried to dissuade these kind people from thinking they could do anything, but I gave them my card and told them they could call me. I didn't expect to hear from them, but within days they called, and they were persistent. We eventually agreed that they would write a letter to Charlie and send it to me to pass on to him. When I received the letter weeks later, I read it. It was remarkable.

Mr. and Mrs. Jennings were a white couple in their mid-seventies from a small community northeast of Birmingham. They were kind and generous people who were active in their local United Methodist church. They never missed a Sunday service and were especially drawn to children in crisis. They spoke softly and always seemed to be smiling but never appeared to be anything less than completely genuine and compassionate. They were affectionate with each other in a way that was endearing, frequently holding hands and leaning into each other. They dressed like farmers and owned ten acres of land, where they grew vegetables and lived simply. Their one and only grandchild, whom they had helped raise, had committed suicide when he was a teenager, and they had never stopped grieving for him. Their grandson struggled with mental health problems during his short life, but he was a smart kid and they had been putting money away to send him to college. They explained in their letter that they wanted to use the money they'd saved for their grandson to help Charlie.

Eventually, Charlie and this couple began corresponding with one another, building up to the day when the Jenningses met Charlie at the juvenile detention facility. They later told me that they "loved him instantly." Charlie's grandmother had died a few months after she first called me, and his mother was still struggling after the tragedy of the shooting and Charlie's incarceration. Charlie had been apprehensive about meeting with the Jenningses because he thought they wouldn't like him, but he told me after they left how much they seemed to care about him and how comforting that was. The Jenningses became his family.

At one point early on, I tried to caution them against expecting too much from Charlie after his release. "You know, he's been through a lot. I'm not sure he can just carry on as if nothing has ever happened. I want you to understand he may not be able to do everything you'd like him to do."

They never accepted my warnings. Mrs. Jennings was rarely disagreeable or argumentative, but I had learned that she would grunt when someone said something she didn't completely accept. She told me, "We've all been through a lot, Bryan, all of us. I know that some have been through more than others. But if we don't expect more from each other, hope better for one another, and recover from the hurt we experience, we are surely doomed."

The Jenningses helped Charlie get his general equivalency degree in detention and insisted on financing his college education. They were there, along with his mother, to take him home when he was released.

Chapter Seven

Justice Denied

Walter's appeal was denied.

The seventy-page opinion from the Alabama Court of Criminal Appeals affirming his conviction and death sentence was devastating. I'd filed a lengthy brief that documented the insufficiency of the evidence and raised every legal deficiency in the trial that I could identify. I argued that there was no credible corroboration of Myers's testimony and that under Alabama law the State couldn't rely exclusively on the testimony of an accomplice. I argued that there was prosecutorial misconduct, racially discriminatory jury selection, and an improper change of venue. I even challenged Judge Robert E. Lee Key's override of the jury's life sentence, though I knew the reduction of an innocent man's death sentence to life imprisonment without parole would still have been an egregious miscarriage of justice. The court rejected all of my arguments.

I didn't think it would turn out this way. At the oral argument months earlier, I'd been hopeful as I walked into the imposing Alabama Judicial Building and stood in the grand appellate courtroom that was formerly a Scottish Rite Freemasonry temple. Constructed in the 1920s, the building was renovated into a cavernous courthouse in the 1940s, complete with marble floors and an impressive domed ceiling. It stood at the end of Dexter Avenue in Montgomery, across the street from the historic Dexter Avenue Baptist Church, where Dr. Martin Luther King Jr. had pastored during the Montgomery Bus Boycott. A block away was the state capitol, adorned with three banners: the American flag, the white and red state flag of Alabama, and the battle flag of the Confederacy.

The Alabama Court of Criminal Appeals courtroom was on the second floor. The chief judge of the court was former governor John Patterson. He had made national news in the 1960s as a fierce opponent of civil rights and racial integration. In 1958, with the backing of the Ku Klux Klan, he defeated George Wallace for governor. His positions were even more pro-segregation than Wallace's (who, having learned his lesson, would become the most famous segregationist in America, declaring in 1963 "segregation now, segregation tomorrow, segregation forever" just a block away from this courthouse). When he was attorney general before becoming governor, Patterson banned the NAACP from operating in Alabama and blocked civil rights boycotts and protests in Tuskegee and Montgomery. As governor, he withheld law enforcement protection for the Freedom Riders—the black and white college students and activists who traveled south in the early 1960s to desegregate public facilities in recognition of new federal laws. When the Freedom Riders' bus traveled through Alabama, they were abandoned by the police. Alone and unprotected, they were beaten violently, and their bus was bombed.

Still, I forced myself to be hopeful. That was all long ago. During my argument, the court's five judges looked at me with curiosity but asked few questions. I chose to interpret their silence as agreement. I hoped they saw so little support for the conviction that they didn't think there was much to discuss. Judge Patterson's only remark during the oral argument came at the end, when he slowly but firmly asked a single question that echoed through the mostly empty courtroom.

"Where are you from?"

I was thrown by the question and hesitated before answering.

"I live in Montgomery, sir."

I had foolishly discouraged McMillian's family from attending the oral argument because I knew that the issues were fairly arcane and that there would be very little discussion of the facts. Supporters would have to take off from work and make the long drive to Montgomery for an early morning argument. Since each side had only thirty minutes to present, I hadn't thought it worth the effort. When I sat down after the argument, I regretted that decision. I would have appreciated some sympathetic faces in the courtroom to signal to the court that this case was different, but there were none.

An assistant attorney general then presented the State's arguments—capital cases on appeal were managed by the attorney general, not the local district attorney. The State's lawyer argued that this was a routine capital murder case and that the death penalty had been appropriately imposed. Following the oral argument, I still had hope that the court would overturn the conviction and sentence because it was so clearly unsupported by reliable facts. State law required credible corroboration of accomplice testimony in a murder case, and there simply wasn't any in Walter's case. I believed that the court would have a hard time affirming a conviction with so little evidence. I was wrong.

I drove to the prison to deliver the news. Walter didn't say anything as I explained the situation, but he had a strange, despairing look on his face. I had tried to prepare him for the possibility that it could take years to get his conviction overturned, but he had gotten his hopes up.

"They aren't ever going to admit they made a mistake," he said glumly. "They know I didn't do this. They just can't admit to being wrong, to looking bad."

"We're just getting started, Walter," I replied. "There is a lot more to do, and we're going to make them confront this."

I was telling the truth: We did have to press on. Our plan was to ask the Court of Criminal Appeals to reconsider its decision, and if that turned out to be a dead end, we would seek review in the Alabama

Supreme Court. And we had uncovered even more evidence of Walter's innocence.

After filing the appeal brief, I'd continued investigating the case intensively. If we hadn't come up with so much new evidence to prove Walter's innocence, I think the court's ruling would have been even more overwhelming. I told Walter before I left the prison, "They don't know what we now know about your innocence. As soon as we present the new evidence to them, they'll think differently." My hopefulness was genuine, in spite of everything that had happened already. But I was underestimating the resistance we would face.

I'd finally been able to hire some additional lawyers for the organization, which gave me more time to investigate Walter's case. One of my new hires was Michael O'Connor, a recent Yale Law School graduate with a passion for helping people in trouble that had been kindled by his own struggles earlier in life. The son of Irish immigrants, Michael had grown up outside of Philadelphia in a tough working-class neighborhood. When his high school friends started experimenting with hard drugs, so did Mike, and he soon developed a heroin addiction. His life descended into a nightmare of drug dependency and chaos, complete with the growing risk of death by overdose. For several years he floated from one crisis to another until the overdose death of a close friend motivated him to crawl his way back to sobriety. Throughout all of this heartache, his family had never abandoned him. They helped him stabilize his life and find his way back to college. At Penn State he revealed himself to be a brilliant student, graduating summa cum laude. His academic credentials got him into Yale Law School, but his heart was still connected to all the brokenness his years on the street had shown him.

When I interviewed him for the job, he was apologetic about the darker episodes in his past, but I thought he was perfect for the kind of staff we were trying to build. He signed up, moved to Montgomery, and without hesitation jumped into the McMillian case with me. We spent days tracking leads, interviewing dozens of people, following wild rumors, investigating different theories. I was increasingly persuaded that we would have to figure out who really had killed Ronda Morrison to win Walter's release. Aside from my appreciation for Michael's invaluable help with the work itself, I was grateful finally to have someone around to share the insanity of the case with—just as I was discovering that it was even crazier than I thought.

After a few months of investigation, we'd uncovered strong evidence to support Walter's innocence. We discovered that Bill Hooks had been paid by Sheriff Tate for his testimony against Walter—we found checks in the county's financial records showing close to $5,000 in payments to Hooks in reward money and "expenses." Sheriff Tate had also paid Hooks money to travel back and forth out of the county around the time of the trial. This information should have been disclosed to Walter's counsel prior to trial so that they could have used it to cast doubt on the credibility of Hooks's testimony.

We also found out that Hooks had been released from jail immediately after giving the police his statement that he'd seen Walter's "low-rider" truck at the cleaners on the day of the murder. We found court records revealing that the D.A. and the sheriff, who are *county* officials, had somehow gotten *city* charges and fines against Hooks dismissed, even though they had no authority in city courts. Under U.S. Supreme Court precedent, that Hooks had charges against him dismissed in exchange for cooperation with authorities was information that the State was obligated to reveal to the defense. But, of course, they hadn't.

We found the white man who was running the store on the day that Ralph Myers came in for the purpose of giving a note to Walter. Walter had tried to persuade his original lawyers to speak to this man, but they had failed to do so. After Walter described the location of the store, we were able to track him down. The storeowner recounted his memory of that day: Myers had sought out Walter—but had to ask the storeowner which of the several black men in the store was Walter McMillian. Months after the crime, the storeowner was adamant that Myers had never seen Walter McMillian before.

In a church basement, Walter's sister found flyers advertising the fish fry held at Walter's house; they confirmed that the event had taken place on the same day as the Morrison murder. A white storeowner who had no relationship to Walter or his family had kept a copy of that flyer for some reason, and he confirmed that he had received it before the Morrison murder. We even tracked down Clay Kast, the white mechanic who had modified Walter's truck and converted it to a low-rider. He confirmed that the work had been done over six months *after* Ronda Morrison was murdered. This proved that McMillian's truck had had no modifications or special features and therefore could not have been the truck described by Myers and Hooks at the trial.

I was feeling very good about the progress we were making when I got a call that would become the most significant break in the case.

The voice said, "Mr. Stevenson, this is Ralph Myers."

Our secretary had told me there was a "Mr. Miles" on the phone, so I was a little shocked to hear Ralph Myers on the other end of the line. Before I could compose myself, he spoke again.

"I think you need to come and see me. I have something I need to tell you," he said dramatically.

Myers was imprisoned at the St. Clair Correctional Facility in Springville, Alabama, and Michael and I made plans to meet him there in three days.

Michael and I had started running a few miles at night after work to help us wind down from the increasingly long work days. Montgomery has a beautiful park that houses the Alabama Shakespeare Festival, which brings nationally acclaimed playwrights and actors to Alabama to perform Shakespeare and modern theatrical productions. The theater is set among hundreds of acres of beautifully maintained parkland with lakes and ponds. There are several trails for running. That evening we spent most of our run speculating about what Myers would tell us.

"Why would Myers call us now?" Michael asked. "Can you imagine just going into a courtroom and straight-up making up a story that

puts an innocent man on death row? I'm not sure we can trust anything he says."

"Well, you may be right, but he had a lot of help in putting together
that testimony. Remember, they also put Myers on death row to coerce some of those statements. Who knows? He may be in touch with
the State now, and this is some kind of setup where they are trying to
mislead us."

I hadn't seriously considered that possibility until our run that
night. I thought again about how sleazy Myers had been during the
trial. "We have to be careful to not reveal information to Myers—just
get information he has. But we have to talk to him because if he re-
cants his trial testimony, the State has nothing on Walter."

We agreed that depending on what he had to say, Myers could
change everything for us. We had made a lot of progress in disproving
the testimony of Bill Hooks; with the appearance of Darnell Houston, the new evidence about the condition of Walter's truck, and the
discovery of the assistance given Hooks by law enforcement, his testimony was now riddled with credibility issues. But getting a recantation from Myers would be a much bigger deal. Myers's bizarre
accusations and testimony were the basis of the State's entire case.

Having read Myers's testimony and reviewed the records that were
available about him, I knew that he had a tragic background and a
complex personality. Walter and his family had described Myers as
pure evil for the lies he had told during the trial. The experience of
being so coldly lied about at trial by someone you don't even know
was one of the most disquieting parts of the trial for Walter. When
Walter called me at the office the next day, I told him we'd heard from
Myers and that we were going to see what he had to say. Walter
warned me: "He's a snake. Be careful."

Michael and I drove two hours to the state prison in Springville, in
St. Clair County. The prison is in a rural area northeast of Birming-

ham, where the Alabama terrain starts to turn rocky and mountain-ous. The maximum-security prison was more recently built than Holman or Donaldson, the other maximum-security prisons in Ala-bama, but no one would suggest that St. Clair was modern. Michael and I cleared security at the prison entrance; the guard who patted us down said he'd been working at the prison for three months, and this was the first time he'd had a legal visit during his shift. We were di-rected down a long corridor that led to a flight of stairs that took us deeper inside the prison. We were admitted through several secure metal doors into the large room that served as the visitation area. It was typical: There were vending machines against the back walls and small rectangular tables where inmates could meet with family mem-bers. The familiarity of the setting did little to calm us. Michael and I put our notepads and pens on one of the tables and then paced around the room, waiting for Myers.

When Myers walked into the visitation area, I was surprised at how old he seemed. His hair was almost completely gray, which made him seem frail and vulnerable. He was also shorter with a much smaller body frame than I was expecting. His testimony had caused so much anguish for Walter and his family that I had created a larger-than-life image of him. He walked toward us but stopped short when he saw Michael and nervously blurted out, "Who is he? You didn't tell me you were bringing anybody with you." Myers had a thick Southern accent. Up close, his scars made him appear more sympathetic than menacing or villainous.

"This is Michael O'Connor. He's a lawyer in my office working with me on this case. Michael is just helping me investigate this case."

"Well, people told me I could trust you. I don't know anything about him."

"I promise, he's fine." I glanced over at Michael, who was trying his best to look trustworthy, before turning back to Myers. "Please have a seat."

He looked at Michael skeptically and then slowly sat down. My plan was to try to ease him into the conversation by letting him know that we just wanted the truth. But before I could say anything, Myers blurted out a full recantation of his trial testimony.

"I lied. Everything I said at McMillian's trial was a lie. I've lost a lot of sleep and have been in a lot of pain over this. I can't be quiet any longer."

"The testimony you gave at trial against Walter McMillian was a lie?" I asked cautiously.

My heart was pounding, but I tried to stay as steady as I could. I was afraid that if I seemed too eager or too surprised—too *anything*—he might retreat.

"It was all a lie. What I'm going to tell you is going to blow your mind, Mr. Stevenson."

He held his stare on me dramatically before turning to Michael. "You, too, Jimmy Connors." It didn't take many conversations with Ralph before it became clear that he had difficulty remembering names.

"Mr. Myers, you know I'm going to want you to not only tell me the truth but also tell the court the truth. Are you willing to do that?"

I was nervous to push so quickly, but I needed to be clear. I didn't want a private performance.

"That's why I called you." He sounded surprised that there could be any question about his intentions. "I've been in a group therapy class here. You're supposed to be real honest. We been talking about honesty for nearly three months. Last week people were talking about all the bad shit that happened to them when they were kids and all the bad things they done."

Myers was picking up steam as he spoke.

"I finally told the group, 'Well, I can top all you sons 'a bitches, I done put a damn man on death row by lying in damn court.'"

He paused dramatically.

"After I told all of 'em what I'd done, everybody said I needed to make it right. That's what I'm tryin' to do." He paused again to let me take it all in. "Hey, y'all gonna buy me a damn soda, or am I just gonna sit here all day looking at them damn vending machines and pouring my heart out?" He smiled for the first time since we'd been together. Michael jumped up and walked over to buy him a drink.

"Hey, Jimmy, Sunkist Orange, if they got it."

For more than two hours, I asked questions and Ralph gave answers. By the end, he did, in fact, blow my mind. He told us about being pressured by the sheriff and the ABI and threatened with the death penalty if he didn't testify against McMillian. He made accusations of official corruption, talked about his involvement in the Pittman murder, and revealed his earlier attempts to recant. He ultimately admitted that he had never known anything about the Morrison murder, had no clue what had happened to her or anything else at all about the crime. He said that he had told lots of people—from the D.A. on down—that he had been coerced to testify falsely against Walter. If even half of what he said was true, there were a lot of people involved in this case who knew, from the mouth of his sole accuser, that Walter McMillian had had nothing to do with the murder of Ronda Morrison.

Ralph was on his third Sunkist Orange when he stopped his stream of confessions, leaned forward, and beckoned us closer. He spoke in a whisper to Michael and me.

"You know they'll try to kill you if you actually get to the bottom of everything."

We would learn that Ralph could never let a meeting end without dropping some final dramatic insight, observation, or prediction. I reassured him that we would be careful.

On the drive back to Montgomery, Michael and I debated how much we could trust Myers. What he told us about the McMillian case all made sense. His story at trial was so implausible that it was easy to believe that he had been pressured to testify falsely. The corruption narrative that he seemed intent to expose was harder to assess. Myers claimed to have committed the Vickie Pittman murder under the di-

rection of another local sheriff; he laid out to us a widespread con-
spiracy involving police, drug dealing, and money laundering. It was
quite a tale.

We spent weeks following up on the leads that Myers had provided.
He admitted to us that he had never met Walter and only knew of him
through Karen Kelly. He also confirmed that he had been spending
time with Karen Kelly and that she was involved in the Pittman murder. So we decided to confirm the story with Kelly herself, now a prisoner at the Tutwiler Prison for Women, where she was serving a
ten-year sentence for the Pittman murder. Tutwiler is one of the
state's oldest prisons and the only prison in the state for women. It has
fewer security restrictions than the men's prisons. When Michael and
I drove up to the gate, we could see incarcerated women hovering
outside the prison entrance with no officers in view. The women eyed
Michael and me carefully before greeting us with curious smiles. We
were subjected to a very cursory pat-down in the prison lobby by a
male officer before being admitted through the barred gate to the
main prison area. We were told to wait for Karen Kelly in a very small
room that was empty except for a square table.

Kelly was a slender white woman in her mid-thirties who walked
into the room wearing no restraints or handcuffs. She seemed surprisingly comfortable, shaking my hand confidently before nodding at
Michael. She was wearing makeup, including a garish shade of green
eye shadow. She sat down and announced that Walter had been framed
and that she was grateful finally to be able to tell someone. When we
began with our questions, she quickly confirmed that Myers had not
known Walter before the Morrison murder.

"Ralph is a fool. He thought he could trust those crooked cops, and
he let them talk him into saying he was involved with a crime he didn't
know anything about. He's done enough bad that he didn't need to go
around making stuff up."

Though she was calm at the outset of our interview, she became
increasingly emotional as she started detailing the events surrounding

the case. She wept more than once. She spoke with remorse about how her life had spiraled out of control when she started abusing drugs.

"I'm not a bad person, but I've made some really foolish, bad decisions."

She was especially upset that Walter was on death row.

"I feel like I'm the reason that he's in prison. He's just not the kind of person that would kill somebody, I know that." Then her tone turned bitter. "I made a lot of mistakes, but those people should be ashamed. They've done just as much bad as I've done. Sheriff Tate only had one thing on his mind. He just kept saying, 'Why you want to sleep with niggers? Why you want to sleep with niggers?' It was awful, and he's awful." She paused and looked down at her hands. "But I'm awful, too. Look at what I've done," she said sadly.

I began getting letters from Karen Kelly after our visit. She wanted me to tell Walter how sorry she was about what had happened to him. She said she still cared about him a great deal. It wasn't clear what we could expect from Karen if we got a new hearing in court, other than to confirm that Ralph had never met Walter. It was clear that she saw Walter as the kind of person who would never kill someone violently, which was consistent with the opinion of everyone who knew him. She hadn't dealt with the police much around the Morrison murder and didn't have useful information pointing to their misconduct, aside from being able to show how they were provoked by her relationship with Walter.

Michael and I decided to spend more time looking into the Pittman murder; we thought it might give us some perspective on the coercion that was leveled against Myers. We now knew that because Myers had recanted his accusations against Walter before the trial, the State might not be entirely surprised to hear that he was denying McMillian's involvement in the crime. We needed as much objective evidence as we could find to confirm the truth of what Myers was now saying.

Understanding the Pittman case and documenting the other demonstrably false things Myers had asserted would strengthen our evidence.

Vickie Pittman's murder had been all but forgotten. Monroe County officials had reduced Myers's and Kelly's sentences in exchange for Myers's testimony against Walter. How they managed to reduce sentences in the Pittman case, which was outside their jurisdiction in another county, was another anomaly. Myers insisted that there were other people besides him and Kelly involved in the Pittman murder, including a corrupt local sheriff. There were still questions about why Vickie Pittman had been killed. Myers told us that her murder had everything to do with drug debts and threats she had made to expose corruption.

We had learned from some of the early police reports that the father of Vickie Pittman, Vic Pittman, had been implicated as a suspect in her death. Vickie Pittman had had two aunts, Mozelle and Onzelle, who had been collecting information and desperately seeking answers to the questions surrounding their niece's death. We reached out to them on the off chance that they'd be willing to speak with us, and we were astounded when they eagerly agreed to talk.

Mozelle and Onzelle were twin sisters—they were also colorful, opinionated talkers who could be bracingly direct. The two middle-aged, rural white women spent so much time together that they could finish each other's sentences without even seeming to notice. They described themselves as "country tough" and presented themselves as fearless, relentless women who could not be intimidated.

"Just so you know: We're gun owners, so don't bring no drama when you come." This was Mozelle's last warning before I hung up the phone with her the first time we talked.

Michael and I traveled to rural Escambia County and were greeted by the twins. They invited us in, sat us at the kitchen table, and wasted no time.

"Did your client kill our baby?" Mozelle asked bluntly.

"No, ma'am, I sincerely believe he did not."

"Do you know who did?"

I sighed. "Well, not completely. We've spoken to Ralph Myers and believe that he and Karen Kelly were involved, but Myers insists that there were others involved as well."

Mozelle looked at Onzelle and leaned back.

"We know there's more involved," said Onzelle. The sisters voiced suspicions about their brother and about local law enforcement but complained that the prosecutor had disrespected and ignored them. (Vic Pittman was never formally charged for the murder.) They said they were turned away even by the state's victims' rights group.

"They treated us like we were low-class white trash. They could not have cared less about us." Mozelle looked furious as she spoke. "I thought they treated victims better. I thought we had some say."

Although crime victims had long complained about their treatment in the criminal justice system, by the 1980s a new movement had emerged that resulted in much more responsiveness to the perspective of crime victims and their families. The problem was that not all crime victims received the same treatment.

Fifty years ago, the prevailing concept in the American criminal justice system was that everyone in the community is the victim when an offender commits a violent crime. The party that prosecutes a criminal defendant is called the "State" or the "People" or the "Commonwealth" because when someone is murdered, raped, robbed, or assaulted, it is an offense against all of us. In the early 1980s, though, states started involving individual crime victims in the trial process and began "personalizing" crime victims in their presentation of cases. Some states authorized the family members of the victim to sit at the prosecutor's table during trial. Thirty-six states enacted laws that gave victims specific rights to participate in the trial process or to make victim impact statements. In many places, prosecutors started introducing themselves as the lawyer representing a particular victim, rather than as a representative of the civic authorities.

In death penalty cases, the U.S. Supreme Court said in 1987 that introducing evidence about the status, character, reputation, or family of a homicide victim was unconstitutional. The prevailing idea for decades had been that "all victims are equal"—that is, the murder of a four-year-old child of a wealthy parent is no more serious an offense than the murder of a child whose parent is in prison or even than the murder of the parent in prison. The Court prohibited jurors from hearing "victim impact" statements because they were too inflammatory and introduced arbitrariness into the capital sentencing process. Many critics argued that such evidence would ultimately disempower poor victims, victims who were racial minorities, and family members who didn't have the resources to advocate for their deceased loved ones. The Court agreed, striking down this kind of evidence in *Booth v. Maryland*.

The Court's decision was widely criticized by prosecutors and some politicians, and it seemed to energize the victims' rights movement. Less than three years later, the Court reversed itself in *Payne v. Tennessee* and upheld the rights of states to present evidence about the character of the victim in a capital sentencing trial.

With the Supreme Court now giving its constitutional blessing to a more visible and protected role for individual victims in the criminal trial process, changes in the American criminal justice process accelerated. Millions of state and federal dollars were authorized to create advocacy groups for crime victims in each state. States found countless ways for individual victims in particular crimes to become decision makers and participants. Victims' advocates were added to parole boards, and in most states they were given a formal role in state and local prosecutors' offices. Victim services and outreach became critical components of the prosecutorial function. Some states made executions more accommodating of victims by increasing the number of people from the victim's family who could watch the execution.

State legislatures enacted harsh new punishments for crimes, naming statutes after particular victims. Megan's Law, for example, which broadened state power to create sex offender registries, was named after Megan Kanka, a seven-year-old girl who was raped and murdered by a man who had previously been convicted of child molestation. Instead of a faceless state or community, crime victims were featured at trial, and criminal cases took on the dynamics of a traditional civil trial, pitting the family of the victim against the offender. Press coverage hyped the personal nature of the conflict between the offender and specific victim. A new formula emerged for criminal prosecution, especially in high-profile cases, in which the emotions, perspectives, and opinions of the victim figured prominently in how criminal cases would be managed.

However, as Mozelle and Onzelle discovered, focusing on the status of the victim became one more way for the criminal justice system to disfavor some people. Poor and minority victims of crime experienced additional victimization by the system itself. The Supreme Court's decision in *Payne* appeared shortly after the Court's decision in *McCleskey v. Kemp*, a case that presented convincing empirical evidence that the race of the victim is the greatest predictor of who gets the death penalty in the United States. The study conducted for that case revealed that offenders in Georgia were eleven times more likely to get the death penalty if the victim was white than if the victim was black. These findings were replicated in every other state where studies about race and the death penalty took place. In Alabama, even though 65 percent of all homicide victims were black, nearly 80 percent of the people on death row were there for crimes against victims who were white. Black defendant and white victim pairings increased the likelihood of a death sentence even more.

Many poor and minority victims complained that they were not getting calls or support from local police and prosecutors. Many weren't included in the conversations about whether a plea bargain was acceptable or what sentence was appropriate. If your family had lost a loved one to murder or had to suffer the anguish of rape or serious assault, your victimization might be ignored if you had loved ones who were incarcerated. The expansion of victims' rights ultimately

made formal what had always been true: Some victims are more protected and valued than others.

More than anything else, it was the lack of concern and responsiveness by police, prosecutors, and victims' services providers that devastated Mozelle and Onzelle. "You're the first two people to come to our
house and spend time with us talking about Vickie," Onzelle told us.
After nearly three hours of hearing their heartbreaking reflections, we
promised to do what we could to find out who else was involved in
their niece Vickie's death.

We were getting to the point where, without access to police records
and files, we wouldn't be able to make more progress. Because the
case was now pending on direct appeal, the State had no obligation to
let us see those records and files. So we decided to file what is known
as a Rule 32 petition, which would put us back in a trial court with the
opportunity to present new evidence and obtain discovery, including
access to the State's files.

Rule 32 petitions are required to include claims that were not raised
at trial or on appeal and that could not have been raised at trial or on
appeal. They are the vehicle to challenge a conviction based on ineffective counsel, the State's failure to disclose evidence, and most important, new evidence of innocence. Michael and I put a petition
together that asserted all of these claims, including police and prosecutorial misconduct, and filed it in the Monroe County Circuit Court.

The document, which alleged that Walter McMillian was unfairly
tried, wrongly convicted, and illegally sentenced, drew a lot of attention in Monroeville. Three years had passed since the trial. The initial
confirmation of Walter's conviction on appeal had generated significant press in the community, and most people now felt that Walter's
guilt was a settled matter. All there was left to do was wait for an execution date. Judge Key had retired, and none of the new Monroe
County judges seemed to want to touch our petition, so it was transferred back to Baldwin County under the theory that the postconvic-

tion appeal should be handled in the same county as the initial trial. This made little sense to us, because a Monroe County judge had presided over the trial, but there was nothing we could do.

Surprisingly, the Alabama Supreme Court agreed to stay our direct appeal process so that the Rule 32 petition could proceed. The general rule was that the direct appeal had to be completed before a postconviction collateral appeal under Rule 32 could be initiated. By staying the case, the Alabama Supreme Court had signaled there was something unusual about Walter's case that warranted further review in the lower courts. The Baldwin County Circuit Court judge was now obligated to review our case and could be forced to grant our discovery motions, which would require disclosure of all police and prosecutorial files. This was a very positive development.

We needed to have another meeting with the district attorney, Tommy Chapman, but this time we'd be going in armed with a court order to turn over police and prosecutorial files. We would also finally meet, in the flesh, the law enforcement officers involved in Walter's prosecution: the D.A.'s investigator, Larry Ikner; ABI agent Simon Benson; and Sheriff Tom Tate.

Chapman suggested that we come to his office in the Monroe County courthouse so that they could turn over all the files together. We agreed. When we arrived, the men were already there. Tate was a tall, heavy-set white man who had come to the meeting in boots, jeans, and a light shirt. Ikner was another white man in his mid-forties, wearing the same outfit. Neither of them smiled much—they greeted Michael and me with the bemused curiosity to which I was getting accustomed. The men knew that we were accusing them of misconduct, but for the most part they remained civil. At one point Tate told Michael that he knew, as soon as he saw him, that he was "a Yankee."

Michael smiled and replied, "Well, actually, I'm a Nittany Lion."

The joke died in the silent room.

Undeterred, Michael continued, "I went to Penn State. The mascot at Penn State is—"

"We kicked your ass in '78." Tate made the statement as if he had just won the lottery. Penn State and the University of Alabama had been football rivals in the 1970s, when both schools had had successful programs and iconic coaches, Bear Bryant at Alabama and Joe Paterno at Penn State. Alabama had defeated the number-one-ranked Penn State team 14–7 to win the 1978 national championship.

Michael, a huge college football fan and a "JoePa" devotee, looked at me as if seeking nonverbal permission to say something reckless. I gave him a cautionary stare; to my great relief, he seemed to understand.

"How much is 'Johnny D' paying y'all?" Tate asked, using the nickname Walter's friends and family had given him.

"We work for a nonprofit. We don't charge the people we represent anything," I said as blandly and politely as I could.

"Well, you're getting money from somewhere to do what you do."

I decided to let that pass and move things forward.

"I thought that it might be a good idea to sign something that verifies these are all the files you all have on this case. Can we index what you're turning over to us and then all sign?"

"We don't need to do anything that formal, Bryan. These men are officers of the court, just like you and I. You should just take the files," Chapman said, apparently sensing that this suggestion had provoked Tate and Ikner.

"Well, there could be files that have inadvertently been missed or documents that dropped out. I'm just trying to document that what we receive is what you give us—same number of pages, same file folder headings, et cetera. I'm not questioning anyone's integrity."

"The hell you ain't." Tate was direct. He looked at Chapman. "We can sign something confirming what we give him. I think we may need a record of that more than he does."

Chapman nodded. We got the files and left Monroeville with a lot of excitement about what we might find in the hundreds of pages of records we'd received. Back in Montgomery, we eagerly started reviewing them, and not just the files from the police and prosecutors. With our discovery order from the court, we were able to collect records from Taylor Hardin, the mental health facility where Myers was sent after he first refused to testify. We got the ABI file from Simon Benson, the only black ABI agent in South Alabama, as he had proudly told us. We got Monroeville city police department records and other city files. We even got Escambia County records and exhibits on the Vickie Pittman murder. The files were astonishing.

We might have been influenced by the pain of Mozelle and Onzelle or drawn in by the elaborate conspiracies that Ralph Myers had described, but we soon started asking questions about some of the law enforcement officers whose names kept coming up around the Pittman murder. We even decided to talk to the FBI about some of what we had learned.

It wasn't long after that when the bomb threats started.

Chapter Eight

All God's Children

UNCRIED TEARS

Imagine teardrops left uncried
From pain trapped inside
Waiting to escape
Through the windows of your eyes

"Why won't you let us out?"
The tears question the conscience
"Relinquish your fears and doubts
And heal yourself in the process."

The conscience told the tears
"I know you really want me to cry
But if I release you from bondage,
In gaining your freedom you die."

The tears gave it some thought
Before giving the conscience an answer

"If crying brings you to triumph
Then dying's not such a disaster."

IAN E. MANUEL, Union Correctional Institution

Trina Garnett was the youngest of twelve children living in the poorest section of Chester, Pennsylvania, a financially distressed municipality outside of Philadelphia. The extraordinarily high rates of poverty, crime, and unemployment in Chester intersected with the worst-ranked public school system among Pennsylvania's 501 districts. Close to 46 percent of the city's children were living below the federal poverty level.

Trina's father, Walter Garnett, was a former boxer whose failed career had turned him into a violent, abusive alcoholic well known to local police for throwing a punch with little provocation. Trina's mother, Edith Garnett, was sickly after bearing so many children, some of whom were conceived during rapes by her husband. The older and sicker Edith became, the more she found herself a target of Walter's rage. He would regularly punch, kick, and verbally abuse her in front of the children. Walter would often go to extremes, stripping Edith naked and beating her until she writhed on the floor in pain while her children looked on fearfully. When she lost consciousness during the beatings, Walter would shove a stick down her throat to revive her for more abuse. Nothing was safe in the Garnett home. Trina once watched her father strangle her pet dog into silence because it wouldn't stop barking. He beat the animal to death with a hammer and threw its limp body out a window.

Trina had twin sisters, Lynn and Lynda, who were a year older than her. They taught her to play "invisible" when she was a small child to shield her from their father when he was drunk and prowling their apartment with his belt, stripping the children naked, and beating them randomly. Trina was taught to hide under the bed or in a closet and remain as quiet as possible.

Trina showed signs of intellectual disabilities and other troubles at a young age. When she was a toddler, she became seriously ill after ingesting lighter fluid when she was left unattended. At the age of five, she accidently set herself on fire, resulting in severe burns over her chest, stomach, and back. She spent weeks in a hospital enduring painful skin grafts that left her terribly scarred.

Edith died when Trina was just nine. Trina's older sisters tried to take care of her, but when Walter began sexually abusing them, they fled. After the older siblings left home, Walter's abuse focused on Trina, Lynn, and Lynda. The girls ran away from home and began roaming the streets of Chester. Trina and her sisters would eat out of garbage cans; sometimes they would not eat for days. They slept in parks and public bathrooms. The girls stayed with their older sister Edy until Edy's husband began sexually abusing them. Their older siblings and aunts would sometimes provide temporary shelter, but the living situation would get disrupted by violence or death, and so Trina would find herself wandering the streets again.

Her mother's death, the abuse, and the desperate circumstances all exacerbated Trina's emotional and mental health problems. She would sometimes become so distraught and ill that her sisters would have to find a relative to take her to the hospital. But she was penniless and was never allowed to stay long enough to become stable or recover.

Late at night in August 1976, fourteen-year-old Trina and her friend, sixteen-year-old Francis Newsome, climbed through the window of a row house in Chester. The girls wanted to talk to the boys who lived there. The mother of these boys had forbidden her children from playing with Trina, but Trina wanted to see them. Once she'd climbed into the house, Trina lit matches to find her way to the boys' room. The house caught fire. It spread quickly, and two boys who were sleeping in the home died from smoke asphyxiation. Their mother accused Trina of starting the fire intentionally, but Trina and her friend insisted that it was an accident.

Trina was traumatized by the boys' deaths and could barely speak when the police arrested her. She was so nonfunctional and listless that her appointed lawyer thought she was incompetent to stand trial.

Defendants who are deemed incompetent can't be tried in adversarial criminal proceedings—meaning that the State can't prosecute them unless they become well enough to defend themselves. Criminally accused people facing trial are entitled to treatment and services. But Trina's lawyer failed to file the appropriate motions or present evidence to support an incompetency determination for Trina. The lawyer, who was subsequently disbarred and jailed for unrelated criminal misconduct, also never challenged the State's decision to try Trina as an adult. As a result, Trina was forced to stand trial for second-degree murder in an adult courthouse. At trial, Francis Newsome testified against Trina in exchange for the charges against her being dropped. Trina was convicted of second-degree murder, and the trial moved to the sentencing phase.

Delaware County Circuit Judge Howard Reed found that Trina had no intent to kill. But under Pennsylvania law, the judge could not take the absence of intent into account during sentencing. He could not consider Trina's age, mental illness, poverty, the abuse she had suffered, or the tragic circumstances surrounding the fire. Pennsylvania sentencing law was inflexible: For those convicted of second-degree murder, mandatory life imprisonment without the possibility of parole was the only sentence. Judge Reed expressed serious misgivings about the sentence he was forced to impose. "This is the saddest case I've ever seen," he wrote. For a tragic crime committed at fourteen, Trina was condemned to die in prison.

After sentencing, Trina was immediately shipped off to an adult prison for women. Now sixteen, Trina walked through the gates of the State Correctional Institution at Muncy, an adult prison for women, terrified, still suffering from trauma and mental illness, and intensely vulnerable—with the knowledge that she would never leave. Prison spared Trina the uncertainty of homelessness but presented new dangers and challenges. Not long after she arrived at Muncy, a male correctional officer pulled her into a secluded area and raped her.

The crime was discovered when Trina became pregnant. As is often the case, the correctional officer was fired but not criminally prosecuted. Trina remained imprisoned and gave birth to a son. Like hundreds of women who give birth while in prison, Trina was completely unprepared for the stress of childbirth. She delivered her baby while handcuffed to a bed. It wasn't until 2008 that most states abandoned the practice of shackling or handcuffing incarcerated women during delivery.

Trina's baby boy was taken away from her and placed in foster care. After this series of events—the fire, the imprisonment, the rape, the traumatic birth, and then the seizure of her son—Trina's mental health deteriorated further. Over the years, she became less functional and more mentally disabled. Her body began to spasm and quiver uncontrollably, until she required a cane and then a wheelchair. By the time she had turned thirty, prison doctors diagnosed her with multiple sclerosis, intellectual disability, and mental illness related to trauma.

Trina had filed a civil suit against the officer who raped her, and the jury awarded her a judgment of $62,000. The guard appealed, and the Court reversed the verdict because the correctional officer had not been permitted to tell the jury that Trina was in prison for murder. Consequently, Trina never received any financial aid or services from the state to compensate her for being violently raped by one of its "correctional" officers.

In 2014, Trina turned fifty-two. She has been in prison for thirty-eight years. She is one of nearly five hundred people in Pennsylvania who have been condemned to mandatory life imprisonment without parole for crimes they were accused of committing when they were between the ages of thirteen and seventeen. It is the largest population of child offenders condemned to die in prison in any single jurisdiction in the world.

In 1990, Ian Manuel and two older boys attempted to rob a couple who were out for dinner in Tampa, Florida. Ian was thirteen years old. When Debbie Baigre resisted, Ian shot her with a handgun given to him by the older boys. The bullet went through Baigre's cheek, shattering several teeth and severely damaging her jaw. All three boys were arrested and charged with armed robbery and attempted homicide.

Ian's appointed lawyer encouraged him to plead guilty, assuring him that he would be sentenced to fifteen years in prison. The lawyer didn't realize that two of the charges against Ian were punishable with sentences of life imprisonment without parole. The judge accepted Ian's plea and then sentenced him to life with no parole. Even though he was thirteen, the judge condemned Ian for living in the streets, for not having good parental supervision, and for his multiple prior arrests for shoplifting and minor property crimes. Ian was sent to an adult prison—the Apalachee Correctional Institution, one of the toughest prisons in Florida. The correctional staff at the prison processing center couldn't find any uniforms that would fit a boy Ian's size, so they cut six inches from the bottom of their smallest pants. Juveniles housed in adult prisons are five times more likely to be the victims of sexual assault, so the staff at Apalachee put Ian, who was small for his age, in solitary confinement.

Solitary confinement at Apalachee means living in a concrete box the size of a walk-in closet. You get your meals through a slot, you do not see other inmates, and you never touch or get near another human being. If you "act out" by saying something insubordinate or refusing to comply with an order given to you by a correctional officer, you are forced to sleep on the concrete floor of your cell without a mattress. If you shout or scream, your time in solitary is extended; if you hurt yourself by refusing to eat or mutilating your body, your time in solitary is extended; if you complain to officers or say anything menacing or inappropriate, your time in solitary is extended. You get three showers a week and are allowed forty-five minutes in a small caged area for exercise a few times a week. Otherwise you are alone, hidden away in your concrete box, week after week, month after month.

In solitary, Ian became a self-described "cutter"; he would take anything sharp on his food tray to cut his wrists and arms just to watch himself bleed. His mental health unraveled, and he attempted suicide several times. Each time he hurt himself or acted out, his time in isolation was extended.

Ian spent eighteen years in uninterrupted solitary confinement.

Once a month, Ian was allowed to make a phone call. Soon after he arrived in prison, on Christmas Eve in 1992, he used his call to reach out to Debbie Baigre, the woman he shot. When she answered the phone, Ian spilled out an emotional apology, expressing his deep regret and remorse. Ms. Baigre was stunned to hear from the boy who had shot her, but she was moved by his call. She had physically recovered from the shooting and was working to become a successful bodybuilder and had started a magazine focused on women's health. She was a determined woman who didn't let the shooting derail her from her goals. That first surprising phone call led to a regular correspondence. Ian had been neglected by his family before the crime took place. He'd been left to wander the streets with little parental or family support. In solitary, he met few prisoners or correctional staff. As he sank deeper into despair, Debbie Baigre became one of the few people in Ian's life who encouraged him to remain strong.

After communicating with Ian for several years, Baigre wrote the court and told the judge who sentenced Ian of her conviction that his sentence was too harsh and that his conditions of confinement were inhumane. She tried to talk to prison officials and gave interviews to the press to draw attention to Ian's plight. "No one knows more than I do how destructive and reckless Ian's crime was. But what we're currently doing to him is mean and irresponsible," she told one reporter. "When this crime was committed, he was a child, a thirteen-year-old boy with a lot of problems, no supervision, and no help available. We are not children."

The courts ignored Debbie Baigre's call for a reduced sentence.

By 2010, Florida had sentenced more than a hundred children to life imprisonment without parole for non-homicide offenses, several of whom were thirteen years old at the time of the crime. All of the youngest condemned children—thirteen or fourteen years of age—were black or Latino. Florida had the largest population in the world of children condemned to die in prison for non-homicides.

The section of South Central Los Angeles where Antonio Nuñez lived was plagued by gang violence. Antonio's mother would force her children to the floor when shooting erupted outside their crowded home, which happened with disturbing regularity. Nearly a dozen of their neighbors were shot and killed after being caught in the crossfire of gun violence.

The difficulties outside Antonio's home were compounded by severe domestic abuse inside the home. From the time Antonio was in diapers, he endured abusive beatings by his father, who hit him with his hand, fist, belt, and extension cords, causing bruises and cuts; he also witnessed terrifying conflicts in which his parents would violently assault each other and threaten to kill one another. The violence was so bad that on more than one occasion Antonio called the police. He began experiencing severe nightmares from which he awoke screaming. Antonio's depressed mother neglected him; when he cried, she just left him alone. The only activity she could recall ever attending for Antonio was his graduation from a Drug Abuse Resistance Education program in elementary school.

"He was excited to take his picture with the police officer," she would later say. "He wanted to be a police officer when he grew up."

In September 1999, a month after he turned thirteen, Antonio Nuñez was riding his bicycle near his home when a stranger shot him in his stomach, side, and arm. Antonio collapsed onto the street. His fourteen-year-old brother José heard him screaming and ran to his aid. José was shot in the head and killed when he responded to his little brother's call for help. Antonio suffered serious internal injuries that hospitalized him for weeks.

When Antonio was released from the hospital, his mother sent him to live with relatives in Las Vegas, where he tried to recover from the tragedy of José's death. Antonio was relieved to be away from the dangers of South Central Los Angeles. He stayed out of trouble, was helpful and obedient at home, and spent evenings doing his home-work with help from his cousin's husband. He put the gangs and vio-lence of South Central behind him and showed remarkable progress. But within a year, California probation authorities ordered him to re-turn to Los Angeles because he was on probation following his adjudi-cation as a ward of the court for a prior offense.

In poor urban neighborhoods across the United States, black and brown boys routinely have multiple encounters with the police. Even though many of these children have done nothing wrong, they are targeted by police, presumed guilty, and suspected by law enforce-ment of being dangerous or engaged in criminal activity. The random stops, questioning, and harassment dramatically increase the risk of arrest for petty crimes. Many of these children develop criminal rec-ords for behavior that more affluent children engage in with impunity.

Forced back to South Central, blocks from where his brother was murdered, Antonio struggled. A court later found that "[l]iving just blocks from where he was shot and his brother was killed, Nuñez suf-fered trauma symptoms, including flashbacks, an urgent need to avoid the area, a heightened awareness of potential threats, and an intensi-fied need to protect himself from real or perceived threats." He got his hands on a gun for self-defense but was quickly arrested for it and placed in a juvenile camp where supervisors reported that he eagerly participated in and positively responded to the structured environ-ment and guidance of staff members.

After returning from the camp, Antonio was invited to a party where two men twice Antonio's age told him that they were planning to fake a kidnapping to get money from a relative who would pay the ransom. They insisted that Antonio join them. Fourteen-year-old Antonio got in a car with the men to pick up the ransom money. The pretend victim sat in the backseat, while Juan Perez drove and Antonio sat in the passenger seat. Before they arrived at their Orange County destination to retrieve the money, they found themselves being followed—and then chased—by two Latino men in a gray van. At some point, Perez and the other man gave Antonio a gun and told him to shoot at the van, and a dangerous high-speed shoot-out unfolded. The men chasing them were undercover police officers—but Antonio didn't know that when he fired. When a marked police car joined the pursuit, Antonio dropped the gun just before the car crashed into some trees. No one was injured, but Antonio and Perez were charged with aggravated kidnapping and attempted murder of the police officers.

Antonio and his twenty-seven-year-old co-defendant were tried together in a joint trial, and both were found guilty. Under California law, a juvenile has to be at least sixteen to be sentenced to life imprisonment without parole for murder. But there is no minimum age for kidnapping, so the Orange County judge sentenced Antonio to imprisonment until death, asserting that he was a dangerous gang member who could never change or be rehabilitated, despite his difficult background and the absence of any significant criminal history. The judge sent him to California's dangerous, overcrowded adult prisons. At fourteen, Antonio became the youngest person in the United States condemned to die in prison for a crime in which no one was physically injured.

Most adults convicted of the kinds of crimes with which Trina, Ian, and Antonio were charged are not sentenced to life imprisonment without parole. In the federal system, adults who unintentionally commit arson-murder where more than one person is killed usually receive sentences that permit release in less than twenty-five years. Many adults convicted of attempted murder in Florida serve less than ten years in prison. Gun violence with no reported injuries frequently result in sentences of less than ten years for adult defendants, even in this era of harsh punishments.

Children who commit serious crimes long have been vulnerable to adult prosecution and punishment in many states, but the development of juvenile justice systems has meant that most child offenders were sent to juvenile detention facilities. Juvenile justice systems vary across the United States, but most states would have kept Trina, Ian, or Antonio in juvenile custody until they turned eighteen or twenty-one. At most, they might have stayed in custody until age twenty-five or older, if their institutional history or juvenile detention record suggested that they were still a threat to public safety.

In an earlier era, if you were thirteen or fourteen when you committed a crime, you would find yourself in the adult system with a lengthy sentence only if the crime was unusually high-profile—or committed by a black child against a white person in the South. For instance, in the infamous Scottsboro Boys case in the 1930s, two of the defendants, Roy Wright and Eugene Williams, were just thirteen years old when they were wrongfully convicted of rape and sentenced to death in Alabama.

In another signature case of juvenile prosecution, George Stinney, a fourteen-year-old black boy, was executed by the State of South Carolina on June 16, 1944. Three months earlier, two young white girls who lived nearby in Alcolu, a small mill town where the races were separated by railroad tracks, had gone out to pick flowers and never returned home. Scores of people across the community went searching for the missing girls. Young George and his siblings joined the search party. At some point, George mentioned to one of the white adult searchers that he and his sister had seen the girls earlier in the day. The girls had approached them while they were playing outside and asked where they could find flowers.

The next day, the dead bodies of the girls were found in a shallow ditch. George was immediately arrested for the murders because he had admitted seeing the girls before they disappeared and was the last person to see them alive. He was subjected to hours of interrogation without his parents or an attorney present. The understandable anger about the death of the girls exploded when word circulated that a black boy had been arrested for the murders. The sheriff claimed that George had confessed to the murders, though no written or signed statement was presented. George's father was summarily fired from his job; his family was told to leave town or else they would be lynched. Out of fear for their lives, George's family fled town late that night, leaving George behind in jail with no family support. Within hours of announcing the alleged confession, a lynch mob formed at the jail-house in Alcolu, but the fourteen-year-old had already been moved to a jail in Charleston.

A month later, a trial was convened. Facing charges of first-degree murder, George sat alone in front of an estimated crowd of fifteen hundred white people who had packed the courtroom and surrounded the building. No African Americans were allowed inside the court-house. George's white court-appointed attorney, a tax lawyer with po-litical aspirations, called no witnesses. The prosecution's only evidence was the sheriff's testimony regarding George's alleged confession. The trial was over in a few hours. An all-white jury deliberated for ten minutes before convicting George of rape and murder. Judge Stoll promptly sentenced the fourteen-year-old to death. George's lawyer said there would be no appeal because his family didn't have the money to pay for it.

Despite appeals from the NAACP and black clergy, who asked that the sentence be converted to life imprisonment, Governor Olin John-ston refused to intervene and George was sent to Columbia to be ex-ecuted in South Carolina's electric chair. Small even for his age, the five foot two, ninety-two-pound Stinney walked up to the chair with a Bible in his hand. He had to sit on the book when prison staff couldn't fit the electrodes to his small frame. Alone in the room, with no family or any people of color present, the terrified child sat in the oversized electric chair. He frantically searched the room for someone to help but saw only law enforcement personnel and reporters. The adult-size mask slid off George's face when the first jolt of electricity struck his body. Witnesses to the execution could see his "wide open, tearful eyes and saliva dripping from his mouth." Eighty-one days after being approached by two young girls about where flowers might be found, George Stinney was pronounced dead. Years later, rumors surfaced that a white man from a prominent family confessed on his deathbed to killing the girls. Recently, an effort has been launched to exonerate George Stinney.

The Stinney execution was horrific and heartbreaking, but it reflected the racial politics of the South more than the way children accused of crimes were generally treated. It was an example of how policies and norms once directed exclusively at controlling and punishing the black population have filtered their way into our general criminal justice system. By the late 1980s and early 1990s, the politics of fear and anger sweeping the country and fueling mass incarceration was turning its attention to children.

Influential criminologists predicted a coming wave of "superpredators" with whom the juvenile justice system would be unable to cope. Sometimes expressly focusing on black and brown children, theorists suggested that America would soon be overcome by "elementary school youngsters who pack guns instead of lunches" and who "have absolutely no respect for human life." Panic over the impending crime wave expected from these "radically impulsive, brutally remorseless" children led nearly every state to enact legislation that increased the exposure of children to adult prosecution. Many states lowered or eliminated the minimum age for trying children as adults, leaving children as young as eight vulnerable to adult prosecution and imprisonment.

Some states also initiated mandatory transfer rules, which took away any discretion from prosecutors and judges over whether a child should be kept in the juvenile system. Tens of thousands of children who had previously been managed by the juvenile justice system, with its well-developed protections and requirements for children, were now thrown into an increasingly overcrowded, violent, and desperate adult prison system.

The predictions of "super-predators" proved wildly inaccurate. The juvenile population in America increased from 1994 to 2000, but the juvenile crime rate declined, leading academics who had originally supported the "super-predator" theory to disclaim it. In 2001, the surgeon general of the United States released a report labeling the "super-predator" theory a myth and stated that "[t]here is no evidence that young people involved in violence during the peak years of the early 1990s were more frequent or more vicious offenders than youths in earlier years." This admission came too late for kids like Trina, Ian, and Antonio. Their death-in-prison sentences were insulated from legal challenges or appeals by a maze of procedural rules, statutes of limitations, and legal barricades designed to make successful postconviction challenges almost impossible.

When I met Trina, Ian, and Antonio years later, they had each been broken by years of hopeless confinement. They were legally condemned children hidden away in adult prisons, largely unknown and forgotten, preoccupied with surviving in dangerous, terrifying environments with little family support or outside help. They weren't exceptional. There were thousands of children like them scattered throughout prisons in the United States—children who had been sentenced to life imprisonment without parole or other extreme sentences. The relative anonymity of these kids seemed to aggravate their plight and their despair. I agreed to represent Trina, Ian, and Antonio, and our office would eventually make challenging death-in-prison sentences imposed on children a major focus of our work. But it became immediately clear that their extreme, unjust sentences were just one of the problems that had to be overcome. They were all damaged and traumatized by our system of justice.

Trina's mental and physical health made her life in prison extremely challenging. She was grateful for our help and showed remarkable improvement when we told her that we were going to fight to get her sentence reduced, but she had many other needs. She talked constantly about wanting to see her son. She wanted to know that she was not alone in the world. We tracked down her sisters and arranged a visit where Trina could see her son, and it seemed to strengthen her in ways I wouldn't have thought possible.

I flew to Los Angeles and drove hundreds of miles through the heart of Central California farmland to meet Antonio at a maximum-security prison dominated by gangs and frequent violence. He was trying to acculturate himself to a world that corrupted healthy human development in every way. Reading had always been challenging for Antonio, but he had a strong desire to learn and was so determined to understand that he would read a passage over and over, looking up unfamiliar words in the dictionary we sent him, until he got it. We recently sent him Darwin's *The Origin of Species,* which he hopes will help him better understand those around him.

It turns out that Ian was very, very bright. Although being smart and sensitive made his extended time in solitary confinement especially destructive, he had managed to educate himself, read hundreds of books, and write poetry and short stories that reflected an eager, robust intellect. He sent me dozens of letters and poems. I'd return to the office after traveling for a few days and often find letters from Ian. Sometimes I'd find within a letter a scrap of wrinkled paper, which, once unfolded, would reveal thoughtful and sobering poems with titles like "Uncried Tears," "Tied Up with Words," "The Unforgiving Minute," "Silence," and "Wednesday Ritual."

We decided to publish a report to draw attention to the plight of children in the United States who had been sentenced to die in prison. I wanted to photograph some of our clients in order to give the life-without-parole sentences imposed on children a human face. Florida was one of the few states that would allow photographers inside a prison, so we asked prison officials if Ian could be permitted out of his solitary, no-touch existence for an hour so that the photographer we hired could take the pictures. To my delight, they agreed and allowed Ian to be in the same room with an outside photographer. As soon as the visit was over, Ian immediately wrote me a letter.

Dear Mr. Stevenson:

I hope this letter reaches you in good health, and everything is going well for you. The focal point of this letter is to thank you for the photo session with the photographer and obtain information from you how I can obtain a good amount of photos.

As you know, I've been in solitary confinement approx. 14.5 years. It's like the system has buried me alive and I'm dead to the outside world. <u>Those photos mean so very much to me right now.</u> All I have is $1.75 in my inmate account right now. If I send you $1.00 of that, how many of the photos will that purchase me?

In my elation at the photo shoot today, I forgot to mention that today June 19th was my deceased mom's birthday. I know it's not a big significance, but reflecting on it afterward it seemed symbolic and special that the photo shoot took place on my mother's birthday!

I don't know how to make you feel the emotion and importance of those photos, but to be real, I want to show the world I'm alive! I want to look at those photos and feel alive! It would really help with my pain. I felt joyful today during the photo shoot. I wanted it to never end. Every time you all visit and leave, I feel saddened. But I capture and cherish those moments in time, replaying them in my mind's eye, feeling grateful for human interaction and contact. But today, just the simple handshakes we shared was a welcome addition to my sensory deprived life.

Please tell me how many photos I can get? I want those photos of myself, <u>almost</u> as bad as I want my freedom.

Thank you for making a lot of the positive occurrences that are happening in my life possible. I don't know exactly how the law led you to me, but I thank God it did. I appreciate everything you and EJI are doing for me. Please send me some photos, okay?

Chapter Nine

I'm Here

Finally, the date for Walter McMillian's hearing had arrived. We would now have an opportunity to present Ralph Myers's new testimony and all the exculpatory evidence we'd discovered in police records that had never been disclosed.

Michael and I had gone over the case a dozen times, thinking through the best way to present the evidence of Walter's innocence. Our biggest concern was Myers, mostly because we knew he would feel incredible pressure once he was brought back to the county courthouse, and he'd broken under pressure before. We were consoled by the fact that so much of our evidence was documentary and could be admitted without the complications and unpredictability that Myers's testimony might introduce.

We now had a paralegal on staff, so we brought her into the case. Brenda Lewis was a former Montgomery police officer who joined us after seeing more abuses of power than she could tolerate at the police department. An African American woman, she was adept even in environments where her gender or race made her an outsider. We had asked her to touch base with our witnesses before the hearing to go over last-minute details and calm their nerves.

Chapman had called in the state attorney general's office to help defend Walter's conviction, and they'd sent Assistant Attorney General Don Valeska, a longtime prosecutor with a reputation for being intense and combative. Valeska was a white man in his forties whose fit, medium frame suggested someone who stayed active; the glasses he wore added to his serious demeanor. His brother Doug was the district attorney in Houston County, and both men were aggressive and unapologetic in their prosecution of "bad guys." Michael and I had reached out to Chapman once more before the hearing to see if we could persuade him to reopen the investigation and independently reexamine whether McMillian was guilty. But by now, Chapman and all of the law enforcement officers had grown tired of us. They seemed increasingly hostile whenever they had to deal with us. I had considered reporting to them the bomb threats and death threats we'd received, since they were likely coming from people in Monroe County, but I wasn't sure anyone in the sheriff's or D.A.'s office would care.

The new judge on the case, Judge Thomas B. Norton Jr., had also grown weary of us. We'd had several pretrial hearings on different motions during which he would sometimes become frustrated because of the bickering between the lawyers. We kept insisting on obtaining all files and evidence the State had in its possession. We had uncovered so much exculpatory evidence that had not been disclosed previously that we were sure there was still more that had not been turned over. The judge finally told us that we were fishing after we'd made our ninth or tenth request for more police and prosecution files. I suspect that Judge Norton had scheduled the final Rule 32 hearing in part because he wanted to get this contentious, complicated case off his docket and out of his court.

In the last pretrial appearance, the judge had asked, "How much time will you need to present your evidence, Mr. Stevenson?"

"We'd like to reserve a week, your honor."

"A week? You've got to be joking. For a Rule 32 hearing? The trial in this case only lasted a day and a half."

"Yes, sir. We believe this is an extraordinary case and there are several witnesses and—"

"Three days, Mr. Stevenson. If you can't make your case in three days after all of this drama you've stirred up, you don't really have anything."

"Judge, I—"

"Adjourned."

After spending another long day in Monroeville tracking down a few final witnesses, Michael and I went back to the office to plot out how to present all of the evidence in the narrow amount of time the judge was giving us. We needed to make the complexity of the case and the multiple ways that Walter's rights had been violated coherent and understandable to the judge. Another concern was Myers and his love of fantastical narration, so we sat down with him a few days before the hearing and tried to make it as plain as possible.

"No long excursions about police corruption," I said. "Just answer the questions accurately and honestly, Ralph."

"I always do," Ralph said confidently.

"Wait, did you just say you *always* do?" Michael asked. "What are you talking about, you *always* do? Ralph, you lied through your ass the entire trial. That's what we're going to expose at this hearing."

"I know," Myers said coolly. "I meant I always tell y'all the truth."

"Don't freak me out, Ralph. Just testify truthfully," Michael said.

Ralph had been calling our office almost daily with an unending stream of strange thoughts, ideas, and conspiracies. I was frequently too busy to talk to him, so Michael had been fielding most of the calls and had become increasingly worried about Ralph's unique perspective on the world. But we could do no more about it.

We arrived at the courthouse the morning of the hearing early and anxious. We were both dressed in dark suits, white shirts, and muted ties. I usually dressed as conservatively as possible for court. I was a young, bearded black man, and even when there was no jury I still tried to meet the court's expectation of what a lawyer looked like, if only for the sake of my clients. We first went to check on Myers to make sure he had arrived safely and was in a stable state of mind before the hearing began. The Baldwin County Sheriff's Department deputies had brought Ralph from the prison in St. Clair County to the courthouse the night before the hearing. The five-hour trip through the nighttime roads of southern Alabama had clearly unnerved Ralph. We met with him in his holding cell; he was palpably anxious. Worse, he was quiet and reserved, which was even more unusual. After we finished that unsettling meeting, I went to see Walter, who was also at the courthouse in one of the holding cells. Being back at the courthouse where his fate had seemingly been sealed four years earlier had shaken him as well, but he forced himself to smile when I walked in.

"Was the trip okay?" I asked.

"Everything is good. Just hoping for something better than the last time I was here."

I nodded sympathetically and reviewed with him what I thought would unfold over the next few days.

The holding cells for prisoners were in the basement of the courthouse, and after meeting with Walter, I made my way upstairs to get ready for court to begin. When I walked into the courtroom, I was shocked by what I saw. Dozens of people from the community—mostly black and poor—had packed the viewing area. On both sides of the hearing room, people from Walter's family, people who had attended the fish fry on the day of the crime, people we'd interviewed over the past several months, people who knew Walter from working with him, even Sam Crook and his posse, were crammed into the courtroom. Minnie and Armelia smiled as I walked into court.

Tom Chapman then walked in with Don Valeska, and they both scanned the room. I could tell from the looks on their faces that they were unhappy about the crowd. Tate, Larry Ikner, and Benson—the law enforcement team primarily responsible for Walter's prosecution—piled in behind the prosecutors and sat down in the courtroom as well. A deputy sheriff escorted the parents of Ronda Morrison to the front of the court just before the hearing began. When the judge took the bench, the crowd of black faces noisily rose as one and sat back down. Many of the black community members looked dressed for church. The men were in suits, and some of the women wore hats. It took them a few seconds to settle into silence, which seemed to annoy Judge Norton. But I was energized by their presence and happy for Walter that so many people had come out to support him.

Judge Norton was a balding white man in his fifties. He wasn't a tall man, but the elevated bench made him as imposing as any judge. He had managed some of our earlier preliminary hearings in a suit, but today he was in his robe, gavel firmly in hand.

"Gentlemen, are we ready to proceed?" Judge Norton asked.

"We are, Your Honor," I replied. "But we intend to call several of the law enforcement officers present in the courtroom, and I would like to invoke the rule of sequestration." In criminal cases, witnesses who will be testifying are required to sit outside the courtroom so they can't alter their testimony based on what other witnesses say.

Valeska was on his feet immediately. "No, Judge. That's not going to happen. These are the investigators who figured out this heinous crime, and we need them in court to present our case."

I stayed on my feet. "The State doesn't bear the burden of presenting a case in these proceedings, Your Honor; we do. This isn't a criminal trial but a postconviction evidentiary hearing."

"Judge, they're the ones that are trying to retry this case and we need our people inside," Valeska countered.

The judge jumped in with, "Well, it does sound like you're trying to retry the case, Mr. Stevenson, so I'm going to allow the State to keep the crime investigators in the courtroom."

It was not a good start. I decided to proceed with an opening statement before calling Myers as our first witness. I wanted the judge to understand that we weren't simply defending Mr. McMillian from a different angle than his original lawyers. I wanted him to know that we had dramatic new evidence of innocence that exonerated Walter and that justice demanded his immediate release. We wouldn't succeed if the judge didn't know how to hear the evidence.

"Your Honor, the State's case against Walter McMillian turned entirely on the testimony of Ralph Myers, who had several prior felony convictions and another capital murder case pending against him in Escambia County at the time of Mr. McMillian's trial. At trial, Mr. McMillian asserted that he is innocent and that he did not know Mr. Myers at the time of this crime. He has maintained his innocence throughout these proceedings."

The judge had been fidgeting and had seemed distracted when I started, so I paused. Even if he didn't agree I wanted him to hear what I was saying. I stopped talking until I was sure that he was paying close attention. Finally he made eye contact with me, so I continued.

"There is no question that Walter McMillian was convicted of capital murder based on the testimony of Ralph Myers. There was no other evidence to establish Mr. McMillian's guilt for capital murder at trial other than Myers's testimony. The State had no physical evidence linking Mr. McMillian to this crime, the State had no motive, the State had no witnesses to the crime, the State had only the testimony of Ralph Myers.

"At trial, Myers testified that he was *unknowingly* and *unwillingly* made part of a capital murder and robbery on November 1, 1986, when Walter McMillian saw him at a car wash and asked him to drive McMillian's truck because his 'arm hurt.' Myers stated that he drove Mr. McMillian to Jackson Cleaners, subsequently went into the cleaners, and saw McMillian with a gun, placing money in a brown bag. Another man, who was white, was also present in the cleaners. Myers testified this man had black-gray hair and allegedly talked to McMillian. Myers asserted that he was shoved and threatened by Mr. McMillian when he went into the cleaners. The mysterious third person, who is circumstantially presumed to be in charge, allegedly instructed McMillian to 'get rid of Myers,' which Mr. McMillian said he couldn't do because he was out of bullets. The white man in charge has never been identified or arrested by the state. The State has not been looking for a third person, a ringleader for this crime, because I think they recognize that this person doesn't exist."

I paused again to let the meaning of this sink in. "Based on the testimony of Ralph Myers, Walter McMillian was convicted of capital murder and sentenced to death. As you're about to hear, the testimony of Ralph Myers was completely false. Again, Your Honor, the testimony of Ralph Myers at trial was completely false."

I took a moment before turning to the bailiff to call Myers to the stand. The courtroom was silent until the deputy opened the door to the holding area and Ralph Myers walked into the courtroom. There was an audible reaction to his presence. Ralph had aged visibly since the last time many of the people in the courtroom had seen him; I could hear murmurs about how his hair had grayed. Dressed in his prison whites, Myers once again appeared small and sad to me as he climbed up onto the witness stand. He looked around the courtroom nervously before raising his hand and swearing an oath to tell the truth. I waited until the courtroom became quiet. Judge Norton was looking at Myers attentively.

I walked over to begin my examination. After asking him to state his name for the record and establishing that he had previously appeared in court and testified against Walter McMillian, it was time to get to the heart of things.

I walked closer to the witness stand.

"Mr. Myers, was the testimony that you gave at Mr. McMillian's trial true?" I was hoping that the judge couldn't see I was holding my breath waiting for Ralph to answer. Ralph looked at me coolly but then spoke very clearly and confidently.

"Not at all." There was more murmuring in the courtroom now, but the crowd quickly quieted to hear more.

"Not at all," I repeated before continuing. I wanted Ralph's recantation to sink in, but I didn't want to hesitate too long because we needed a lot more.

"Did you see Mr. McMillian on the day that Ronda Morrison was murdered?"

"Absolutely not." Ralph looked steady as he spoke.

"Did you drive his truck into Monroeville on that day?"

"Absolutely not."

"Did you go into Jackson Cleaners when Ronda Morrison was murdered?"

"No. Never did."

I didn't want the court to think that Ralph was robotically denying everything I asked him, so I asked a question that required an affirmative answer. "Now, at Mr. McMillian's trial, did you give some testimony that there was a white man inside the cleaners when you went inside?"

"Yes, I did."

I had gone as long as I dared asking Ralph yes/no questions. "What was that testimony, please?"

"As I can recall, the testimony was that I had overheard Walter McMillian saying something to this guy, and I had also recalled saying that I had seen the back part of his head, but that's just about all I can recall on that."

"Was that testimony true, Mr. Myers?"

"No, it wasn't." Now the judge leaned in to listen with rapt attention.

"Were any of the allegations you made against Walter McMillian as being involved in the Ronda Morrison murder true?"

Ralph paused and looked around the courtroom before he answered. For the first time there was emotion in his voice, regret or remorse.

"No."

It seemed that everyone in the courtroom had been holding their breath but now there was an audible buzz from many of Walter's supporters.

I had a copy of the trial transcript and took Ralph through every sentence of his testimony against Walter. Statement by statement he acknowledged that his previous testimony was entirely false. Myers was direct and persuasive. He would frequently turn his head to look Judge Norton directly in the eye as he spoke. When I made him repeat the parts of his testimony about being coerced to testify falsely, Ralph remained calm and conveyed absolute sincerity. Even during the lengthy cross-examination by Chapman, Myers was unwavering. After relentless questioning about why he was changing his testimony and Chapman's suggestion that someone was putting him up to this, Ralph became indignant. He looked at the prosecutor and said:

> Me, I can simply look in your face and anybody else's face dead eye to eyeball and tell you that that's all I—anything that was told about McMillian was a lie. . . . As far as I know, McMillian didn't have any-thing to do with this because on the day, on the day they say this happened, I didn't even see McMillian. And that's exactly what I told lots of people.

On re-direct examination, I asked Ralph to acknowledge once again that his trial testimony was false and that he had knowingly put an in-nocent man on death row. Then I took a moment and walked over to the defense table to make sure I hadn't forgotten anything. I reviewed my notes and then glanced at Michael. "Are we okay?"

Michael looked astonished. "Ralph was great. He was really, really great."

I looked at Walter and only then realized that his eyes were moist. He was shaking his head from side to side in disbelief. I put my hand on his shoulder before announcing to the court that Myers could be excused. We had no further questions.

Myers stood up to leave the courtroom. As the deputies led him to a side door, he looked apologetically at Walter before being escorted out. I'm not sure Walter saw him.

People in the courtroom started whispering again. I heard one of Walter's relatives, in a muted tone, say, "Thank you, Jesus!"

The next challenge was to rebut the testimony of Bill Hooks and

Joe Hightower, who had claimed to see Walter's modified "low-rider" truck pulling out from the cleaners about the time Ronda Morrison was murdered.

I called Clay Kast to the stand. The white mechanic testified that McMillian's truck was not a low-rider in November 1986 when Ronda Morrison was murdered. Kast had records and clearly remembered modifying Walter's truck in May 1987, over six months after the day when Hooks and Hightower claimed they'd seen a low-rider truck at the cleaners. We finished the day with Woodrow Ikner, a Monroeville police officer who testified that he was the first on the scene and that the body of Ronda Morrison was not where Myers had testified it was. Ikner said it was clear from his observation of the murder scene that Morrison had been shot in the back after a struggle that had started in the bathroom and ended in the rear of the cleaners, where the body was found. Ikner's description of the scene contradicted the assertion that Myers had made at trial about seeing Morrison near the front counter. More significantly, Ikner testified that he'd been asked by Pearson, the trial prosecutor, to testify that Morrison's body had been dragged through the store from the front counter to the spot where it was found. Ikner was indignant on the stand as he recalled the conversation. He knew that such testimony would be false and had told the prosecutors that he refused to lie. He was soon after discharged from the police department.

Evidentiary hearings, like jury trials, can be exhausting. I had done the direct examination of all of the witnesses and was surprised when I realized that it was already 5:00 P.M. The hearing was going well. I was excited and energized to be able, finally, to lay out all of the evidence proving Walter's innocence. I kept an eye on Judge Norton to make sure he was still engaged, and he seemed visibly affected by the proceedings. I believed the concerned look on his face revealed confusion about what he was going to do in light of this evidence, and I considered the judge's newfound confusion and concern to be real progress.

All of the witnesses we called during the first day were white, and none had any loyalties to Walter McMillian. It seemed that Judge Norton had not expected that. When Clay Kast acknowledged that the truck the state witnesses described as a "low-rider" wasn't modified until close to seven months after the crime took place, the judge furiously scribbled notes, the worry lines on his face deepening. When Woodrow Ikner announced that he had been fired for trying to be honest about the evidence against McMillian, the judge seemed shaken. This was the first evidence we presented that suggested that people in law enforcement had been so focused on convicting Walter that they were prepared to ignore or even hide evidence that contradicted their case.

After Woodrow Ikner completed his testimony, it was deep into the afternoon. The judge looked at the clock and called it a day. I wanted to keep going, to continue until midnight if necessary, but I realized that that wasn't going to happen. I walked over to Walter.

"We have to stop now?" he asked worriedly.

"Yes, but we'll just pick up and keep going tomorrow morning." I smiled at him, and I was pleased when he smiled back.

Walter looked at me excitedly. "Man, I can't tell you how I'm feeling right now. All this time I've been waiting for the truth and been hearing nothing but lies. Right now feels incredible. I just—" A uniformed deputy walked over and interrupted us.

"We need to take him back to the holding cell, you'll have to talk there." The middle-aged white officer seemed provoked. I didn't pay it much attention and told Walter I'd come down later.

As people filed out of the courtroom you could see hope growing among Walter's family. They came up to me and gave me hugs. Walter's sister Armelia, his wife Minnie, and his nephew Giles were all talking excitedly about the evidence we'd presented.

When we got back to the hotel, Michael was pumped up, too. "Chapman should just call you and say he wants to drop the charges against Walter and let him go home."

"Let's not hold our breath waiting for that call," I replied.

Chapman had seemed troubled as we left the courthouse. I still had some hope that he might turn around on this and even help us, but we definitely couldn't plan on that.

I arrived at the courthouse early the next morning to visit Walter in his basement cell before the proceedings began. When I headed upstairs, I was confused to see a throng of black folks sitting outside the courtroom in the courthouse lobby. It was just about time for the proceedings to begin. I went up to Armelia, who was sitting with the others outside the courtroom, and she looked at me with concern.

"What's wrong?" I asked. "Why aren't y'all inside the courtroom?"

I looked around the lobby. If there had been a huge crowd yesterday, today's hearing had brought more people, including several clergy members and older people of color I'd never seen before.

"They won't let us in, Mr. Stevenson."

"What do you mean they won't let you in?"

"We tried to go in earlier, and they told us we couldn't come in."

A young man in a deputy sheriff's uniform was standing in front of the entrance to the courtroom. I walked over to him and he put his arm up to stop me.

"I want to go into the courtroom," I said firmly.

"You can't come in."

"What do you mean I can't come in? There is a hearing scheduled and I want to go inside."

"I'm sorry, sir, you can't come into the courtroom."

"Why not?" I asked.

He stood there silently. Finally, I added, "I'm the defense attorney. I think I have to be able to go inside the courtroom."

He looked at me closely and was clearly perplexed. "Um, I don't know. I'll have to go and check." He disappeared inside the courtroom. He came back a few moments later and grinned at me tentatively. "Um, you can come in."

I pushed by the deputy, opened the door, and saw that the entire courtroom had been altered. Inside the courtroom door they had placed a large metal detector, on the other side of which was an enormous German shepherd held back by a police officer. The courtroom was already half filled. The benches that had been filled by Walter's supporters the previous day were now mostly occupied by older white people. Clearly the people here were supporting the Morrisons and the prosecution. Chapman and Valeska were already sitting at the prosecutor's table, acting as if nothing was going on. I was livid.

I walked over to Chapman, "Who told the deputies not to let the folks outside come into the courtroom?" I asked. They looked at me as if they didn't know what I was talking about. "I'm going to speak to the judge about this."

I spun on my heel and went directly to the judge's chambers, and the prosecutors followed me. When I explained to Judge Norton that McMillian's family and supporters had been told that they couldn't come into the courtroom, even though the State's supporters had been let in, the judge rolled his eyes and looked annoyed.

"Mr. Stevenson, your people will just have to get here earlier," he said dismissively.

"Judge, the problem isn't that they weren't here early. The problem is they were told they couldn't come into the courtroom."

"No one is being denied entrance to the courtroom, Mr. Stevenson."

He turned to his bailiff, who left the room. I followed the bailiff and saw him whisper something to the deputy outside the courtroom. McMillian's supporters would be let into the courtroom—now that half the courtroom was already filled.

I walked over to where two ministers had assembled all of Walter's supporters and tried to explain the situation.

"I'm sorry, everyone," I said. "They've done something really inappropriate today. They'll let you in now, but the courtroom is already half filled with people here to support the State. There won't be enough seats for everyone."

One of the ministers, a heavyset African American man dressed in a dark suit with a large cross around his neck, walked over to me.

"Mr. Stevenson, it's okay. Please don't worry about us. We'll have a few people be our representatives today and we will be here even earlier tomorrow. We won't let nobody turn us around, sir."

The ministers began selecting people to be representatives in the courtroom. They told Minnie, Armelia, Walter's children, and several others to go on in. When the ministers called out Mrs. Williams, everyone seemed to smile. Mrs. Williams, an older black woman, stood up and prepared herself to enter the courtroom. She took great care in fixing her hair just right. On top of her gray hair she wore a small hat whose placement she precisely adjusted. She then pulled out a long blue scarf that she delicately wrapped around her neck. Only then did she slowly begin to make her way to the courtroom door where the line of McMillian supporters had formed. I found her dignified ritual riveting, but when the spell was broken I realized that I needed to get going myself. I hadn't spent the morning preparing for witnesses as I had intended but had instead been drawn into this foolish mistreatment of McMillian's supporters. I walked past the line of patient people and went inside to begin preparing for the hearing.

I was standing at counsel's table when out of the corner of my eye I saw that Mrs. Williams had made it to the courtroom door. She was quite elegant in her hat and scarf. She wasn't a large woman, but there was something commanding about her presence—I couldn't help but watch her as she moved carefully through the doorway toward the metal detector. She walked more slowly than everyone else, but she held her head high with an undeniable grace and dignity. She reminded me of older women I'd been around all my life—women whose lives were hard but who remained kind and dedicated themselves to building and sustaining their communities. Mrs. Williams glanced at the available rows to see where she would sit, and then turned to walk through the metal detector—and that's when she saw the dog.

I watched all her composure fall away, replaced by a look of absolute fear. Her shoulders dropped, her body sagged, and she seemed paralyzed. For over a minute she stood there, frozen, and then her body began to tremble and then shake noticeably. I heard her groan.

Tears were running down her face and she began to shake her head sadly. I kept watching until she turned around and quickly walked out of the courtroom.

I felt my own mood shift. I didn't know exactly what had happened to Mrs. Williams, but I knew that here in Alabama, police dogs and black folks looking for justice had never mixed well.

I was trying to shake off the dark feeling that the morning's events had conjured when the officers brought Walter into the courtroom. Because there was no jury, the judge had not permitted me to give him street clothes to wear, so Walter was wearing his prison uniform. They allowed him to be in the courtroom without handcuffs but had insisted on keeping his ankles shackled. Michael and I conferred briefly about the order of witnesses as the rest of McMillian's family and supporters slowly filed through the metal detector, past the dog, and into the courtroom.

Despite the State's early-morning maneuvers and the bad omen of the dog and Mrs. Williams, we had another good day in court. Evidence from the state mental health workers who had dealt with Myers after he initially refused to testify in the first trial and was sent to the Taylor Hardin Secure Medical Facility for evaluation confirmed Myers's testimony from the day before. Dr. Omar Mohabbat explained that Myers had told him then "that the police had framed him to accept the penalty for the murder case that he is accused of or 'to testify' that 'the man did.'" Mohabbat reported that Myers "categorically denied having anything to do with the alleged crime. He claimed, 'I don't know the name of this girl, I don't know the time of the alleged crime, I don't know the date of the alleged crime, I don't know the place of the alleged crime.'" Mohabbat testified that Myers had told him, "They told me to say what they wanted me to say."

Evidence from other doctors further confirmed this testimony. Dr. Norman Poythress from Taylor Hardin explained that Myers had told him that "his prior 'confessions' are bogus and were coerced out of him by the police through keeping him physically and psychologically isolated."

We presented evidence from Taylor Hardin staffer Dr. Kamal Nagi, who said that Myers had told him of "another murder that occurred in 1986 where a girl was shot in the Laundromat. [He] said that the 'police and also my lawyer want me to say that I had driven these people to the Laundromat and they shot the girl, but I won't do it.'" Myers also told Nagi, "They threatened me. They want me to say what they want to hear and if I don't then they tell me, 'You're going to the electric chair.'"

We had evidence from a fourth doctor to whom Myers confided that he was being pressured to give false testimony against Walter McMillian. Dr. Bernard Bryant testified that Myers told him "he did not commit the crime and that at the time he was incarcered for the crime, he was threatened and harassed by the local police authorities into confessing he committed a crime."

We emphasized to the court throughout the day's hearing that all of these statements were made by Myers *before* the initial trial. Not only did these statements make Myers's recantation more credible but they had also been documented in medical records that had never been turned over to Walter's trial lawyers, as the law required. The U.S. Supreme Court has long required that the prosecution disclose to the defendant anything that is exculpatory or that may be helpful to the defendant in impeaching a witness.

The supporters whom the State had brought to court and the victim's family seemed confused by the evidence we were presenting—it complicated the simple narrative they had fully embraced about Walter's guilt and the need for swift and certain punishment. State supporters began to leave the courtroom as the day went on, and the number of black people who were let into the room grew. By the end of that second day, I felt very hopeful. We had maintained a good pace and the cross-examinations had been shorter than I had expected. I thought we could finish our case in one more day.

I was tired but feeling pleased as I walked to my car that evening. To my surprise, I noticed Mrs. Williams sitting outside the courthouse on a bench, alone. She stood when our eyes met. I walked over, remembering how unsettled I had been to see her leave the courtroom.

"Mrs. Williams, I'm so sorry they did what they did this morning. They should not have done it, and I'm sorry if they upset you. But, so you know, things went well today. I feel like we had a good day—"

"Attorney Stevenson, I feel so bad. I feel so bad," she said and grabbed my hands.

"I should have come into that courtroom this morning. I was supposed to be in that courtroom this morning," she said and began to weep.

"Mrs. Williams, it's all right," I said. "They shouldn't have done what they did. Please don't worry about it." I put my arm around her and gave her a hug.

"No, no, no, Attorney Stevenson. I was meant to be in that courtroom, I was supposed to be in that courtroom."

"It's okay, Mrs. Williams, it's okay."

"No, sir, I was supposed to be there and I wanted to be there. I tried, I tried, Lord knows I tried, Mr. Stevenson. But when I saw that dog—" She shook her head and stared away with a distant look. "When I saw that dog, I thought about 1965, when we gathered at the Edmund Pettus Bridge in Selma and tried to march for our voting rights. They beat us and put those dogs on us." She looked back to me sadly. "I tried to move, Attorney Stevenson, I wanted to move, but I just couldn't do it."

As she spoke it seemed like a world of sadness surrounded her. She let go of my hand and walked away. I watched her get into a car with some other people I had seen in the courtroom earlier.

I drove back to the motel in a more somber mood to start preparing for the last day of hearings.

I arrived at the court early the next morning to make sure there were no problems. As it turned out, very few people showed up to support the State. And though the metal detector and the dog were still there, no deputy stood at the door to block black people from entering the courtroom. Inside the courtroom, I noticed one of the women I'd seen leave with Mrs. Williams the night before. She came up to me and introduced herself as Mrs. Williams's daughter. She thanked me for trying to console her mother.

"When she got home last night, she was so upset. She didn't eat anything, she didn't speak to anybody, she just went to her bedroom. We could hear her praying all night long. This morning she called the Reverend and begged him for another chance to be a community representative at the hearing. She was up when I got out of bed, dressed and ready to come to court. I told her she didn't have to come, but she wouldn't hear none of it. She's been through a lot and, well, on the trip down here she just kept saying over and over, 'Lord, I can't be scared of no dog, I can't be scared of no dog.'"

I was apologizing again to the daughter for what the court officials had done the day before when suddenly there was a commotion at the courtroom door. We both looked up and there stood Mrs. Williams. She was once again dressed impeccably in her scarf and hat. She held her handbag tight at her side and seemed to be swaying at the entrance. I could hear her speaking to herself, repeating over and over again: "I ain't scared of no dog, I ain't scared of no dog." I watched as the officers allowed her to move forward. She held her head up as she walked slowly through the metal detector, repeating over and over, "I ain't scared of no dog." It was impossible to look away. She made it through the detector and stared at the dog. Then, loud enough for everyone to hear, she belted out: "I ain't scared of no dog!"

She moved past the dog and walked into the courtroom. Black folks who were already inside beamed with joy as she passed them. She sat down near the front of the courtroom and turned to me with a broad smile and announced, "Attorney Stevenson, I'm here!"

"Mrs. Williams, it's so good to see you here. Thank you for coming."

The courtroom filled up, and I started getting my papers together. They brought Walter into the courtroom, the signal that the hearing was about to begin. That's when I heard Mrs. Williams call my name.

"No, Attorney Stevenson, you didn't hear me. I said I'm here." She spoke very loudly, and I was a little confused and embarrassed. I turned around and smiled at her.

"No, Mrs. Williams, I did hear you, and I'm so glad you're here." When I looked at her, though, it was as if she was in her own world.

The courtroom was packed, and the bailiff brought the court to order as the judge walked in. Everyone rose, as is the custom. When the judge took the bench and sat down, everyone else in the courtroom sat down as well. There was an unusually long pause as we all waited for the judge to say something. I noticed people staring at something behind me, and that's when I turned around and saw that Mrs. Williams was still standing. The courtroom got very quiet. All eyes were on her. I tried to gesture to her that she should sit, but then she leaned her head back and shouted, "I'm here!" People chuckled nervously as she took her seat, but when she looked at me, I saw tears in her eyes.

In that moment, I felt something peculiar, a deep sense of recognition. I smiled now, because I knew she was saying to the room, "I may be old, I may be poor, I may be black, but I'm here. I'm here because I've got this vision of justice that compels me to be a witness. I'm here because I'm supposed to be here. I'm here because you can't keep me away."

I smiled at Mrs. Williams while she sat proudly. For the first time since I started working on the case, everything we were struggling to achieve finally seemed to make sense. It took me a minute to realize that the judge was calling my name, impatiently asking me to begin.

The last day of hearings went well. There were a half-dozen people who had been jailed or imprisoned with Ralph Myers whom Ralph had told he was being pressured to give false testimony against Walter McMillian. We found most of them and had them testify. They were consistent in what they related. Isaac Dailey, who had been falsely accused by Myers of committing the Pittman murder, explained how Myers had falsely implicated Walter in the Pittman crime. Myers had confided to Dailey after he was arrested that he and Karen had discussed pinning the Pittman murder on Walter. "He related to us that he and Karen did the killing and, ah, plotted together to put it off on Johnny D."

Another inmate who wrote letters for Myers at the Monroe County Jail explained that Myers didn't know McMillian, had no knowledge of the Morrison murder, and was being pressured by police to testify falsely against McMillian.

We saved the most powerful evidence for the end. The tapes that Tate, Benson, and Ikner had made when they interrogated Myers were pretty dramatic. The multiple recorded statements Myers gave to the police featured Myers repeatedly telling the police that he didn't know anything about the Morrison murder or Walter McMillian. They included the officers' threats against Myers and Myers's resistance to framing an innocent man for murder. Not only did the tapes confirm Myers's recantation and contradict his trial testimony, they exposed the lie that Pearson had told the court, the jury, and McMillian's trial counsel—that there were only two statements provided by Myers. In fact, Myers gave at least six additional statements to the police that were largely consistent with his testimony at the Rule 32 hearing that he had no information about Walter McMillian committing the Ronda Morrison murder. All of these recorded statements were typed, exculpatory, and favorable to Walter McMillian, and none of them had been disclosed to McMillian's attorneys, as was required.

I called on McMillian's trial lawyers, Bruce Boynton and J. L. Chestnut, to testify about how much more they could have done to win an acquittal if the State had turned over the evidence it had suppressed. We finished the presentation of our evidence and, to our surprise, the State put on no rebuttal case. I didn't know what they could have presented to rebut our evidence, but I'd assumed they would present *something*. The judge seemed surprised, too. He paused and then said he wanted the parties to submit written briefs arguing what ruling he should make. We had hoped for this, and I was relieved that the court would give us time to explain the significance of all the evidence in writing and assist him in preparing his order, an order I hoped would set Walter free. At the end of three days of intense litigation, the judge adjourned the proceedings in the late afternoon.

Michael and I had been in a rush the final morning of the hearing and hadn't checked out of our hotel before leaving for the courthouse. We said our farewells to the family in the courtroom and went back to the hotel, feeling exhausted but satisfied.

Bay Minette, where the hearing took place, is about thirty minutes from the beautiful beaches on the Gulf of Mexico. We had started a tradition of bringing our staff down to the beach each September, and we'd all fallen in love with the clear warm waters of the Gulf. The white sand and pleasantly underdeveloped beachfront were spectacular and soothing. The view was slightly spoiled by the massive offshore oil rigs you could see in the distance, but if you could make yourself forget about them, you'd think you were in paradise. Dolphins loved this part of the Gulf and could be spotted in the early mornings, playfully making their way through the water. I'd often thought we should move our office to right there on the beach.

It was Michael's idea to hit the beach before heading back to Montgomery. I wasn't sure it was a good idea, but the day was warm and the coast was so close, I couldn't resist. We jumped in the car, trailing the last hours of sunlight to the beautiful shores near Fort Morgan, Alabama. As soon as we got there, Michael changed from his suit to swim trunks and went sprinting into the ocean. I was too tired to race into the sea, so I put on some shorts and sat down at the water's edge. It would soon be dusk, but the heat persisted. My head was full of everything that had transpired in court: I was replaying what witnesses had said and worrying about whether things had gone exactly right. I was trawling through every detail in my mind, every possible misstep, until I caught myself. It was over; there was no point in making myself crazy by overthinking it now. I decided to dive into the ocean and, for a moment at least, forget it all.

Recently, stranded at the airport with nothing else to read, I had read an article about shark attacks. As I approached the waves at Fort Morgan, now lit by the sunset, I remembered that sharks feed at dusk and at dawn. I watched Michael swimming far off shore, and as fun as it looked, I knew I'd be the more vulnerable target if a shark showed up. Michael swam like a fish while I barely stayed afloat.

Michael waved at me and shouted: "B-man, come on out!" I cautiously ventured into the water far enough to explain my concerns about sharks to him. He laughed at me. The water felt warm and wonderful, comforting in a way I hadn't expected. A school of fish zipped by my legs, and I stared at them in wonder until I realized that they might be fleeing some larger predator. I carefully made my way back to the shore.

I sat on the sandy shore and watched the brilliant white pelicans gliding effortlessly over the still waters in search of food. Small fiddler crabs scurried around me, too fearful to get close but curious enough to linger nearby. I thought about Walter making his way back to Holman, shackled in the back of the van again. I wanted him to be hopeful but grounded enough to manage whatever the court decided. I thought about his family and all the people who had come to court. They'd kept the faith through the five years that had passed since Walter was first arrested, and now they had cause to feel energized and encouraged. I thought about Mrs. Williams. She had come up to me after the hearings and had given me a sweet kiss on the cheek. I told her how happy I was she'd come back to court. She looked at me playfully. "Attorney Stevenson, you *know* I was going to be here, and you *know* I wasn't going to let these people keep me out." Her words had made me smile.

Michael got out of the water looking worried.

"What did you see?" I joked. "Shark? Eel? Poisonous jellyfish? Stingray? Piranha?"

He was out of breath. "They've threatened us, lied to us, there are people who have told us that some folks in the county are so unnerved by what we're doing that they're going to kill us. What do you think they're going to do now that they know how much evidence we have to prove Walter's innocence?"

I had given this some thought, too. Our opponents had done everything they could to frame Walter—in order to kill him. They'd lied to us and subverted the judicial process. More than a few people had passed on to us that they'd heard angry people in the community make threats on our lives because they believed we were trying to help a guilty murderer get off death row.

"I don't know," I told Michael, "but we have to press on, man, we have to press on."

We both sat there in silence, watching the sun fade into darkness. More fiddler crabs emerged from their holes, scurrying crazily and getting closer to where we sat. I turned to Michael in the approaching darkness.

"We should go."

Chapter Ten

Mitigation

America's prisons have become warehouses for the mentally ill. Mass incarceration has been largely fueled by misguided drug policy and excessive sentencing, but the internment of hundreds of thousands of poor and mentally ill people has been a driving force in achieving our record levels of imprisonment. It's created unprecedented problems.

I first met Avery Jenkins over the telephone. He called me, but he was pretty incoherent. He couldn't explain what he had been convicted of or even clearly describe what he wanted me to do. He complained about the conditions of his confinement until a random thought caused him to abruptly switch topics. He sent letters, too, but they were just as hard to follow as his phone calls, so I decided to speak with him in person to see if I could make better sense of how to help.

For over a century, institutional care for Americans suffering from serious mental illness shifted between prisons and hospitals set up to manage people with mental illness. In the late nineteenth century, alarmed by the inhumane treatment of incarcerated people suffering from mental illness, Dorothea Dix and Reverend Louis Dwight led a successful campaign to get the mentally ill out of prison. The numbers of incarcerated people with serious mental illness declined dramatically, while public and private mental health facilities emerged to provide care to the mentally distressed. State mental hospitals were soon everywhere.

By the middle of the twentieth century, abuses within mental institutions generated a lot of attention, and involuntary confinement of people became a significant problem. Families, teachers, and courts were sending thousands to institutions for eccentricities that were less attributable to acute mental illness than resistance to social, cultural, or sexual norms. People who were gay, resisted gender norms, or engaged in interracial dating often found themselves involuntarily committed. The introduction of antipsychotic medications like Thorazine held great promise for many people suffering from some severe mental health disorders, but the drug was overused in many mental institutions, resulting in terrible side effects and abuses. Aggressive and violent treatment protocols at some facilities generated horror stories that fueled a new campaign, this time to get people out of institutional mental health settings.

In the 1960s and 1970s, laws were enacted to make involuntary commitment much more difficult. Deinstitutionalization became the objective in many states. Mental health advocates and lawyers succeeded in winning a series of Supreme Court cases that forced states to transfer institutional residents to community programs. Legal rulings empowered people with developmental disabilities to refuse treatment and created rights for the mentally disabled that made forced institutionalization much less common. By the 1990s, several states had a deinstitutionalization rate of over 95 percent, meaning that for every hundred patients who had been residents in state hospitals before deinstitutionalization programs, fewer than five were residents when the study was conducted in the 1990s. In 1955, there was one psychiatric bed for every three hundred Americans; fifty years later, it was one bed for every three thousand.

While these reforms were desperately needed, deinstitutionalization intersected with the spread of mass imprisonment policies— expanding criminal statutes and harsh sentencing—to disastrous effect. The "free world" became perilous for deinstitutionalized poor people suffering from mental disabilities. The inability of many disabled, low-income people to receive treatment or necessary medication dramatically increased their likelihood of a police encounter that would result in jail or prison time. Jail and prison became the state's strategy for dealing with a health crisis created by drug use and dependency. A flood of mentally ill people headed to prison for minor offenses and drug crimes or simply for behaviors their communities were unwilling to tolerate.

Today, over 50 percent of prison and jail inmates in the United States have a diagnosed mental illness, a rate nearly five times greater than that of the general adult population. Nearly one in five prison and jail inmates has a serious mental illness. In fact, there are more than three times the number of seriously mentally ill individuals in jail or prison than in hospitals; in some states that number is ten times. And prison is a terrible place for someone with mental illness or a neurological disorder that prison guards are not trained to understand.

For instance, when I still worked in Atlanta, our office sued Louisiana's notorious Angola Prison for refusing to modify a policy that required prisoners in segregation cells to place their hands through bars for handcuffing before officers entered to move them. Disabled prisoners with epilepsy and seizure disorders would sometimes need assistance while convulsing in their cells, and because they couldn't put their hands through the bars, guards would mace them or use fire extinguishers to subdue them. This intervention aggravated the health problems of the prisoners and sometimes resulted in death.

Most overcrowded prisons don't have the capacity to provide care and treatment to the mentally ill. The lack of treatment makes compliance with the myriad rules that define prison life impossible for many disabled people. Other prisoners exploit or react violently to the behavioral symptoms of the mentally ill. Frustrated prison staff frequently subject them to abusive punishment, solitary confinement, or the most extreme forms of available detention. Many judges, prosecutors, and defense lawyers do a poor job of recognizing the special needs of the mentally disabled, which leads to wrongful convictions, lengthier prison terms, and high rates of recidivism.

I once represented a mentally ill man on Alabama's death row named George Daniel. George had suffered brain damage in a car accident that knocked him unconscious late one night in Houston, Texas. When he woke up, he was in an upside-down car on the side of the road. He went home that night and never sought medical assistance. His girlfriend later told his family that at first he just seemed a little off. Then he started hallucinating and exhibiting increasingly bizarre and erratic behavior. He stopped sleeping regularly, complained about hearing voices, and on two occasions ran out of the house naked because he thought he was being chased by wasps. Within a week of the accident he had stopped speaking in sentences. Just before his mother, who lived in Montgomery, was summoned to help persuade him to go to a hospital, George boarded a Greyhound bus in the middle of the night. He traveled as far as the money he had in his pocket would take him.

Disoriented and uncommunicative, he was forced off the bus in Hurtsboro, Alabama, after unnerving some passengers by talking loudly to himself and gesturing wildly at objects he imagined were flying around him. The bus had gone through Montgomery, where he had family, but he stayed on until he was thrown off, with no money and wearing jeans, a T-shirt, and no shoes in the middle of January. He wandered around Hurtsboro and eventually stopped at a house. He knocked on the door, and when the homeowner opened it, George walked inside without being invited and roamed around until he found the kitchen table, where he sat down. The alarmed homeowner called her son, who came and physically removed George from the house. George went to another home owned by an older woman and did the same thing. She called the police. The officer who responded had a reputation for being aggressive, and he forcefully removed George from the home. George started resisting while being pulled to the police car, and the two men began wrestling and fell to the ground. The officer pulled his weapon and the two were grappling over the gun when it discharged, shooting the officer in the stomach. He died from the gunshot wound.

George was arrested and charged with capital murder. While in the Russell County jail, he became acutely psychotic. Officers reported that he wouldn't leave his cell. He was observed eating his own feces. His mother visited him, but he didn't recognize her. He couldn't speak in complete sentences. The two lawyers who were appointed to represent him at his capital trial were primarily concerned that only one of them would be paid the $1,000 for out-of-court time that Alabama provided lawyers appointed in capital cases. They began squabbling with each other, and one filed a civil suit against the other about who could claim the money. Meanwhile, the judge sent George to Bryce Hospital in Tuscaloosa for a competency examination. Ed Seger, the doctor who examined George, mysteriously concluded that he was not mentally ill but was "malingering" or faking symptoms of mental illness.

Based on that evaluation, the judge allowed the capital murder trial to proceed. George's lawyers bickered with one another, presented no defense, and called no witnesses. The State called Dr. Seger, who persuaded the jury that there was nothing mentally wrong with George, even as he continuously spit in a cup and made loud clucking noises throughout the trial. George's family members were distraught. George had been working at a Pier 1 furniture store in Houston before his car accident. He left town without picking up his check, which had been ready for collection for over two days before his departure.

His mother, a poor woman who knew the value of a dollar to some-one like George, found this behavior more demonstrative of mental illness than anything else she could point to, and she authorized the lawyers to obtain the unclaimed check in the hope that they could present it at the trial to confirm George's confused mental state. The lawyers, who were still bickering over the money, cashed the check to pay themselves instead of using it as evidence.

George was convicted and given the death penalty. By the time we at EJI got involved, he had been on death row for several years, moving inexorably toward execution. When I met him, prison doctors were heavily medicating him with psychotropic drugs, which at least stabilized his behavior. It was so abundantly clear that George was mentally ill that it came as no shock when we discovered that the doctor who had examined him at Bryce Hospital was a fraud with no medical training. "Dr. Ed Seger" had made up his credentials. He had never graduated from college but had fooled hospital officials into believing he was a trained physician with expertise in psychiatry. He had masqueraded at the hospital for *eight years* conducting competency evaluations on people accused of crimes before his fraud was uncovered.

I represented George in his federal court proceedings. There, the State acknowledged that Seger was an imposter but wouldn't agree that George was entitled to a new trial. We eventually won a favorable ruling from a federal judge who overturned his conviction and sentence. Because of his mental illness and incompetency, George was never retried or prosecuted. He has been at a mental institution ever since. But there are likely hundreds of other people imprisoned after an evaluation by "Dr. Seger" whose convictions have never been reviewed.

A lot of my clients on death row have had serious mental illnesses, but it wasn't always obvious that their history of mental illness predated their time in prison, since symptoms of their disabilities could be episodic and were frequently stress-induced. But Avery Jenkins's letters, handwritten in print so small I needed a magnifying glass to read them, convinced me that he had been very ill for a long time.

I looked up his case and began to piece together his story. It turned out he'd been convicted of the very disturbing and brutal murder of an older man. The multiple stab wounds inflicted on the victim strongly suggested mental illness, but the court records and files never referenced anything about Jenkins suffering from a disability. I thought I'd find out more by meeting him in person.

When I pulled into the prison parking lot, I noticed a pickup truck there that looked like a shrine to the Old South: It was completely covered with disturbing bumper stickers, Confederate flag decals, and other troubling images. Confederate flag license plates are everywhere in the South, but some of the bumper stickers were new to me. A lot were about guns and Southern identity. One read, IF I'D KNOWN IT WAS GOING TO BE LIKE THIS, I'D HAVE PICKED MY OWN DAMN COTTON. Despite growing up around images of the Confederate South and working in the Deep South for many years, I was pretty shaken by the symbols.

I'd always been especially interested in the post-Reconstruction era of American history. My grandmother was the daughter of people who were enslaved. She was born in Virginia in the 1880s, after federal troops had been withdrawn and a reign of violence and terror had begun, designed to deny any political or social rights for African Americans. Her father told her stories of how the recently emancipated black people were essentially re-enslaved by former Confederate officers and soldiers, who used violence, intimidation, lynching, and peonage to keep African Americans subordinate and marginalized. My grandmother's parents were deeply embittered by how the promise of freedom and equality following slavery ended when white Southern Democrats reclaimed political power through violence.

Terrorist groups like the Ku Klux Klan cloaked themselves in the symbols of the Confederate South to intimidate and victimize thousands of black people. Nothing unnerved rural black settlements more than rumors about nearby Klan activity. For a hundred years, any sign of black progress in the South could trigger a white reaction that would invariably invoke Confederate symbols and talk of resistance. Confederate Memorial Day was declared a state holiday in Alabama at the turn of the century, soon after whites rewrote the state constitution to ensure white supremacy. (The holiday is still celebrated today.) When black veterans returned to the South after World War II, Southern politicians formed a "Dixiecrat" bloc to preserve racial segregation and white domination out of fear that military service might encourage black veterans to question racial segregation. In the 1950s and 1960s, civil rights activism and new federal laws inspired the same resistance to racial progress and once again led to a spike in the use of Confederate imagery. In fact, it was in the 1950s, after racial segregation in public schools was declared unconstitutional in *Brown v. Board of Education,* that many Southern states erected Confederate flags atop their state government buildings. Confederate monuments, memorials, and imagery proliferated throughout the South during the Civil Rights Era. It was during this time that the birthday of Jefferson Davis, the president of the Confederacy, was added as a holiday in Alabama. Even today, banks, state offices, and state institutions shut down in his honor.

At a pretrial hearing, I once argued against the exclusion of African Americans from the jury pool. In this particular rural Southern community, the population was about 27 percent black, but African Americans made up only 10 percent of the jury pool. After presenting the data and making my arguments about the unconstitutional exclusion of African Americans, the judge complained loudly.

"I'm going to grant your motion, Mr. Stevenson, but I'll be honest. I'm pretty fed up with people always talking about minority rights. African Americans, Mexican Americans, Asian Americans, Native Americans . . . When is someone going to come to my courtroom and protect the rights of Confederate Americans?" The judge had definitely caught me off guard. I wanted to ask if being born in the South or living in Alabama made me a Confederate American, but I thought better of it.

I stopped in the prison yard to take a closer look at the truck. I couldn't help walking around it and reading the provocative stickers. I turned back toward the front gate of the prison, trying to regain my focus, but I couldn't make myself indifferent to what I perceived were symbols of racial oppression. I had been to this prison often enough to be familiar to many of the correctional officers, but as I entered I was met by a correctional officer I'd never seen before. He was a white man of my height—about six feet tall—with a muscular build. He looked to be in his early forties and wore a short military haircut. He was staring coldly at me with steel-blue eyes. I walked toward the gate that led to the lobby of the visitation room, where I expected a routine pat-down before entering the visitation area. The officer stepped in front of me and blocked me from proceeding.

"What are you doing?" he snarled.

"I'm here for a legal visit," I replied. "It was scheduled earlier this week. The people in the warden's office have the papers." I smiled and spoke as politely as I could to defuse the situation.

"That's fine, that's fine, but you have to be searched first."

It was difficult to ignore his clearly hostile attitude, but I did my best.

"Okay, do you need me to take my shoes off?" The hardcore officers would sometimes make me remove my shoes before going inside.

"You're going to go into that bathroom and take everything off if you expect to get into my prison."

I was shocked, but spoke as nicely as I could. "Oh, no, sir. I think you might be confused. I'm an attorney. Lawyers don't have to get strip-searched to come in for legal visits."

Instead of calming him, this seemed to make him angrier. "Look, I don't know who you think you are, but you're not coming into my prison without complying with our security protocols. Now, you can get into that bathroom and strip, or you can go back to wherever you came from."

I'd had some difficult encounters with officers getting into prisons from time to time, mostly in small county jails or places where I'd never been before, but this was highly unusual.

"I've been to this prison many times, and I've never been required to submit to a strip search. I don't think this is the procedure," I said more firmly.

"Well, I don't know and don't care what other people do, but this is the protocol I use." I thought about trying to find an assistant warden but realized that that might be difficult, and anyway, an assistant warden would be unlikely to tell an officer he was wrong in front of me. I had driven two hours for this visit and had a very tough schedule over the next three weeks; I wouldn't be able to get back to the prison any time soon if I didn't get in now. I went inside the bathroom and removed my clothes. The officer came in and gave me an unnecessarily aggressive search before mumbling that I was clear. I put my suit back on and walked out.

"I'd like to get inside the visitation room now." I tried to reclaim some dignity by speaking more forcefully.

"Well, you have to go back and sign the book."

He said it coolly, but he was clearly trying to provoke me. There was a visitation log that the prison used for family visits, but it was not used for legal visits. I'd already signed the attorney book. It would make no sense to sign a second book.

"Lawyers don't have to sign that book—"

"If you want to come in my prison, you'll sign the book." He seemed to be smirking now. I tried hard to keep my composure.

I turned around and went over to the book and signed my name. I walked back to the visitation room and waited. There was a padlock on the glass door that had to be unlocked before I could enter the space where I'd meet my client. The officer finally pulled out his keys to unlock the door. I stood silently hoping to get inside without more drama. When he opened the door, I stepped forward, but he grabbed my arm to stop me. He lowered his voice as he spoke to me.

"Hey, man, did you happen to see a truck out in the visitation yard with a lot of bumper stickers, flags, and a gun rack?"

I spoke cautiously. "Yes, I saw that truck."

His face hardened before he spoke. "I want you to know, that's my truck." He released my arm and allowed me to walk inside the prison. I felt angry at the guard, but I was even more irritated by my own powerlessness. I was distracted from my thoughts when the back door of the visitation room opened and Mr. Jenkins was led in by another officer.

Jenkins was a short African American man with close-cropped hair. He grasped my hand with both of his and smiled broadly as he sat down. He seemed unusually happy to see me.

"Mr. Jenkins, my name is Bryan Stevenson. I'm the attorney you spoke—"

"Did you bring me a chocolate milkshake?" He spoke quickly.

"I'm sorry, what did you say?"

He kept grinning. "Did you bring me a chocolate milkshake? I want a chocolate milkshake."

The trip, the Confederate truck, the harassment from the guard, and now a request for a milkshake—this was becoming a bizarre day. I didn't hide my impatience.

"No, Mr. Jenkins, I didn't bring you a chocolate milkshake. I'm an attorney. I'm here to help you with your case and try to get you a new trial. Okay? That's why I'm here. Now I need to ask you some questions and try to understand what's going on."

I saw the grin fade quickly from the man's face. I started asking questions and he gave single-word answers, sometimes just grunting out a yes or no. I realized that he was still thinking about his milkshake. My time with the officer had made me forget how impaired this man might be. I stopped the interview and leaned forward.

"Mr. Jenkins, I'm really sorry. I didn't realize you wanted me to bring you a chocolate milkshake. If I had known that, I would absolutely have tried. I promise that the next time I come, if they let me bring you in a chocolate milkshake, I'll definitely do it. Okay?"

With that, his smile returned, and his mood brightened. His prison records revealed that he often experienced psychotic episodes in which he would scream for hours. He was generally kind and gentle in our meeting, but he was clearly ill. I couldn't understand why his trial records made no reference to mental illness, but after the George Daniel case, nothing surprised me. When I returned to my office, we began a deeper investigation into Mr. Jenkins's background. What we found was heartbreaking. His father had been murdered before he was born, and his mother had died of a drug overdose when he was a year old. He'd been in foster care since he was two years old. His time in foster care had been horrific; he'd been in nineteen different foster homes before he turned eight. He began showing signs of intellectual disability at an early age. He had cognitive impairments that suggested some organic brain damage and behavioral problems that suggested schizophrenia and other serious mental illness.

When he was ten, Avery lived with abusive foster parents whose rigid rules kept him in constant turmoil. He couldn't comply with all of the requirements imposed on him, so he was frequently locked in a closet, denied food, and subjected to beatings and other physical abuse. When his behavior didn't improve, his foster mother decided to get rid of him. She took him out into the woods, tied him to a tree, and left him there. He was found, in very poor health, by hunters three days later. After recovering from serious medical problems relating to his abandonment, he was turned over to authorities, who placed him back into foster care. By the time he was thirteen, he had started abusing drugs and alcohol. By fifteen, he was having seizures and experiencing psychotic episodes. At seventeen, he was deemed incapable of management and was left homeless. Avery was in and out of jail until he turned twenty, when in the midst of a psychotic episode he wandered into a strange house, thinking he was being attacked by demons. In the house, he brutally stabbed to death a man he'd believed to be a demon. His lawyers did no investigation of Mr. Jenkins's history prior to trial, and he was quickly convicted of murder and sentenced to death.

The prison would not let me bring Mr. Jenkins a milkshake. I tried to explain this to him, but at the start of every visit, he'd ask me if I'd brought one. I'd tell him that I would keep trying—I had to, just to get him to focus on anything else. Months later, we were finally scheduled to go to court with the evidence about his profound mental illness, material that should have been presented at trial. We contended that his attorneys had failed to provide effective assistance of counsel at trial when they didn't uncover Avery's history or present his disabilities as relevant to his criminal culpability and sentence.

When I got to the court where the hearing would take place, about a three-hour drive from the prison, I went to see Avery in the court's basement holding cell. After going through my usual protocol about the milkshake, I tried to get him to understand what would happen in court. I was concerned that seeing some of the witnesses—people who had dealt with him when he was in foster care—might upset him. The testimony the experts would provide would also be very direct in characterizing his disabilities and illness. I wanted him to understand why we were doing that. He was pleasant and agreeable, as always.

When I went upstairs to the courtroom, I spotted the correctional officer who had given me such a hard time when I had first met Avery. I hadn't seen the officer since that initial ugly encounter. I had asked another client about the guard and was told that he had a bad reputation and usually worked the late shift. Most people tried to steer clear of him. He must have been the officer assigned to transport Avery to the hearing, which made me worried about how Avery might have been treated on the trip, but he had seemed his usual self.

Over the next three days we presented our evidence about Avery's background. The experts who spoke about Avery's disabilities were terrific. They weren't partial or biased, just very persuasive in detailing how organic brain damage, schizophrenia, and bipolar disorder can conspire to create severe mental impairment. They explained that the psychosis and other serious mental health problems that burdened

Mr. Jenkins could lead to dangerous behavior, but this behavior was a manifestation of serious illness, not a reflection of his character. We also put forth evidence about the foster care system and how it had failed Avery. Several of the foster parents with whom Avery had been placed were later convicted of sexual abuse and criminal mismanagement of foster children. We discussed how Avery had been passed from one unhappy situation to the next, until he was drug-addicted and homeless.

Several former foster parents admitted to being very frustrated by Avery because they weren't equipped to deal with his serious mental health problems. I argued to the judge that not taking Avery's mental health issues into consideration at trial was as cruel as saying to someone who has lost his legs, "You must climb these stairs with no assistance, and if you don't, you're just lazy." Or to say to someone who is blind, "You should get across this busy interstate highway unaided, or you're just cowardly."

There are hundreds of ways we accommodate physical disabilities—or at least understand them. We get angry when people fail to recognize the need for thoughtful and compassionate assistance when it comes to the physically disabled, but because mental disabilities aren't visible in the same way, we tend to be dismissive of the needs of the disabled and quick to judge their deficits and failures. Brutally murdering someone would, of course, require the State to hold that person accountable and to protect the public. But to completely disregard a person's disability would be unfair in evaluating what degree of culpability to assign and what sentence to impose.

I went back home feeling very good about the hearing, but the truth was that a state postconviction hearing rarely resulted in a favorable ruling. If relief was to come, it would most likely be on appeal. I wasn't expecting any miracle rulings. About a month after the hearing, before judgment was rendered, I decided to go to the prison and see Avery. We hadn't had much time to talk after the hearing, and I wanted to make sure he was okay. Throughout most of the hearing he had sat pleasantly, but when some of his former foster parents had come into the court, I could see him become upset. I thought a post-hearing visit would be helpful.

When I pulled into the parking lot, I once again saw that loathsome truck, with its flags, stickers, and menacing gun rack. I feared another encounter with the guard. Sure enough, after checking in with the warden's secretary and heading toward the visitation room, I saw him approaching me. I braced myself, preparing for the encounter. And then something surprising happened.

"Hello, Mr. Stevenson. How are you?" the guard asked. He sounded earnest and sincere. I was skeptical.

"Well, I'm fine. How are you?" He was looking at me differently from how he had before; he wasn't glaring and seemed genuinely to want to interact. I decided to play along.

"Look, I'll step into the bathroom to get ready for your search."

"Oh, Mr. Stevenson, you don't have to worry about that," he quickly replied. "I know you're okay." Everything about his tone and demeanor was different.

"Oh, well, thank you. I appreciate that. I'll go back and sign the book, then."

"Mr. Stevenson, you don't have to do that. I saw you coming and signed your name in for you. I've taken care of it." I realized that he actually looked nervous.

I was confused by the shift in his attitude. I thanked him and walked to the visitation room door with the officer following behind me. He turned to unlock the padlock so that I could go inside. As I started to walk past him to enter, he placed his hand on my shoulder.

"Hey, um, I'd like to tell you something."

I wasn't sure where he was going with this.

"You know I took ole Avery to court for his hearing and was down there with y'all for those three days. And I, uh, well, I want you to know that I was listening." He removed his hand from my shoulder and looked past me, as if staring at something behind me. "You know, I—uh, well, I appreciate what you're doing, I really do. It was kind of difficult for me to be in that courtroom to hear what y'all was talking about. I came up in foster care, you know. I came up in foster care, too." His face softened. "Man, I didn't think anybody had it as bad as me. They moved me around like I wasn't wanted nowhere. I had it pretty rough. But listening to what you was saying about Avery made me realize that there were other people who had it as bad as I did. I guess even worse. I mean, it brought back a lot of memories, sitting in that courtroom."

He reached into his pocket to pull out a handkerchief to wipe the perspiration that had formed on his brow. I noticed for the first time that he had a Confederate flag tattooed on his arm.

"You know, I guess what I'm trying to say is that I think it's good what you're doing. I got so angry coming up that there were plenty of times when I really wanted to hurt somebody, just because I was angry. I made it to eighteen, joined the military, and you know, I've been okay. But sitting in that courtroom brought back memories, and I think I realized how I'm still kind of angry."

I smiled. He continued: "That expert doctor you put up said that some of the damage that's done to kids in these abusive homes is permanent; that kind of made me worry. You think that's true?"

"Oh, I think we can always do better," I told him. "The bad things that happen to us don't define us. It's just important sometimes that people understand where we're coming from."

We were both speaking softly to one another. Another officer walked by and stared at us. I went on: "You know, I really appreciate you saying to me what you just said. It means a lot, I really mean that. Sometimes I forget how we all need mitigation at some point."

He looked at me and smiled. "You kept talking about mitigation in that court. I said to myself, 'What the hell is wrong with him? Why does he keep talking about "mitigation" like that?' When I got home I looked it up. I wasn't sure what you meant at first, but now I do."

I laughed. "Sometimes I get going in court, and I'm not sure I know what I'm saying, either."

"Well, I think you done good, real good." He looked me in the eye before he extended his hand. We shook hands and I started toward the door again. I was just about inside when he grabbed my arm again.

"Oh, wait. I've got to tell you something else. Listen, I did something I probably wasn't supposed to do, but I want you to know about it. On the trip back down here after court on that last day—well, I know how Avery is, you know. Well anyway, I just want you to know that I took an exit off the interstate on the way back. And, well, I took him to a Wendy's, and I bought him a chocolate milkshake."

I stared at him incredulously, and he broke into a chuckle. Then he locked me inside the room. I was so stunned by what the officer said, I didn't hear the other officer bring Avery into the room. When I realized Avery was already in the room, I turned and greeted him. When he didn't say anything, I was a little alarmed.

"Are you okay?"

"Yes, sir, I'm fine. Are you okay?" he asked.

"Yes, Avery, I'm really doing well." I waited for our ritual to begin. When he didn't say anything, I figured I'd just play my part. "Look, I tried to bring you a chocolate milkshake, but they wouldn't—"

Avery cut me off. "Oh, I got a milkshake. I'm okay now."

As I began discussing the hearing, he grinned. We talked for an hour before I had to see another client. Avery never again asked me for a chocolate milkshake. We won a new trial for him and ultimately got him off death row and into a facility where he could receive mental health treatment. I never saw the officer again; someone told me he quit not long after that last time I saw him.

Chapter Eleven

I'll Fly Away

It was the third bomb threat in two months. As we quickly cleared the office and waited for the police to arrive, the entire staff was nervous. We now had five attorneys, an investigator, and three administrative staff members. Law students had started arriving for short-term internships, which provided us with additional legal assistance and critically needed investigative help. But none of them had signed on for bomb threats. It was tempting to ignore them, but two years earlier an African American civil rights lawyer in Savannah, Georgia, named Robert "Robbie" Robinson was murdered when a bomb sent to his law office exploded. Around the same time, a federal appeals court judge, Robert Vance, was killed in Birmingham by a mail bomb. Days later a third bomb was sent to a civil rights office in Florida and a fourth to a courthouse in Atlanta. The bomber seemed to be attacking legal professionals connected to civil rights. We were warned that we could be targets, and for weeks we carefully hauled our mail packages to the federal courthouse for X-ray screenings before opening them. After that, bomb threats were no joke.

Everyone fled the building while we discussed the likelihood of an actual bombing. The caller had described our building precisely when making his threat. Sharon, our receptionist, had scolded the caller. She was a young mother of two small children and had grown up in a poor, rural white family. She spoke to people plainly and directly.

"Why are you doing this? You're scaring us!"

She said the man had sounded middle-aged and Southern, but she couldn't give any more of a description. "I'm doing you a favor," he said threateningly. "I want y'all to stop doing what you're doing. My first option is not to kill everybody, so you better get out of there now! Next time there won't be a warning."

It had been a month since the McMillian hearing. The first time the office was threatened the caller had made racist remarks about the need to teach us a lesson. Around the same time I got threatening calls at home. One typical caller said, "If you think we're going to let you help that nigger get away with killing that girl, you've got another thing coming. You're both going to be dead niggers!"

Although I was handling other cases, I was certain the calls were in response to the McMillian case. Leading up to the hearing, Michael and I had been followed several times while doing investigative work in Monroe County. A scary man had called me late one night to tell me that someone had offered him a lot of money to kill me, but he said he wasn't going to do it because he respected what we did. I expressed my appreciation for his support and politely thanked him. It was hard to know how seriously to take any of it, but it was definitely unnerving.

After we cleared the building, the police went through the office with dogs. No bomb was found, and when the building didn't blow up after an hour and a half, we all filed back inside. We had work to do.

A few days later, I received a different kind of bombshell, this time a call from the clerk's office in Baldwin County. The clerk was calling to let me know that Judge Norton had ruled in the McMillian case—she needed my fax number to send me a copy of the ruling. I gave it to her and sat nervously by the fax machine. When only three sheets of paper came through the machine I was concerned.

The pages contained a tersely worded order from Judge Norton denying us relief. I was more disappointed than devastated. I had suspected that this would be Judge Norton's response. For all his interest at the hearing, he had never seemed particularly engaged over the basic question of whether Walter was guilty or innocent. He was locked into a maintenance role: He was a custodian for the system who was unlikely to overturn the previous judgment, even if there was compelling evidence of innocence.

What was surprising, however, was how superficial, insubstantial, and uninterested the court's two-and-a-half-page order read. The judge addressed only the testimony of Ralph Myers and none of the legal claims we'd presented or any of the testimonies of the other dozen-plus witnesses. In fact, there was no case law cited in the entire order:

Ralph Meyers took the stand before this Court, swore to tell the truth and proceeded to recant most, if not all, of the relevant portions of his testimony at trial. Clearly, Ralph Meyers has either perjured himself at trial or has perjured himself in front of this Court.

The following areas of concern were considered in reaching this decision: The demeanor of the witness; the opportunity of the witness to have knowledge of the facts which he testified to at trial; the rationale, as stated by the witness for his testimony at the first trial; the rationale, as stated by the defendant, for his recantation; the evidence of external pressures brought to bear on the witness prior to and after both trial and recantation; the actions of the witness that lend credence to his trial testimony and the actions of the witness that lend credence to his recantation; evidence adduced at trial in contradiction of the witness' testimony on details, and due to the nature of this case, any evidence from any source concerning the inability of the witness to have known the facts to which he testified to at trial.

Since the trial of this matter was conducted before the Honorable R. E. L. Key, Circuit Judge, Retired, this court did not have the opportunity to compare the demeanor of the witness during trial testimony and his recantation testimony.

A review of the other factors set out above does not provide conclusive evidence that the witness, Ralph Meyers, perjured himself at the original trial. There is ample evidence that pressure has been brought to bear on Ralph Meyers since his trial testimony which could tend to discredit his recantation. There is absolutely no evidence in the trial record or the recantation testimony that places Ralph Meyers somewhere other than the scene of the crime at the time it was committed.

This cause having been remanded to the Court for a determination of whether there is evidence to support the theory that Ralph Meyers perjured himself at the original trial and this court having determined that there is insufficient evidence to support that theory, it is therefore ORDERED, ADJUDGED and DECREED that the trial testimony of Ralph Myers is not found to have been perjured testimony.

Done this 19th day of May, 1992.

THOMAS B. NORTON, JR.
Circuit Judge

While Chapman had suggested that Myers must have been pressured to recant, the district attorney presented no actual evidence to support that claim, which made the judge's ruling hard to understand. I had advised Walter and his family that we would likely need to go to an appellate court for any real chance of relief, despite how positive everyone thought the hearing had been.

I was optimistic about what our evidence might accomplish in the Alabama Court of Criminal Appeals. We were now regularly arguing cases in front of that court. Following my first McMillian argument, we had filed almost two dozen death penalty appeals, and the court was starting to respond to our advocacy. We had won four reversals in death penalty cases in 1990, four more in 1991, and by the end of 1992, we'd won relief for another eight death row prisoners. The court frequently complained about being forced to order new trials or grant relief, but nonetheless ruled in our favor. In a few years, some of the appellate court judges would be attacked and replaced in partisan judicial elections by candidates who complained about the court's rulings in death penalty cases. But we persisted and continued raising reversible errors in capital cases. We were pushing the court to enforce the law in these cases, and when they refused, we were having success getting the Alabama Supreme Court and federal courts to grant relief.

Based on this recent experience, I thought we could win relief for McMillian on appeal. Even if the court was unwilling to rule that Walter was innocent and should be released, the withholding of exculpatory evidence was extreme enough that the court would have a hard time avoiding the case law requiring a new trial. Nothing could be assured, but I explained to Walter that we were only just now getting to a court where our claims would be seriously considered.

Michael had stayed long past the two years he had committed to us, but he was now scheduled to move to San Diego to start a job as a federal public defender. He agonized about leaving our office, although he was less conflicted about leaving Alabama.

I assigned one of our new attorneys, Bernard Harcourt, to replace Michael on Walter's case. Bernard was a lot like Michael in that he was smart, determined, and extremely hardworking. He had first worked with me when he was a law student at Harvard Law School. He became so engaged in the work that he asked the federal judge he was clerking for after law school if he could cut short his two-year clerkship to join us in Alabama. The judge agreed, and Bernard arrived shortly before Michael left. Raised in New York City by French parents, he had attended the Lycée Français de New York in Manhattan, a high school that was unapologetic about its European perspective on education. After graduating from Princeton, Bernard worked in banking before pursuing his law degree. He had been preparing for a traditional legal career until he came down to work with us one summer and became fascinated by the issues that death penalty cases presented. He and his girlfriend, Mia, moved to Montgomery and were intrigued by life in Alabama. Bernard's quick immersion in the McMillian case intensified his cultural adventure more than he could have ever imagined.

The community's presence at the hearing got people talking about what we had presented in court, and that encouraged more people to come forward with helpful information. All sorts of people were contacting us with wide-ranging claims of corruption and misconduct. Only a few things here and there were useful to us in our efforts to free Walter, but all of it was interesting. Bernard and I continued to track leads and interview people who had insights to share about life in Monroe County.

The threats we received made me worry about the hostility that Walter would face if he was ever released. I wondered how safely he could live in the community if everyone was persuaded that he was a dangerous murderer. We began discussing the idea of reaching out to a few people who might help us publicly dramatize the injustice of Mr. McMillian's wrongful conviction as a way of setting the stage for his possible release. If the public could only know what we knew, it might ease his re-entry into freedom. We wanted people to understand this simple fact: *Walter did not commit that murder.* His freedom wouldn't be based on some tricky legal loophole or the exploitation of a technicality. It would be based on simple justice—he was an innocent man.

On the other hand, I didn't think media attention would help win the case now pending in the Court of Criminal Appeals. In fact, the chief judge on the court, John Patterson, had famously sued *The New York Times* over their coverage of the Civil Rights Movement when he was Alabama's governor. It was a common tactic used by Southern politicians during civil rights protests: Sue national media outlets for defamation if they provide sympathetic coverage of activists or if they characterize Southern politicians and law enforcement officers unfavorably. Southern state court judges and all-white juries were all too willing to rule in favor of "defamed" local officials, and state authorities had won millions of dollars in judgments this way. More important, the defamation lawsuits chilled sympathetic coverage of civil rights activism.

In 1960, *The New York Times* printed an advertisement titled "Heed Their Rising Voices" that attempted to raise money to defend Dr. Martin Luther King Jr. against perjury charges in Alabama. Southern officials responded by going on the offensive and suing the newspaper. Public Safety Commissioner L. B. Sullivan and Governor Patterson claimed defamation. A local jury awarded them half a million dollars, and the case was appealed to the U.S. Supreme Court.

In a landmark ruling, *New York Times v. Sullivan* changed the standard for defamation and libel by requiring plaintiffs to prove malice—that is, evidence of actual knowledge on the part of the publisher that a statement is false. The ruling marked a significant victory for freedom of the press, and it liberated media outlets and publishers to talk more honestly about civil rights protests and activism. But in the South it generated even more contempt for the national press, and that animosity has lingered beyond the Civil Rights Era. I had no doubt that national press coverage of Walter's case would not help our cause at the Court of Criminal Appeals.

But I did think getting a more informed view of Walter's conviction and the murder would make his life after release less dangerous—assuming we could ever get his conviction overturned. We felt that we had to take our chances and get the story out. I was concerned about the inability of people in the local community to get a fair picture of what was going on. Aside from the hostility we feared he would face if Walter was released, we were worried about what would happen if a new trial was ordered. All of the prejudicial media coverage would make a fair trial nearly impossible. The local press in Monroe County and Mobile had demonized Walter and had defiantly maintained that his conviction was reliable and his execution necessary.

Local papers had painted Walter as a dangerous drug dealer who had possibly murdered several innocent teenagers. Monroeville and Mobile newspapers freely printed assertions that Walter was a "drug kingpin," a "sexual predator," and a "gang leader." When he was first arrested, local headlines emphasized the absurd sexual misconduct charges involving Ralph Myers. "McMillian Charged with Sodomy" was a common headline. In covering the hearings, the *Monroe Journal* focused on the danger Walter posed: "Those entering the courtroom had to pass through a metal detector, as has been the case throughout the court proceedings against McMillian, and officers were stationed throughout the courtroom." Despite all of the evidence presented at our hearing showing that Walter had nothing to do with the Pittman murder, the local press invoked the case to scare up more fear about Walter. "Convicted Slayer Wanted in East Brewton Murder" was an early headline in the Brewton paper. "Ronda Wasn't the Only Girl Killed" was the headline in the *Mobile Press Register* after our hearing. The Mobile paper reported after the hearing: "Myers and McMillian were part of a burglary, theft, forgery and drug smuggling ring that operated in several counties in South Alabama, according to law enforcement officers. McMillian was the leader of the operation." From its focus on his pretrial placement on death row to the extra security surrounding his court appearances, the narrative in the press was clear: This man was extremely dangerous.

At this point, people seemed uninterested in the truth surrounding the crime. During the most recent hearing in Baldwin County, the State's local supporters walked out of the courtroom rather than hear the evidence that supported Walter's innocence. It was risky, but we hoped that national press coverage of our side of the story would change the narrative.

A *Washington Post* journalist, Walt Harrington, had come to Alabama to do a piece on our work a year earlier and had heard me describe the McMillian case. He passed that information to a journalist friend of his, Pete Earley, who contacted me and became immediately interested. After reading the transcripts and files we provided him, he jumped into the case, spent time with several of the players, and quickly came to share our astonishment that Walter had been convicted on such unreliable evidence.

I'd given a speech at Yale Law School earlier in the year that was attended by a producer from the popular CBS investigative program *60 Minutes*, and he also called me. We'd gotten calls from various news magazine programs over the previous few years that expressed interest in covering our work, but I was wary. My general attitude was that press coverage rarely helped our clients. Beyond the general anti-media sentiments in the South, the death penalty was particularly polarizing. It's such a politically charged topic that even sympathetic pieces about people on death row usually triggered a local backlash that created more problems for the client and the case. Even though the clients sometimes wanted press attention, I was extremely resistant to media interviews about pending cases. I knew of too many cases where a favorable profile in the media had provoked an expedited execution date or retaliatory mistreatment that made things much worse.

We filed our appeal in the Court of Criminal Appeals that summer. With no small amount of lingering uncertainty, I decided to move forward with the *60 Minutes* piece. Veteran reporter Ed Bradley and his producer David Gelber came down from New York City to Monroeville on a 100-degree day in July and interviewed many of the people whose testimony we'd presented at our hearing. They spoke with Walter, Ralph Myers, Karen Kelly, Darnell Houston, Clay Kast, Jimmy Williams, Walter's family, and Woodrow Ikner. They confronted Bill Hooks at his job and conducted an extensive interview with Tommy Chapman. Word got around quickly that news celebrity Ed Bradley was in town, upsetting local officials. The *Monroe Journal* wrote:

> Too many of these [out-of-town] writers express open scorn for the people and institutions they encounter here, making no more than a superficial effort to gather facts. Worse, a few have been demonstrably inaccurate. We could do without any more news coverage of the "big-time reporter comes to hick town" genre.

Even before the piece was broadcast, the local media seemed to be urging the community to distrust anything they heard reported about the case. In "CBS Examines Murder Case," a local reporter for the *Monroe Journal* wrote, "Monroe County District Attorney Tommy Chapman said he believes researchers for the CBS television news-magazine program *60 Minutes* had their minds made up before ever coming here." Chapman had taken to using a photo of Walter obtained at the time of his arrest that showed him with long bushy hair and a beard, which Chapman thought made it clear that he was a dangerous criminal. "The person they interviewed at Holman prison is not the same person arrested by Sheriff Tate for this murder," Chapman explained. The *Journal* added that Chapman offered CBS the photograph of the "real" McMillian taken at the time of his arrest, but they were "not interested." Prisoners in Alabama are required to remain clean-shaven, so of course Walter looked different when interviewed on camera.

When the *60 Minutes* piece aired months later, local officials were quick to discredit it. The *Mobile Press Register* headline was "DA: TV Account of McMillian's Conviction a 'Disgrace'"; the article quoted Chapman: "For them to hold themselves up as a reputable news show is beyond belief, and irresponsible." The publicity was characterized as further injuring Ronda Morrison's parents. The local writers complained that the Morrisons had to worry and deal with the stress that new publicity "could lead many people to think McMillian is innocent."

The local media were eager to join the prosecutors in criticizing the *60 Minutes* piece because it implicated their coverage, which had largely presented only the prosecution's theory and characterization of Walter and the crime. But people in the community watched *60 Minutes* all the time and generally trusted it. Despite the local media reaction, the CBS coverage gave the community a summary of the evidence we'd presented in court and created questions and doubts about Walter's guilt. Some influential community leaders also thought it made Monroeville look backward and possibly racist in a way that was not good for the community's image or efforts at recruiting business, and business leaders started asking tough questions of Chapman and law enforcement about what was going on in the case.

People in the black community were thrilled to see honest coverage of the case. They had been whispering about Walter's wrongful conviction for years. The case had so traumatized the black community that many had become preoccupied with each court development and ruling. We frequently got calls from people simply seeking an update. Some callers sought clarification of a particular point in the case that had been the subject of serious debate in a barbershop or at a social gathering. For many black people in the region, watching the evidence that we had presented in court now laid out on national television was therapeutic.

In the *60 Minutes* interview with Chapman, he dismissed as silly the suggestion of any racial bias in Walter McMillian's prosecution. He calmly professed his complete confidence and certainty that McMillian was guilty and that he should be executed as soon as possible. He expressed contempt for Walter's attorneys and "people who try to second-guess juries."

We later found out that privately, despite the confidence expressed in his statements to local media and to *60 Minutes*, Chapman had begun to worry about the reliability of the evidence against Walter. He couldn't ignore the problems in the case that had been exposed at the hearing. Given our success in other death penalty cases, he must have feared the very real possibility of the appellate court's overturning Walter's conviction. Chapman had become the public face defending the conviction, and he realized that he'd put his own credibility on the line by relying on the work of local investigators—work that was now revealed as almost farcically flawed.

Chapman called Tate, Ikner, and Benson together shortly after the hearing and expressed his concerns. When he asked the local investigators to explain the contradictory evidence we had presented, he wasn't impressed with what he heard. Not long after that, he formally asked ABI officials in Montgomery to conduct another investigation into the murder to confirm Mr. McMillian's guilt.

Chapman never informed us directly about the new investigation, even though for over two years we'd sought just such a re-examination of the evidence. When the new ABI investigators, Tom Taylor and Greg Cole, called me, I eagerly agreed to share case files and information. After meeting with them, I was even more hopeful about what might come out of the investigation. They both seemed like no-nonsense, experienced investigators who were interested in doing credible and reliable work.

Within a few weeks, Taylor and Cole seemed to doubt that McMillian was guilty. They were not connected to any of the players in South Alabama. We gave them files, memoranda, and even some original evidence because we had nothing to hide. I was nervous that if we won a reversal and had to retry the case, we might be disadvantaged by disclosing so much information to state investigators—who would then be better prepared to smear or undermine our evidence—but I was still confident that any reasonable, honest investigation would reveal the absurdity of the charges against Walter.

By January, six months had passed since we had filed our appeal at the Court of Criminal Appeals, and a ruling was due any week. That's when Tom Taylor called and said that he and Cole wanted to meet with us again. We'd talked a few times during their investigation, but this time we'd be discussing their findings. When they arrived, Bernard and I sat down with them in my office and they wasted no time.

"There is no way Walter McMillian killed Ronda Morrison." Tom Taylor spoke plainly and directly. "We're going to report to the attorney general, the district attorney, and anyone who asks that McMillian had nothing to do with either of these murders and is completely innocent."

I tried not to look as thrilled as I felt. I didn't want to scare away this good news. "That's terrific," I said, trying to sound unsurprised. "I'm pleased to hear that and I have to say I'm extremely grateful that you've looked at the evidence in this case thoroughly and honestly."

"Well, confirming that McMillian had nothing to do with this wasn't that hard," Taylor replied. "Why would a drug kingpin live in the conditions he was living in and work fifteen hours a day cutting timber on difficult terrain? What we were told by local law enforcement about McMillian didn't make much sense, and the story Myers told at trial definitely made no sense. I still can't believe a jury ever convicted him."

Cole spoke up. "You'll be very interested to know that both Hooks and Hightower have admitted that their trial testimony was false."

"Really?" I couldn't hide my surprise at this.

"Yes. When we were asked to investigate this case, we were told that you should be investigated because Hooks had said that you had offered him money and a condo in Mexico if he changed his testimony." Taylor was dead serious.

"A condo in Mexico?"

"On a beach, I think," Cole added nonchalantly.

"Wait, me? I was going to give Bill Hooks a beach condo in Mexico if he changed his testimony against Walter?" It was difficult to contain my shock.

"Well, I know it must sound crazy to you, but believe me there were people down there who were raring to get you indicted. But when we talked to Hooks, it didn't take very long before he not only acknowledged that he'd never spoken to you and that you had never bribed him, but he also admitted that his trial testimony against McMillian was completely made up."

"Well, we've never had any doubts that Hooks was lying."

Cole chuckled. "We started polygraphing people, and things fell apart pretty quickly."

Bernard asked the obvious question, "Well, what happens now?"

Taylor looked over at his partner and then at us. "Well, we're not completely done. We'd like to solve this crime, and we have a suspect.

I'm wondering if you might be willing to help us. I know you're not trying to get anybody on death row, but we thought you might at least consider providing some help to identify the real killer. People will be a lot more accepting of Mr. McMillian's innocence if they know who really committed this crime."

While it was ridiculous to think that Walter's freedom depended on the arrest of someone else, I had imagined that a successful investigation might get to this—and I couldn't dispute that even if an ABI investigation cleared Walter, people would still think he'd gotten away with murder until the actual killer was identified. We had long ago concluded that finding the real murderer might be the most effective way to free Walter, but without the power and authority of law enforcement officers, we were limited in what we could discover.

We did have a strong theory. Several witnesses had told us that around the time of the crime, a white man had been seen leaving the cleaners. We had learned that before her death, Ronda Morrison had been receiving menacing calls and that there was a man who had been avidly and inappropriately pursuing her—stopping by unannounced at the cleaners, maybe even stalking her. We had not initially been able to identify this strange man.

But we did have our suspicions. We had been contacted by a white man who seemed intensely interested in the case. He would call wanting to talk at length about what we were investigating. He would hint at having information that could help us, but he was coy and slow to share anything concrete. He repeatedly told us that he knew that McMillian was innocent and he would help us prove it. Eventually, after several calls and hours of conversation, he claimed to know where the murder weapon, which had never been recovered, might be located.

We tried to get as much information out of him as we could. We also checked his background. He told us that he'd had some conflicts with another man in town and that the more he talked the more he blamed this other man for the shooting death of Morrison. When we investigated this theory, we weren't impressed. The other man didn't match the eyewitness descriptions of the person seen leaving the cleaners, and he didn't have our caller's history of stalking, violence against women, and preoccupation with the Morrison murder. We began to think that our caller could be the person who had murdered Ronda Morrison. We had dozens of phone conversations with him and even met him a couple of times. We were less and less convinced that the man he was accusing of committing the crime was involved. At some point we asked him some direct questions about where he was on the day of the murder, which must have alarmed him because we heard from him less often after that.

Before I could tell any of this to the ABI investigators, Taylor said, "We think you may have interviewed our suspect and may have collected a good bit of information from this guy. We were hoping you might allow us to have access to that information and those interviews." He named our suspect.

I told them we would give them access to the information we had collected. None of it was protected by attorney-client privilege; we had never represented this man or obtained anything confidentially. I told Taylor and Cole to give us a few days to organize the information, and then we would turn it over.

"We want to get Walter out of prison as soon as possible," I insisted.

"Well, I think the attorney general and the lawyers would like to maintain the status quo for a few more months, until we can make an arrest of the actual killer."

"Right, but you do understand that the status quo is a problem for us? Walter has been on death row for nearly six years for a crime he didn't commit."

Taylor and Cole looked at each other uncomfortably. Taylor responded, "We're not lawyers so I can't really understand where they're coming from. If I was in prison for something I didn't do and you were my lawyer, I hope to hell you'd get me out as soon as you could."

When they left, Bernard and I were very excited, but we remained troubled by this plan to "maintain the status quo." I decided I would call the attorney general's office and see if they would concede legal error in the pending appeal, which would ensure relief at the appellate court and perhaps expedite Walter's release.

Another lawyer from the attorney general's office named Ken Nunnelly had taken over the appeal. I had dealt with Nunnelly in several other death penalty cases. I told him that I'd met with the ABI investigators and that I understood there were some case developments that favored Mr. McMillian. It became clear that the state lawyers had been discussing this case quite a bit.

"Bryan, it's all going to work out, but you'll need to wait a few more months. He's been on the row for years, so a few more months are not going to make that much of a difference."

"Ken, every day makes a difference when you're locked down on death row, and you've been wrongly convicted." I tried to get a commitment but he offered nothing. I asked to meet with the attorney general or whatever official had final decision-making authority, and he said that he would see what he could do. Within a few days the State submitted a peculiar pleading to the Court of Criminal Appeals. The attorney general's motion asked the court to stay the litigation and not issue a ruling because they "may have uncovered exculpatory evidence favorable to Mr. McMillian that could entitle him to a new trial," but they needed more time to complete their investigation.

I was furious that the State would try to prolong any order granting relief to Walter. It was consistent with everything that had happened over the last six years, but it was still maddening. We quickly filed a response opposing the State's motion. We told the court that there was overwhelming evidence that Mr. McMillian's rights had been violated, and that he was entitled to immediate relief. Delaying relief would add further injury to a man who had been wrongfully convicted and condemned to death row for a crime he did not commit. We urged the court to deny the State's request and rule quickly.

I was talking to Minnie and the family every week now, keeping everyone updated about the new state investigation.

"I feel like something good is about to happen, Bryan," Minnie said to me. "They've kept him for years. Now it's time they let him go. They have to let him go."

I appreciated her optimism, but I worried, too. We'd been disappointed so often before. "We have to remain hopeful, Minnie."

"I've always told people 'no lie can live forever,' and this has always been one big lie."

I wasn't exactly sure how to manage the family's expectations. I felt I was supposed to be the cautionary voice that prepared family members for the worst even while I urged them to hope for the best. It was a task that was growing in complexity as I handled more cases and saw the myriad ways that things could go wrong. But I was developing a maturing recognition of the importance of hopefulness in creating justice.

I'd started addressing the subject of hopefulness in talks to small groups. I'd grown fond of quoting Václav Havel, the great Czech leader who had said that "hope" was the one thing that people struggling in Eastern Europe needed during the era of Soviet domination.

Havel had said that people struggling for independence wanted money and recognition from other countries; they wanted more criticism of the Soviet empire from the West and more diplomatic pressure. But Havel had said that these were things they *wanted*; the only thing they *needed* was hope. Not that pie in the sky stuff, not a preference for optimism over pessimism, but rather "an orientation of the spirit." The kind of hope that creates a willingness to position oneself in a hopeless place and be a witness, that allows one to believe in a better future, even in the face of abusive power. That kind of hope makes one strong.

Havel prescribed exactly what our work seemed to require. Walter's case had needed it more than most. So I didn't discourage Minnie. Together, we hoped.

On February 23, nearly six weeks after getting the ABI's report, I received a call from the clerk of the court informing us that the Court of

Criminal Appeals had ruled in the McMillian case and that we could pick up the opinion.

"You're going to like this," she said cryptically.

I ran over to the courthouse and was out of breath by the time I sat down to read the thirty-five-page ruling. The clerk was right. The ruling invalidated Walter's conviction and death sentence. The court didn't conclude that he was innocent and must be released, but it ruled in our favor on every other claim and ordered a new trial. I didn't realize how much I had feared that we would lose until we finally won.

I jumped into the car and raced down to death row to tell Walter in person. I watched him take it all in. He leaned back and gave me a familiar chuckle.

"Well," he said slowly, "you know, that's good. That's good."

"Good? It's great!"

"Yeah, it is great." He was grinning now with a freedom I hadn't seen before. "Whew, man, I can't believe it, I can't believe it. . . . Whew!"

His smile started to fade, and he began slowly shaking his head.

"Six years, six years gone." He looked away with a pained expression. "These six years feel like fifty. Six years, just gone. I've been so worried they were going to kill me, I haven't even thought about the time I've lost."

His troubled look sobered me, too. "I know, Walter, and we're not clear yet," I said. "The ruling only gives you a new trial. Given what the ABI has said, I can't believe they would try to prosecute you again, but with this crowd reasonable conduct is never guaranteed. I'm going to try and get you home as soon as humanly possible."

With thoughts of home, his mood lightened and we started talking about things we'd been too afraid to discuss since we'd met. He said, "I want to meet everybody who has helped me in Montgomery. And I want to go around with you and tell the world what they did to me. There are other people here who are as innocent as I am." He paused and started smiling again. "Man, I want some good food, too. I ain't had no real good food in so long that I can't even remember what it tastes like."

"Whatever you want, it will be my treat," I said proudly.

"From what I hear, you might not be able to afford the kind of meal I want," he teased. "I want steak, chicken, pork, maybe some good cooked coon."

"Coon?"

"Oh, don't pretend. You know you like grilled raccoon. Please don't sit there and tell me you ain't never had no good coon when I know you grew up in the country just like I did. There has been many a time when me and my cousin would be driving, and a coon would run cross the road and he'd say, 'Stop the car, stop the car!' And I'd stop the car and he'd jump out and go running into the woods and come back minutes later with a raccoon he done caught. We would take it home, skin it, and fry or barbecue that meat. Maaaan . . . what you talking about? That would be some good eatin'."

"You've got to be joking. I grew up in the country, but I never chased any kind of wild animal into the woods to take home and eat."

We relaxed and laughed a lot. We had laughed before today—Walter's sense of humor hadn't failed him despite his six years on death row. And this case had given him lots of fodder. We would often talk about situations and people connected to the case that, for all the damage they had caused, had still made us laugh at their absurdity. But the laughter today felt very different. It was the laughter of liberation.

I drove back to Montgomery and thought about how to expedite Walter's release. I called Tommy Chapman and told him that I intended to file a motion to dismiss all charges against Walter in light of the appellate court's ruling, and I hoped he would consider joining the motion or at least not oppose it. He sighed. "We should talk when this is all over. Once you file your motion, I'll get back to you about whether I'll join it. We certainly won't oppose it."

A hearing on the motion was set. The State did, in fact, join our motion to dismiss the charges, and I didn't expect the final hearing to last more than a few minutes. The night before, I'd driven down to

Minnie's to get a suit for Walter to wear at the hearing, since he would finally be able to walk out of court a free man. When I arrived at her house, she gave me a long hug. It looked like she had been crying and hadn't slept. We sat down, and she told me again how happy she was that they were letting him out. But she looked troubled. Finally, she turned to me.

"Bryan, I think you need to tell him that maybe he shouldn't come back here. It's just all been too much. The stress, the gossip, the lies, everything. He doesn't deserve what they put him through, and it will hurt me to my heart the rest of my life what they did to him, and the rest of us. But I don't think I can go back to the way things were."

"Well, you all should talk when he gets home."

"We want to have everybody over when he gets out. We want to cook some good food, and everybody will want to celebrate. But after that, maybe he should go to Montgomery with you."

I had already talked with Walter about not staying his first few nights in Monroeville, for security reasons. We had talked about him spending time with family members in Florida while we monitored the local reaction to his release. But I hadn't discussed his future with Minnie.

I kept urging Minnie to talk with Walter when he got home, but it was clear she didn't have the heart for that. I drove back to Montgomery, sadly realizing that even as we stood on the brink of victory and what should have been a glorious release for Walter and his family, this nightmare would likely never be completely over for him. For the first time I fully reckoned with the truth that the conviction, the death sentence, and the heartbreak and devastation of this miscarriage of justice had created permanent injuries.

State, local, and national media outlets were crowded outside the courthouse when I arrived the next morning. Dozens of Walter's family members and friends from the community were there to greet him when he came out. They had made signs and banners, which surprised me. They were such simple gestures, but I found myself deeply moved. The signs gave a silent voice to the crowd: "Welcome Home, Johnny

D," "God Never Fails," "Free at Last, Thank God Almighty, We Are Free at Last."

I went down to the jail and brought Walter his suit. I told him that a celebration was planned at his house after the hearing. The prison had not allowed Walter to bring his possessions to the courthouse, refusing to acknowledge that he might be released, so we would have to go back to Holman Prison to get his things before the homecoming at his house. I also told him that I'd reserved a hotel room for him in Montgomery and that it would probably be safest to spend the next few nights there.

I reluctantly talked to him about my conversation with Minnie. He seemed surprised and hurt but didn't linger on it.

"This is a really happy day for me. Nothing can really spoil getting your freedom back."

"Well, y'all should talk at some point," I urged.

I went upstairs to find Tommy Chapman waiting for me in the courtroom. "After we're done, I'd like to shake his hand," he told me. "Would that be all right?"

"I think he'd appreciate that."

"This case has taught me things I didn't even know I had to learn."

"We've all learned a lot, Tommy."

There were deputy sheriffs everywhere. When Bernard arrived, we consulted briefly at the counsel table before a bailiff asked us to go back to the judge's chambers. Judge Norton had retired weeks before the ruling from the Court of Criminal Appeals. The new judge, Pamela Baschab, greeted me warmly. We made small talk and then discussed what would happen during the hearing. Everyone was strangely pleasant.

"Mr. Stevenson, if you'll just present the motion and provide a brief summary, I don't need any arguments or statements, I intend to grant the motion immediately so you all can get home. We can get this done quickly." We went into the courtroom. There seemed to be more black deputies in the courtroom for this hearing than I'd ever seen in my appearances in that courthouse. There was no metal detector, no menacing dog. The courtroom was packed with Walter's family members and supporters. There were more cheering black folks outside the courthouse who couldn't get in. A horde of television cameras and journalists spilled out of the crowded courtroom.

They finally brought Walter into the courtroom wearing the black suit and white shirt I'd brought him. He looked handsome and fit, like a different man. The deputies didn't handcuff Walter or shackle him, so he walked into court waving to family and friends. His family had not seen him dressed in anything but his white prison uniform since the trial six years earlier, and many in the crowd gasped when he walked into the courtroom in a suit. For years Walter's family members and supporters had been confronted with menacing stares and threats of expulsion whenever they expressed some spontaneous opinion during court proceedings, but today the deputies accepted their expressive cheerfulness in silence.

The judge took the bench, and I stepped forward to speak. I gave a brief history of the case and informed the court that both the defendant and the State were moving the court to dismiss all charges. The judge quickly granted the motion and asked if there was anything further. All of sudden, I felt strangely agitated. I'd expected to be exuberant. Everyone was in such a good mood. The judge and the prosecutor were suddenly generous and accommodating. It was as if everyone wanted to be sure there were no hard feelings or grudges.

Walter was rightfully ecstatic, but I was confused by my suddenly simmering anger. We were about to leave court for the last time, and I started thinking about how much pain and suffering had been inflicted on Walter and his family, the entire community. I thought about how if Judge Robert E. Lee Key hadn't overridden the jury's verdict of life imprisonment without parole and imposed the death penalty, which brought the case to our attention, Walter likely would have spent the rest of his life incarcerated and died in a prison cell. I thought about how certain it was that hundreds, maybe thousands of other people were just as innocent as Walter but would never get the help they need. I knew this wasn't the place or time to make a speech or complain, but I couldn't stop myself from making one final comment.

"Your Honor, I just want to say this before we adjourn. It was far too easy to convict this wrongly accused man for murder and send him to death row for something he didn't do and much too hard to win his freedom after proving his innocence. We have serious problems and important work that must be done in this state."

I sat down and the judge pronounced Walter free to go. Just like that he was a free man.

Walter hugged me tightly, and I gave him a handkerchief to wipe the tears from his eyes. I led him over to Chapman, and they shook hands. The black deputies who had hovered nearby ushered us toward a back door that led downstairs, where a throng of reporters waited. One of the deputies patted me on the back, declaring, "That's awesome, man. That's awesome." I asked Bernard to tell the family and supporters that we would meet them out front.

Walter stood very close to me as we answered questions from the press. I could tell he was feeling overwhelmed, so I cut off the questions after a few minutes, and we walked to the front door of the courthouse. TV camera crews followed us. As we walked outside, dozens of people cheered and waved their signs. Walter's relatives ran up to him to hug him, and they hugged me, too. Walter's grandchildren grabbed his hands. Older people I hadn't previously met came up to hug him. Walter couldn't believe how many people were there for him. He hugged everyone. Even when some of the men came up to shake his hand, he gave them a hug. I told everyone that Bernard and I had to take Walter to the prison and that we would come to the house directly from there. It took nearly an hour to get through the crowd and into the car.

On the drive to the prison, Walter told me that the men on death row had held a special service for him on his last night. They had come to pray for him and give him their final hugs. Walter said he felt guilty leaving them behind. I told him not to—they were all thrilled to know he was going home. His freedom was, in a small way, a sign of hope in a hopeless place.

Despite my assurances that we'd be at the house shortly, everyone followed us to the prison. The press, the local TV crews, the family, everyone. When we got to Holman, a caravan of media and well-wishers trailed behind us. I parked and walked to the front gate to explain to the guard in the tower that I didn't have anything to do with all of the people—I knew that the warden had strict policies about the presence of people who didn't have business at the prison. But the guard waved us inside. No one tried to get the crowd to leave.

We went to the prison office to collect Walter's possessions: his legal materials and correspondence with me, letters from family and supporters, a Bible, the Timex watch he was wearing when he was arrested, and the wallet he had had with him back in June 1987 when his nightmare began. The wallet still had $23 in it. Walter had given to other death row prisoners his fan, a dictionary, and the food items he had in his cell. I saw the warden peering at us from his office as we collected Walter's things, but he didn't come out.

A few guards watched as we walked out the front gate of the prison. Lots of people were still gathered outside. I saw Mrs. Williams. Walter went up to her and gave her a hug. When their embrace released, she looked over and winked at me. I couldn't help but laugh.

Men in their cells could see the crowd outside and started shouting encouragement to Walter as he walked away. We couldn't see them from outside the prison, but their voices rang out just the same—the voices were haunting because they were disembodied, but they were full of excitement and hopefulness. One of the last voices we heard was a man shouting, "Stay strong, man. Stay strong!"

Walter shouted back, "All right!"

As he walked to the car, Walter raised his arms and gently moved them up and down as if he meant to take flight. He looked at me and said, "I feel like a bird, I feel like a bird."

Chapter Twelve

Mother, Mother

On a cool, crisp mid-March evening, Marsha Colbey stepped out onto the streets of New York City in an elegant royal blue gown with her husband beside her. She had dreamed of a moment like this for years. She took in the sights and sounds with great curiosity as they strolled down the busy sidewalks. Enormous buildings stretched to the sky in the distance while raucous traffic whizzed through Greenwich Village streets. The clusters of New York students and artisans paid them no mind as they made their way through Washington Square Park. She noticed an amateur jazz trio laboring through standards on a park corner. It all seemed like something out of a movie.

A white woman from a poor rural Alabama town, Marsha had never been to New York, but she was about to be honored at a dinner with two hundred guests. It was all exciting, but she was experiencing something unusual as she made her way to the venue. She soon sorted out what she was feeling. Freedom. She was wandering the streets of the world's most dazzling city with her husband, and she was free. It was a glorious feeling. Everything in the last three months since her release had been magical. It was beyond what she would have imagined even before she was sentenced to life imprisonment without parole at the Julia Tutwiler Prison for Women.

When Hurricane Ivan hit coastal Alabama and blew chaos and calamity into Marsha's life, she thought things were as bad as they could get. Ivan spawned 119 tornadoes and created over $18 billion dollars in damage. With six children to protect, she had no time to panic over the loss of their home or the violent destruction of everything around them. It was the uncertainty that worried Marsha. Where would she or her husband find work? How long would the kids be out of school? What would they do for money? What would they do for food? Everyone on the Gulf Coast was feeling vulnerable in the face of such an uncertain future. The constant wave of tropical storms and hurricanes that menaced coastal Louisiana, Alabama, Mississippi, and Florida in the summer of 2004 turned their relaxed Southern coastal life into an apocalyptic struggle for survival.

Marsha and Glen Colbey were living in a crowded trailer with their children, and they knew they were at risk when the hurricane warnings were announced. They weren't alone; plenty of other families shared their situation, which offered some consolation. But when Ivan destroyed the Colbey home in September, there was little comfort in finding herself in line with thousands of other people seeking assistance from the Federal Emergency Management Agency (FEMA). Aid eventually came. The Colbeys were given a FEMA camper trailer as temporary housing, and they put it on their property so the kids could stay in their nearby schools. Marsha and Glen had found construction work and roofing jobs at the start of the summer, but now it would be weeks before rebuilding jobs would be available.

Marsha could also tell that she was pregnant. She was forty-three years old and hadn't planned on having another child. All she could think about was how in a few months the pregnancy would limit her ability to do construction work. Her worry sometimes tipped over into a deeper anxiety that triggered an old temptation: drugs. But there were too many people depending on her, and there was too much to manage to give in. Five years earlier, police were called after nurses had found cocaine in her system when she was pregnant with her youngest son, Joshua, and the authorities had terrified her with accusations and threats of criminal prosecution, imprisonment, and the seizure of her children. She was not going to risk that again.

She and Glen were dirt poor, but Marsha had always compensated for the things she couldn't give her kids by giving them all of her heart. She read to them, talked to them, played with them, hugged and kissed them constantly, and kept them close at all times. Against all odds, she nurtured a precious family bonded by an intense love. Her older boys, even her nineteen-year-old, stayed close to her at home despite the many distractions that emerged as they finished high school. Marsha liked being a mom. It's why she didn't worry about having so many kids. Getting pregnant with a seventh was not what she had expected or preferred, but she would love this child as she had loved each one before.

By winter, things in Baldwin County had settled down. Jobs had returned, and Glen finally found more steady work. The family was still struggling financially, but most of the kids were back in school, and it seemed as if they had survived the worst of the destruction.

Marsha knew that a pregnancy at her age was very risky, but she couldn't afford to see a doctor. She just didn't have the money to spare. Having endured six previous deliveries, she knew what to expect and thought she'd make the best of it without prenatal care. She tried not to worry even though she'd been experiencing some pains and problems with this pregnancy that she didn't remember having before. There had been bleeding; if she could have afforded an examination, a doctor would have found signs of placental abruption.

Their old trailer sat next to the new FEMA camper and was largely uninhabitable, but it still had running water and a bathtub, which afforded Marsha a quiet getaway from time to time. One day, she wasn't feeling well and thought a long hot bath would do her good. She settled into a tub of hot water minutes before a violent labor began. She sensed it was happening too fast and before she knew it, she'd delivered a stillborn son. She desperately tried to revive the infant, but he never took a breath.

Although she'd initially fretted about the pregnancy, Marsha mourned the baby's death and insisted on giving him a name and a family burial. They named him Timothy and buried him in a marked grave beside their small camper home. The baby's stillbirth might have remained a private tragedy for Marsha and her family had it not been for a nosy neighbor who had long been suspicious of the Colbeys.

Debbie Cook noticed that Marsha Colbey was no longer pregnant but did not have a baby, which stirred her interest in the details of the stillbirth. Marsha didn't trust the woman and was evasive when she made inquiries. Cook, who worked at the elementary school attended by Mrs. Colbey's children, eventually instructed one of the school cafeteria workers to call the police about the absent infant. Officer Kenneth Lewellen spoke with Ms. Cook and then went to Ms. Colbey's home. Marsha, still grieving the loss of her baby and frustrated by the meddling, reacted badly to the police questioning. She initially attempted to misdirect the officer and the investigators in an effort to protect her privacy. It wasn't a smart thing to do, but she was outraged by their prodding. When Lewellen noticed the marked grave beside the Colbey's home, Marsha admitted it was the burial site for her recently delivered stillborn son.

Kathleen Enstice, a forensic pathologist who worked for the state, was summoned to exhume the infant's body. Marsha was shocked that law enforcement would do something so upsetting without justification. As soon as the baby was exhumed but before she had an opportunity to formally examine the body, Enstice told an investigator that she believed that the baby had been born alive. She later conceded that she had no basis for such an opinion and that without an autopsy and tests there was no way she could know if a baby had been born alive. As it turned out, Enstice had a history of prematurely and incorrectly declaring deaths to be homicides without adequate supporting evidence.

The pathologist subsequently performed an autopsy at the Department of Forensic Sciences laboratory in Mobile. She not only concluded that Marsha Colbey's baby was born alive but also asserted that the child would have survived with medical attention. Even though most experts agree that forensic pathologists—who primarily deal with dead people—are not qualified to estimate survival chances, the State allowed prosecutors to pursue criminal charges.

Unbelievably, Marsha Colbey—a few short weeks after delivering her stillborn son—found herself arrested and charged with capital murder. Alabama is among the growing list of states that make the murder of a person under the age of fourteen a capital offense punishable by the death penalty. The child-victim category resulted in a tremendous increase in the number of young mothers and juveniles who were sent to death row. All five women on Alabama's death row were condemned for the unexplained deaths of their young children or the deaths of abusive spouses or boyfriends—all of them. In fact, nationwide, most women on death row are awaiting execution for a family crime involving an allegation of child abuse or domestic violence involving a male partner.

At trial, Kathleen Enstice testified that Timothy was born alive and had died by drowning. She testified that her conclusion of a live birth was a "diagnosis of exclusion"—that is, she could not find evidence that the baby was stillborn and did not have another explanation for his death. Her testimony was exposed as unreliable by the State's own expert witness, Dr. Dennis McNally, an obstetrician/gynecologist who examined Mrs. Colbey two weeks after the stillbirth. Dr. McNally testified that Mrs. Colbey's pregnancy was at high risk for "unexplained fetal death" because of her age and lack of prenatal care. Enstice's conclusion was further discredited by Dr. Werner Spitz, who had authored the medical treatise Enstice had relied on in her forensic pathology training. Dr. Spitz testified for the defense that he would "absolutely not" declare a live birth, let alone a homicide, under the circumstances of this case.

With no credible scientific evidence that a crime had occurred, the State introduced inflammatory evidence that Marsha was poor, a prior drug user, and obviously a bad mother for not seeking prenatal care. Police investigators went into her home and took photographs of an unflushed toilet and a beer can on the floor, which were waved in front of the jury as evidence of neglect and bad parenting.

Mrs. Colbey consistently maintained during multiple interrogations that the baby was stillborn. She told investigators that her son was born dead and never took a breath, despite her efforts to revive him. Mrs. Colbey rejected the State's offer of a plea agreement, pursuant to which she would have gone to prison for eighteen years, because she was adamant that she had done nothing wrong.

The prosecution of Marsha Colbey eventually caught the attention of the press, which was titillated by another "dangerous mother" story. The crime was sensationalized by the local media, which lauded the police and prosecutor for coming to the aid of a defenseless infant. Demonizing irresponsible mothers had become a media craze by the time Marsha's trial was scheduled. Tragic narratives of mothers killing their children were national sensations. When Andrea Yates drowned her five children in Texas in 2001, the tragedy became a national story. Susan Smith's effort to blame random black men for the death of her children in South Carolina before later admitting to murdering them fascinated crime-obsessed Americans. In time, media interest in these kinds of stories grew into a national preoccupation. *Time* magazine called the prosecution of Casey Anthony, the young Florida mother ultimately acquitted in the death of her two-year-old daughter, the "social media trial of the century" after the story generated nonstop coverage on cable networks.

The murder of a child by a parent is horrific and is usually complicated by serious mental illness, as in the Yates and Smith cases. But these cases also tend to create distortions and bias. Police and prosecutors have been influenced by the media coverage, and a presumption of guilt has now fallen on thousands of women—particularly poor women in difficult circumstances—whose children die unexpectedly. Despite America's preeminent status among developed nations, we have always struggled with high rates of infant mortality—much higher than in most developed countries. The inability of many poor women to get adequate health care, including prenatal and post-partum care, has been a serious problem in this country for decades. Even with recent improvements, infant mortality rates continue to be an embarrassment for a nation that spends more on health care than any other country in the world. The criminalization of infant mortality and the persecution of poor women whose children die have taken on new dimensions in twenty-first-century America, as prisons across the country began to bear witness.

Communities were on the lookout for bad moms who should be put in prison. About the same time as Marsha's prosecution, Bridget Lee gave birth to a stillborn baby in Pickens County, Alabama. She was charged with capital murder and wrongfully imprisoned. Lee, a church pianist, mother of two, and bank bookkeeper, had gotten pregnant after an extramarital affair. Scared and depressed, the thirty-four-year-old hid her pregnancy and hoped to secretly put the child up for adoption. But she went into labor five weeks before her due date, and the baby was stillborn. She didn't tell her husband about the stillbirth, which aroused suspicion. The disreputable circumstances surrounding Lee's pregnancy were enough to influence the pathologist who conducted the autopsy to conclude that the stillborn baby was born alive and was then suffocated by Lee. Months after Lee was arrested and charged with capital murder, six additional pathologists examined the body and unanimously concluded that neonatal pneumonia had killed the child—it was a classic stillbirth with very common features. This new information led the prosecutor to drop the charges, sparing Ms. Lee a capital trial and, potentially, the death penalty. The discredited pathologist left Alabama but continues to serve as a practicing medical examiner in Texas.

In hundreds of other cases, falsely accused women never received the forensic help they needed to avoid wrongful convictions. A few years earlier, before representing Marsha Colbey, we took on the case of Diane Tucker and Victoria Banks. An intellectually disabled black woman living in Choctaw County, Alabama, Ms. Banks was accused of killing her newborn child even though police had no credible basis for believing she had ever been pregnant. Banks had allegedly told a deputy sheriff that she was pregnant to avoid time in jail for an unrelated matter. When she was seen months later with no child, police accused her of killing her infant. Disabled and without adequate legal assistance, Ms. Banks was coerced into pleading guilty to killing a child who had never existed along with her sister, Ms. Tucker. Because she was facing capital murder charges and a potential death sentence, she made a deal to accept a prison sentence of twenty years. Law enforcement officials refused to investigate her claims of innocence prior to sending her to prison. We won her freedom after establishing that she had had a tubal ligation five years prior to her arrest, which made it biologically impossible for her to conceive, let alone give birth to, a child.

In addition to unexplained deaths of infants parented by poor women, other kinds of "bad parenting" have also been criminalized. In 2006, Alabama passed a law that made it a felony to expose a child to a "dangerous environment" in which the child could encounter drugs. This "child chemical endangerment statute" was ostensibly passed to protect children living in households where there were meth labs or drug-trafficking operations. But the law was applied much more broadly, and soon thousands of mothers with children living in poor, marginalized communities where drugs and drug addiction are rampant were at risk of prosecution.

In time, the Alabama Supreme Court interpreted the term *environment* to include the womb and the term *child* to include a fetus. Pregnant women could now be criminally prosecuted and sent to prison for decades if there was any evidence that they had used drugs at any point during their pregnancy. Dozens of women have been sent to prison under this law in recent years, rather than getting the help they needed.

The hysteria surrounding bad mothers made a fair trial for Marsha Colbey very difficult. During jury selection, numerous jurors announced that they could not be impartial toward Mrs. Colbey. Some jurors indicated that they found allegations of killing a child so disturbing that they could not honor the presumption of innocence. Several revealed that they had such a close relationship with one of the state investigators—a key State witness who had been especially vocal about identifying bad mothers—that they would give him "instant credibility" and would "believe everything [he] said was credible." Another juror admitted trusting law enforcement witnesses he knew to the point where he would "believe anything they say."

The trial court allowed almost all of these jurors to remain on the jury panel despite defense objections. Ultimately, a jury who brought many presumptions and biases to the trial of Marsha Colbey was selected to decide her fate.

The jury returned a verdict of guilty on one count of capital murder. Prior to rendering a verdict, jurors expressed concerns about Mrs. Colbey being subject to the death penalty, so the State agreed not to pursue an execution if she was found guilty. This concession yielded an immediate conviction. The trial court sentenced Mrs. Colbey to life imprisonment without the possibility of parole, and a short while later she found herself shackled in a prison van heading to the Julia Tutwiler Prison for Women.

Built in the 1940s, Tutwiler Prison is situated in Wetumpka, Alabama. Named after a woman who promoted the education of prisoners and championed humane conditions of confinement, Tutwiler has become an overcrowded, dangerous nightmare for the women trapped there. Courts have repeatedly found the prison unconstitutionally overcrowded, with almost twice the number of women incarcerated as it was designed to hold. In the United States, the number of women sent to prison increased 646 percent between 1980 and 2010, a rate of increase 1.5 times higher than the rate for men. With close to two hundred thousand women in jails and prisons in America and over a million women under the supervision or control of the criminal justice system, the incarceration of women has reached record levels.

At Tutwiler, women are crammed into dormitories and improvised living spaces. Marsha was shocked by the overcrowding. As the only state prison for women, Tutwiler has no way to meaningfully classify and assign women to appropriate dorms. Women battling serious mental illness or severe emotional problems are thrown in with other women, making dorm life chaotic and stressful for everyone. Marsha could never quite get used to hearing women screaming and hollering inexplicably throughout the night in a crowded dorm.

Most incarcerated women—nearly two-thirds—are in prison for nonviolent, low-level drug crimes or property crimes. Drug laws in particular have had a huge impact on the number of women sent to prison. "Three strikes" laws have also played a considerable role. I started challenging conditions of confinement at Tutwiler in the mid-1980s as a young attorney with the Southern Prisoners Defense Committee. At the time, I was shocked to find women in prison for such minor offenses. One of the first incarcerated women I ever met was a young mother who was serving a long prison sentence for writing checks to buy her three young children Christmas gifts without sufficient funds in her account. Like a character in a Victor Hugo novel, she tearfully explained her heartbreaking tale to me. I couldn't accept the truth of what she was saying until I checked her file and discovered that she had, in fact, been convicted and sentenced to over ten years in prison for writing five checks, including three to Toys"R"Us. None of the checks was for more than $150. She was not unique. Thousands of women have been sentenced to lengthy terms in prison for writing bad checks or for minor property crimes that trigger mandatory minimum sentences.

The collateral consequences of incarcerating women are significant. Approximately 75 to 80 percent of incarcerated women are mothers with minor children. Nearly 65 percent had minor children living with them at the time of their arrest—children who have become more vulnerable and at-risk as a result of their mother's incarceration and will remain so for the rest of their lives, even after their mothers come home. In 1996, Congress passed welfare reform legislation that gratuitously included a provision that authorized states to ban people with drug convictions from public benefits and welfare. The population most affected by this misguided law is formerly incarcerated women with children, most of whom were imprisoned for drug crimes. These women and their children can no longer live in public housing, receive food stamps, or access basic services. In the last twenty years, we've created a new class of "untouchables" in American society, made up of our most vulnerable mothers and their children.

Marsha wandered through her first days at Tutwiler in a state of disbelief. She met other women like herself who had been imprisoned after having given birth to stillborn babies. Efernia McClendon, a young black teenager from Opelika, Alabama, got pregnant in high school and didn't tell her parents. She delivered at just over five months and left the stillborn baby's remains in a drainage ditch. When they were discovered, she was interrogated by police until she acknowledged that she couldn't be 100 percent sure the infant hadn't moved before death, even though the premature delivery made viability extremely unlikely. Threatened with the death penalty, she joined a growing community of women imprisoned for having unplanned pregnancies and bad judgment.

The lives and the suffering of the women got tangled together at Tutwiler. For Marsha, it was impossible not to notice that some women never got visits. She tried at first but couldn't remain indifferent to the people around her who seemed in acute distress—those who cried more than usual or who suffered the greatest anxiety about the children or parents they'd left behind or who seemed especially down or depressed. Knitted together as they were, a horrible day for one woman would inevitably become a horrible day for everyone. The only consolation in such an arrangement was that joyous moments were shared as well. A grant of parole, the arrival of a hoped-for letter, a visit from a long-absent family member would lift everyone's spirits.

If the struggles of the other women had been Marsha's biggest challenge at Tutwiler, her years there would have been difficult but manageable. But there were bigger problems, coming from the correctional staff itself. Women at Tutwiler were being raped by prison guards. Women were being sexually harassed, exploited, abused, and assaulted by male officers in countless ways. The male warden allowed the male guards entry into the showers during prison counts. Officers leered at the naked women and made crude comments and suggestive threats. Women had no privacy in the bathrooms, where male officers could watch them use the toilet. There were dark corners and hallways—terrifying spaces at Tutwiler where women could be beaten or sexually assaulted. EJI had asked the Department of Corrections to install security cameras in the dorms, but they refused. The culture of sexual violence was so pervasive that even the prison chaplain was sexually assaulting women when they came to the chapel.

Shortly after Marsha arrived at Tutwiler, we won the release of Diane Jones, who had been wrongly convicted and sentenced to die in prison for a crime she had not committed. Diane had been wrongly implicated in a drug-trafficking operation that involved her former boyfriend. She was convicted of multiple charges that triggered a sentence of mandatory life imprisonment without parole. We challenged her conviction and sentence and ultimately won her release. The release of Diane Jones, a condemned lifer, gave hope to all of the other lifers at Tutwiler. I received letters from women I'd never met thanking me for helping her. While working on her case, I'd go to Tutwiler to meet with Diane, who would tell me how the women were desperate for help.

"Bryan, I have about nine notes people want me to pass to you. It was too many to get past the guards so I didn't bring them, but these women want your help."

"Well, don't try to smuggle notes. They can write us."

"Well, some say they have written."

"We're swamped, Diane. I'm sorry, but we'll try to reply."

"I'm mostly worried about the lifers. They're the ones who will die in here."

"We're trying—there is only so much we can do."

"I tell them that, I know. They're just desperate, like I was desperate before y'all helped me. Marsha, Ashley, Monica, Patricia are sweatin' me to have you send someone to help."

We met Marsha Colbey shortly after that and began working on her appeal. We decided to challenge the State's case and the way the jury had been selected. Charlotte Morrison, a Rhodes Scholar and former student of mine, was now a senior attorney at EJI. She and staff attorney Kristen Nelson, a Harvard Law grad who had worked at the Public Defender Service for the District of Columbia, the nation's premier public defender office, met with Marsha repeatedly. She would talk about her case, the challenge of keeping her family together while she was in prison, and a range of other problems. But it was the sexual violence at Tutwiler that most frequently came up during these visits.

Charlotte and I took on the case of another woman who had filed a federal civil suit after she was raped at Tutwiler. She had had no legal help; because of defects in her pleadings and the allegations she made in her complaint, we could secure only a small settlement judgment for her. But the details of her experience were so painful that we could no longer look past the violence. We started an investigation for which we interviewed over fifty women; we were truly shocked to see how widespread the problem of sexual violence had become. Several women had been raped and become pregnant. Even when DNA testing confirmed that male officers were the fathers of these children, very little was done about it. Some officers who had received multiple sexual assault complaints were temporarily reassigned to other duties or other prisons, only to wind up back at Tutwiler, where they continued to prey on women. We eventually filed a complaint with the U.S.

Department of Justice and released several public reports about the problem, which received widespread media coverage. Tutwiler made a list of the ten worst prisons in America compiled by *Mother Jones;* it was the only women's facility to be so dishonored. Legislative hearings and policy changes at the prison followed. Male guards are now banned from the shower areas and toilets, and a new warden has taken over the facility.

Marsha held on despite these challenges and started advocating for some of the younger women. We were devastated when the Court of Criminal Appeals issued a ruling affirming her conviction and sentence. We sought review in the Alabama Supreme Court and won a new trial based on the trial judge's refusal to exclude people from jury service who were biased and could not be impartial. Marsha and our team were thrilled, local officials in Baldwin County less so. They were threatening re-prosecution. We involved expert pathologists and persuaded local authorities that there was no basis on which to convict Marsha of murder. It took two years to settle the legal case and then another year of wrangling with the Department of Corrections to give Marsha full credit for the time she'd served before she was finally freed in December 2012 after ten years of wrongful imprisonment.

We had started holding annual benefit dinners each March in New York City to raise money for EJI. We usually honored a luminary in public service and a client. We'd previously honored Marian Wright Edelman, the heroic civil rights lawyer and founder of the Children's Defense Fund. In 2011, we honored retired U.S. Supreme Court Justice John Paul Stevens. I had met Justice Stevens at a small conference when I was a young lawyer, and he had been extremely kind to me. By the time he retired, he'd become the Court's most vocal critic of excessive punishment and mass incarceration. In 2013, along with Marsha Colbey, we decided to honor the charismatic former director of the NAACP Legal Defense Fund, Elaine Jones, and the progressive ice-cream icons Ben (Cohen) and Jerry (Greenfield). Roberta Flack, the legendary singer and songwriter, agreed to perform. She sang the

George Harrison tune "Isn't It a Pity" before it was time to present our award to Marsha.

In my introduction, I told the audience how, on the day of her release from Tutwiler, Marsha had come to the office to thank everyone. Her husband and her two daughters had picked her up at Tutwiler. Her youngest daughter, who was about twelve, had reduced most of our staff to tears because she refused to let go of her mother the entire time she was in the office. She clung to Marsha's waist, kept hold of her arm, and leaned into her as if she intended never to let anyone physically separate them ever again. We took pictures with Marsha and some of the staff, and her daughter is in every shot because she refused to let her mother go. That told us a lot about what kind of mom Marsha Colbey was. Marsha took the podium in her lovely blue dress.

"I want to thank all of you for recognizing me and what I've been through. Y'all are being very kind to me. I'm just happy to be free." She spoke to the large audience calmly and with a great deal of composure. She was articulate and charming. She became emotional only when she talked about the women she'd left behind.

"I am lucky. I got help that most women can't get. It's what bothers me the most now, knowing that they are still there and I'm home. I hope we can do more to help more people." Her gown sparkled in the lights, and the audience rose to applaud Marsha as she wept for the women she'd left behind.

Following her, I couldn't think of what to say. "We need more hope. We need more mercy. We need more justice."

I then introduced Elaine Jones, who began with, "Marsha Colbey— isn't she a beautiful thing?"

Chapter Thirteen

Recovery

Events in the days and weeks following Walter's release were completely unexpected. *The New York Times* covered his exoneration and homecoming in a front-page story. We were flooded with media requests, and Walter and I gave television interviews to local, national, and even international press who wanted to report the story. Despite my general reluctance about media on pending cases, I believed that if people in Monroe County heard enough reports that Walter had been released because he was innocent, there would be less resistance to accepting him when he returned home.

Walter was not the first person to be released from death row after being proved innocent. Several dozen innocent people who had been wrongly condemned to death row had been freed before him. The Death Penalty Information Center reported that Walter was the fiftieth person to be exonerated in the modern era. Yet few of the earlier cases drew much media attention. Clarence Brantley's 1990 release in Texas attracted some coverage—his case had also been featured on *60 Minutes*. Randall Dale Adams inspired a compelling, award-winning documentary film by Errol Morris called *The Thin Blue Line*. The movie had played a role in Adams's exoneration, and he was released from Texas's death row not long after its release. But there had never been anything like the coverage surrounding Walter's exoneration.

In 1992, the year before Walter's release, thirty-eight people were executed in the United States. This was the highest number of executions in a single year since the beginning of the modern death penalty era in 1976. That number rose to ninety-eight in 1999. Walter's release coincided with increased media interest in the death penalty, triggered by the increasing pace of executions. His story was a counternarrative to the rhetoric of fairness and reliability offered by politicians and law enforcement officials who wanted more and faster executions. Walter's case complicated the debate in very graphic ways.

Walter and I traveled to legal conferences and spoke about his experience and about the death penalty. The U.S. Senate Judiciary Committee scheduled hearings on innocence and the death penalty a few months after Walter's release, and we both testified. Pete Earley's book *Circumstantial Evidence* was published a few months after Walter was freed, and it provided a detailed account of the case. Walter enjoyed the travel and the attention, even though he didn't much like speaking in public. Politicians would sometimes say provocative things—such as that his exoneration just proved the system works—which irritated and angered me. My own speaking would sometimes take on an edge of combativeness. But Walter remained calm, jovial, and earnest, and it was very effective—watching Walter tell his story with such good humor, intelligence, and sincerity heightened the horror our audiences felt, that the State had been determined to execute this man in all of our names. It was a compelling presentation. We spent a good bit of time together, and Walter would occasionally share with me that he was still troubled by the cases of the men he'd left behind on death row. He thought of the guys on the row as his friends. Behind his gentle presentations, Walter had become fiercely opposed to capital punishment, an issue he readily admitted he had never thought about until his own experience confronting it.

A few months after winning his freedom, I was still nervous about Walter's return to Monroe County. The big feast immediately following his release had brought hundreds of people to his home to cele-brate his freedom, but I knew that not everyone in the community was overjoyed. I didn't tell Walter about the death threats and bomb threats we'd received until he was free, and then I told him that we needed to be careful. He spent his first week out of prison in Mont-gomery. He then moved to Florida to live with his sister for a couple of months. We still talked almost every day. He'd accepted that Min-nie wanted to move forward without him and seemed mostly happy and hopeful. But that didn't mean there were no aftereffects from his time in prison. He started telling me more and more about how un-bearable it had been to live under the constant threat of execution on death row. He admitted fears and doubts he hadn't told me about when he was incarcerated. He had witnessed six men leave for execu-tion while he was on the row. At the time of the executions, he coped as the other prisoners did—through symbolic protests and private mo-ments of anguish. But he told me that he didn't realize how much the experience had terrified him until he left prison. He was confused about why that would bother him now that he was free.

"Why do I keep thinking about this?"

He sometimes complained of nightmares. A friend or a relative might say something about how they supported the death penalty—just not for Walter—and he would find himself shaken.

All I could tell him was that it would get better.

After a few months, Walter very much wanted to return to the place he'd spent his whole life. It made me nervous, but he went ahead and put a trailer on property he owned in Monroe County and resettled there. He returned to logging work while we made plans to file a civil lawsuit against everyone involved in his wrongful prosecution and conviction.

Most people released from prison after being proved innocent re-ceive no money, no assistance, no counseling—nothing from the state that wrongly imprisoned them. At the time of Walter's release, only ten states and the District of Columbia had laws authorizing compensation to people who have been wrongly incarcerated. The number has since grown, but even today almost half of all states (twenty-two) offer no compensation to the wrongly imprisoned. Many of the states that do authorize some monetary aid severely limit the amount of compensation. No matter how many years an innocent person has been wrongly incarcerated, New Hampshire caps compensation at $20,000; Wisconsin has a $25,000 cap; Oklahoma and Illinois limit the total amount an innocent person can recover to under $200,000, even if the person has spent decades in prison. While other states have caps of more than a million dollars, and many have no cap at all, several states impose onerous eligibility requirements. In some jurisdictions, if the person lacks the support of the prosecuting attorney who wrongly convicted him, compensation will be denied.

At the time Walter was set free, Alabama was not among the handful of states that provided aid to innocent people released from prison. The Alabama legislature could pass a special bill granting compensation to a person wrongly convicted, but that almost never happened. A local legislator introduced a bill seeking compensation on Walter's behalf that prompted the local press to report that Walter was seeking $9 million. The proposed legislation, of which Walter had no prior knowledge, went nowhere. But the news coverage about the possible $9 million payoff outraged people in Monroeville who still questioned his innocence and titillated some of Walter's friends and family, a few of whom started soliciting him aggressively for financial help. One woman even filed a paternity suit falsely claiming that Walter was the father of her child, a child that was born less than eight months after Walter's release. DNA tests confirmed that he was not the father.

Walter at times expressed frustration that people didn't believe him when he told them he had received nothing. We pressed ahead in our efforts to get compensation for him through a lawsuit, but there were obstacles. Our civil suit ran up against laws that give police, prosecutors, and judges special immunity from civil liability in criminal justice matters. While Chapman and the state officers connected with the case now readily acknowledged Walter's innocence, they were unwilling to accept any responsibility for his wrongful prosecution and death sentence. Sheriff Tate, who seemed most active in Walter's wrongful pretrial placement on death row and whose racist threats and intimidation tactics seemed the most actionable in a civil suit, reportedly accepted Walter's innocence upon his release but then started telling people that he still believed Walter was guilty.

Rob McDuff, an old friend of mine from Jackson, Mississippi, agreed to join our team for the civil litigation. Rob is a white native Mississippian whose Southern charm and manner enhanced his outstanding litigation skills in Alabama courts. He had recently asked me to help him with an Alabama civil rights case involving law enforcement misconduct. That case involved a police raid on a nightclub in Chambers County during which black residents had been illegally detained, mistreated, and abused by local authorities who refused to accept any responsibility for their misconduct. We ended up taking the case all the way to the U.S. Supreme Court, and we ultimately won a favorable ruling.

Walter's civil case would also go to the U.S. Supreme Court. We sued almost a dozen state and local officials and agencies. As expected, the defendants all claimed immunity for the conduct that had resulted in Walter's wrongful conviction. The immunity from civil liability given to prosecutors and judges is even greater than the protections provided to law enforcement officers. So even though it was clear that Ted Pearson, the prosecutor who had tried the case against Walter, had illegally withheld evidence that directly resulted in Walter's wrongful conviction, we would likely not succeed in a civil action against him. As he was the person most in charge of Walter's wrongful prosecution and conviction, it was hard to reconcile his immunity with his culpability in the whole affair, but there was little we could do. State and federal courts have persistently insulated prosecutors from accountability for egregious misconduct that results in innocent people being sent to death row.

In 2011, the U.S. Supreme Court again reinforced the protections that shield prosecutors from accountability. A month before an inmate named John Thompson was scheduled to be executed in Louisiana, a crime lab report was uncovered that contradicted the State's case against him for a robbery-murder that had taken place fourteen years earlier. State courts overturned his conviction and death sentence, and he was subsequently acquitted of all charges and released. He filed a civil suit, and a New Orleans jury awarded Thompson $14 million. The jury found that the district attorney, Harry Connick Sr., had illegally suppressed evidence of Thompson's innocence and had allowed him to spend fourteen years in prison for a crime he had not committed. Connick appealed the judgment, and the U.S. Supreme Court overturned the award in a bitterly divided 5–4 decision. As a result of immunity law, the Court held that a prosecutor cannot be held liable for misconduct in a criminal case, even if he intentionally and illegally withheld evidence of innocence. The Court's decision was strongly criticized by scholars and Court observers, and Justice Ruth Bader Ginsburg wrote a compelling dissent, but Thompson did not get any money.

We faced similar obstacles in Walter's case. After a year of depositions, hearings, and pretrial litigation, we eventually reached a settlement with most of the defendants that would provide Walter with a few hundred thousand dollars. Walter's claim against Monroe County for Sheriff Tate's misconduct could not be settled, so we appealed the case to the U.S. Supreme Court. Law enforcement officers generally have no personal resources to pay damages to victims of misconduct, so the city, county, or agency that employs them is typically the target of any civil action that seeks compensation. That's why we had sought relief from Monroe County for the misconduct of its sheriff. The county took the position that even though the sheriff's jurisdiction is limited to the county, he's elected by people only in the county, and he's paid by the county, he's not an employee of the county. The county sheriff was an employee of the State of Alabama, the county claimed.

State governments are broadly shielded from recovery for their employees' misconduct unless the employee works for an agency that can be sued. If Tate was a state officer, Monroe County would have no liability for his misconduct and no recovery would be possible from the State of Alabama. Unfortunately for Walter, the Supreme Court ruled that county sheriffs in Alabama *are* state officers, again in a close 5–4 decision, which limited our ability to recover damages for the most egregious misconduct in Walter's case. We ultimately reached settlement with all parties, but I was disappointed that we couldn't get more for Walter. Adding insult to injury, Tate went on to be re-elected sheriff, and he remains in office today; he has been sheriff continuously for more than twenty-five years.

While the money wasn't as much as we would have liked, it did allow Walter to restart his logging business. He loved getting back into the woods and cutting timber. He told me that it was working from morning until night, being outdoors, that made him feel normal again. Then one afternoon, tragedy struck. He was cutting a tree when a branch dislodged and struck him, breaking his neck. It was a serious injury that left Walter in very poor condition for several weeks. He didn't have a lot of care available, so he came to live with me in Montgomery for several months until he recovered. He eventually regained his mobility, although the injury put an end to his ability to cut trees and perform difficult landscape work. I marveled at how he seemed to take it in stride.

"I'll figure out something else to do when I get back on my feet," he told me.

After a few months, he went back to Monroe County and started collecting car parts for resale. He owned the plot of land where he'd put his trailer and had become convinced, on the advice of some friends, that he could generate income with a junk business—collecting discarded vehicles and car parts and reselling them. The work was less physically demanding than logging and allowed him to be outdoors.

Before long his property was littered with busted vehicles and scrap metal.

In 1998, Walter and I were asked to go to Chicago to attend a national conference where exonerated former death row prisoners were planning to gather. By the late 1990s, the evolution of DNA evidence had helped expose dozens of wrongful convictions. In many states, the number of exonerations exceeded the number of executions. The problem was so significant in Illinois that in 2003, Governor George Ryan, a Republican, citing the unreliability of capital punishment, commuted the death sentences of all 167 people on death row. Concerns about innocence and the death penalty were intensifying, and support for the death penalty in opinion polls began to drop. Abolitionists were becoming hopeful that more profound death penalty reform or possibly a moratorium might be achievable. Our time in Chicago with other exonerated former death row prisoners was energizing for Walter, who seemed more motivated than ever to talk about his experience.

Around the same time, I started teaching at the New York University School of Law. I would travel to New York to teach my classes and then fly back to Montgomery to run EJI. I asked Walter to come to New York each year to talk with students, and it was always a powerful moment when he walked into the classroom. He was a survivor of a criminal justice system that had proven, in his case, just how brutally unfair and cruel it could be. His personality, presence, and witness said something extraordinary about the humanity of people directly impacted by systemic abuse. His firsthand perspective on the plight of people wrongfully convicted was deeply meaningful to students, who often seemed overwhelmed by Walter's testimony. He usually spoke very briefly and would give short answers to the questions posed to him. But he had an enormous effect on the students who met him. He would laugh and joke and tell them he wasn't angry or bitter, just grateful to be free. He would share how his faith had helped him survive his hundreds of nights on death row.

One year, Walter got lost on the trip to New York, and he called to tell me that he couldn't make it. He seemed confused and couldn't offer a coherent explanation of what had happened at the airport. When I got back home, I went to see him and he seemed his usual self, just a little down. He told me that his junkyard business wasn't going great. When he described his finances, it became clear he was spending the money we'd secured for him more quickly than seemed prudent. He was buying equipment to make his collection of cars simpler, but he wasn't generating the kind of revenue necessary to support the costs. After an hour or two of anxious talk, he relaxed a bit and seemed to return to the jovial Walter I'd come to know. We agreed that we would travel together on any future trips.

Walter wasn't the only one who was facing new financial pressures. When a conservative majority took power in Congress in 1994, legal aid to death row prisoners became a political target, and federal funding was quickly eliminated. Most of the capital representation resource centers around the country were forced to close. We had never received state support for our work, and without the federal dollars we faced serious financial challenges. We scraped along and found enough private support to continue our work. Teaching and increased fund-raising responsibilities got piled on top of my bulging litigation docket, but somehow things progressed. Our staff was overextended, but I was thrilled with the talented lawyers and professionals we had working with us. We were assisting clients on death row, challenging excessive punishments, helping disabled prisoners, assisting children incarcerated in the adult system, and looking at ways to expose racial bias, discrimination against the poor, and the abuse of power. It was overwhelming but gratifying.

I received a surprising call one day from the Swedish Ambassador to the United States, who told me that EJI had been selected for the Olof Palme International Human Rights Award. They invited me to Stockholm to receive it. I had studied Sweden's progressive approach to the rehabilitation of criminal offenders as a graduate student and had long marveled at how focused on recovery their system appeared. Their punishments were humane, and their policymakers took rehabilitation of criminal offenders very seriously, which made me excited about the award and the trip. That they were giving an award named after a beloved prime minister who had been tragically murdered by a deranged man to someone who represented people on death row revealed a lot about their values. The trip to Stockholm was planned for January. They sent a film crew to interview me a month or two before the trip, and the crew also wanted to speak with a few clients. I made arrangements for them to interview Walter.

"I can come down for this interview," I told Walter.

"No, you don't need to do that. I don't have to travel, so I'm okay to talk to them. Don't spend time driving all the way down here."

"Do you want to go to Sweden?" I asked, half-joking.

"I don't know exactly where that is, but if you have to fly a long way to get there, no, I'm not too interested. I think I'd like to stay on the ground from now on." We laughed and he sounded fine.

He then became quiet and asked one final question before we hung up. "Maybe you can come and see me when you get back? I'm okay, but we can just hang out."

It was an unusual request from Walter so I eagerly agreed. "Sure, that would be great. We can go fishing," I teased. I'd never gone fishing in my life, and Walter found that so scandalous that he never stopped questioning me about it. When we traveled together, I never ordered fish to eat, and he was sure I didn't eat fish because I'd never caught a fish. I tried to follow his logic and made promises, but we had never gotten around to taking a fishing trip.

The Swedish film crew was eager to meet the challenge of finding Walter's trailer in the backwoods of South Alabama. I told them how to get there. I'd always been with Walter when he spoke to the press, but I felt like this was probably safe.

"He doesn't give speeches. He's usually very direct and succinct," I told the interviewers. "He's great, but you should ask him good questions. And it's probably better if you talk to him outside, too. He prefers to be outdoors." They nodded sympathetically but seemed confused by my anxiety. I called Walter before leaving for Sweden, and he told me that the interview had gone fine, which was reassuring.

Stockholm was beautiful, despite the constant snow and frigid temperatures. I gave some speeches and attended a few dinners. It was a short, cold trip, but the people were lovely and unusually kind to me. I was surprised at how gratifying I found their enthusiasm for our work. Most everyone I met offered support and encouragement. A couple of years earlier, I had been invited to Brazil to talk about punishment and the unjust treatment of disfavored people. I had spent a lot of time in local communities, mostly in the *favelas* outside São Paulo, where I met hundreds of desperately poor people who were intensely interested in talking. I spent hours in conversation with all sorts of people, from struggling mothers to impoverished children who sniffed glue to help them cope with hunger and police brutality. The cross-cultural conversations with those people, who had shared a lot of the same history and struggle as my clients in America, had a huge impact on me. In Sweden, the people I met were equally interested and responsive, even though they hadn't experienced profound need or shared struggle with an abusive justice system. People all over the country seemed motivated to connect from a common place of tremendous compassion.

The organizers asked me to speak at a high school on the outskirts of Stockholm. Kungsholmens Gymnasium is in an extraordinarily beautiful section of Stockholm, an island surrounded by seventeenth-century architecture. As an American with limited experience outside the United States, I was dazzled by the age of the buildings and marveled at their ornate architecture. The school itself was nearly a hundred years old. I was escorted through the school to a narrow, winding staircase with handcrafted railings that led up to a cavernous auditorium. Several hundred high school students packed the room, waiting for my presentation. The domed ceiling of the enormous hall was covered with delicate hand paintings and Latin phrases written in decorative script. Floating angels and trumpet-wielding infants danced all over the walls and ceiling. A large balcony packed with more students seemed to ascend elegantly into the drawings.

While the room was very old, the acoustics were perfect, and there was a balance and precision to the space that seemed almost magical. I studied the hundreds of Scandinavian teenagers seated in the hall while I was being introduced. I was impressed by how eager they appeared. I spoke for forty-five minutes to the strangely silent and attentive group of teens. I knew English wasn't their first language and had real doubts about how much they were even following what I said, but when I finished, they erupted into vigorous applause. Their response actually startled me. They were so young but so interested in the plight of my condemned clients thousands of miles away. The headmaster joined me onstage to thank me and suggested to the students that they offer their own thanks with a song. The school had an internationally famous music program and student choir. The headmaster asked the choir students to stand wherever they were in the auditorium and briefly sing something. About fifty giggling kids stood up and looked around at each other.

After a minute of uncertainty, a seventeen-year-old boy with strawberry blond hair stood on his chair and said something to his choirmates in Swedish. The students laughed, but they became more sober. As they became still and perfectly quiet, the boy hummed a note in a beautiful tenor voice. His pitch was perfect. Then he slowly waved his arms to prompt these extraordinary children to sing. Their voices bounced off the walls and ceiling of this ancient hall and fell into a glorious harmony the likes of which I'd never heard. After starting his classmates in song, the young man stepped off his chair and joined them in performing a heartbreaking melody with tremendous care and precision. I could not understand a word of the Swedish lyrics, but it sounded angelic. Dissonance and harmonic tension slowly resolved into warm chords—the sound was transcendent. The singing built gloriously with each line.

Standing on a stage above the singers with the headmaster beside me, I looked up at the ceiling—at the majestic artwork. My mother had died a few months before this trip. She'd been a church musician most of her life and had worked with dozens of children's choirs. When I looked up and saw the drawings of angels on the domed ceiling I thought of her. I quickly realized I would never recover my composure looking up there, so I looked back at the students and forced a smile. When the students finished their song, the rest of the students cheered and applauded wildly. I joined the applause and tried to hold myself together. When I left the stage, students came up to thank me for the talk, ask questions, and take pictures. I was completely charmed.

It was a long and exhausting but beautiful day. When I got back to the hotel I was grateful for the two-hour break before my next speaking commitment. I don't know what prompted me to turn on the television, but I'd been away from home for four days and hadn't seen any headlines. The local news blasted into my room. The unfamiliar Swedish TV anchors were chatting away when I heard my name. It was the piece the crew had filmed with me; familiar images filled the screen. I watched myself walking with the reporter into Dr. Martin Luther King Jr.'s church on Dexter Avenue in Montgomery, then up the street to the Civil Rights Memorial. The scene then switched to Walter, standing in overalls amid his pile of discarded cars down in Monroeville.

Walter gently put down a little kitten he'd been holding as he started to answer the reporters' questions. He'd mentioned to me previously that all kinds of cats had sought shelter in his field of abandoned metal. He said things I'd heard him say dozens of times before. Then I watched his expression change, and he began talking with more animation and excitement than I'd ever heard from him.

He became uncharacteristically emotional. "They put me on death row for six years! They threatened me for six years. They tortured me with the promise of execution for six years. I lost my job. I lost my wife. I lost my reputation. I lost my—I lost my dignity."

He was speaking loudly and passionately and looked to be on the verge of tears. "I lost everything," he continued. He calmed himself and tried to smile, but it didn't work. He looked soberly at the camera. "It's rough, it's rough, man. It's rough." I watched worriedly while Walter crouched down close to the ground and began to sob violently. The camera stayed on him while he cried. The report switched back to me saying something abstract and philosophical, and then it was over. I was stunned. I wanted to call Walter, but I couldn't figure out how to dial him from Sweden. I knew it was time to get back to Alabama.

Chapter Fourteen

Cruel and Unusual

On the morning of May 4, 1989, Michael Gulley, fifteen, and Nathan McCants, seventeen, convinced thirteen-year-old Joe Sullivan to accompany them when they broke into an empty house in Pensacola, Florida. The three boys entered the home of Lena Bruner in the morning, while no one was there. McCants took some money and jewelry. The three boys then left. That afternoon, Ms. Bruner, an older white woman in her early seventies, was sexually assaulted in her home. Someone knocked on her door, and as she went to open it, another person who had entered through the back of her home grabbed her from behind. It was a violent and shocking rape; Ms. Bruner never even saw her attacker clearly. She could describe him only as "quite a dark colored boy" with "curly type hair." Gulley, McCants, and Sullivan are all African American.

Within minutes of the assault, Gulley and McCants were apprehended together. McCants had Ms. Bruner's jewelry on him. Facing serious felony charges, Gulley—who had an extensive criminal history involving at least one sexual offense—accused Joe of the sexual battery. Joe was not apprehended that day, but he voluntarily turned himself in the next day after learning that Gulley and McCants had implicated him. Joe admitted helping the older boys with the burglary earlier in the day but adamantly denied any knowledge of or involvement in the sexual assault.

The prosecutor chose to indict thirteen-year-old Joe Sullivan in adult court for sexual battery and other charges. There was no review of whether Joe should be tried in juvenile or adult court. Florida is one of a few states that allows the prosecutor to decide to charge a child in adult court for certain crimes and has no minimum age for trying a child as an adult.

At trial, Joe testified that he had participated in the earlier burglary but had not committed sexual battery. The prosecution relied primarily on the self-serving stories of McCants and Gulley, including Gulley's claim that Joe had confessed the rape to him in a detention facility before trial. After implicating Joe, McCants was sentenced as an adult to four-and-one-half years and served just six months. Gulley, despite admitting his involvement in some twenty prior burglaries and a prior sex crime, was adjudicated and sentenced as a juvenile and spent only a short period of time in a juvenile detention facility.

The only physical evidence to implicate Joe was a latent partial palm-print that the state's examiner testified matched him. This was consistent with Joe's admitted presence in the bedroom prior to the rape. The police had collected seminal fluid and blood, but the state chose not to present it in court and then destroyed it before it could be tested by the defense. The prosecution also presented testimony from a police officer who got a "glimpse" of an African American youth running from the victim's house after he observed Joe Sullivan at the police station being interrogated as the suspect in the sexual assault. He identified Joe as the fleeing youth.

Finally, the prosecution presented testimony from the victim, who, despite being coached through a rehearsal of her testimony outside the presence of the jury, could not affirmatively identify Joe Sullivan as the perpetrator. Joe was made to say in court what the victim remembered her assailant saying to her, but she testified that Joe's voice "could very easily be" that of the perpetrator.

Joe was convicted by a six-person jury after a trial that lasted only one day. Opening statements began sometime after 9 A.M., and the jury returned its verdict at 4:55 P.M. Joe's appointed counsel was later suspended from practice in Florida and never reinstated. The defense lawyer had filed no written pleadings and uttered no more than twelve transcript lines at sentencing. There was a great deal to say that was never said.

At the time of his arrest in 1989, Joe Sullivan was a thirteen-year-old boy with mental disabilities who read at a first-grade level, had experienced repeated physical abuse by his father, and had suffered severe neglect. His family had disintegrated into what state officials described as "abuse and chaos." From age ten until his arrest, Joe had no stable home; he had no fewer than ten different addresses within this three-year period. He spent most of his time on the streets, where police stopped him for violations including trespassing, stealing a bike, and property crimes committed with his older brother and other older teens.

Joe had been brought to court and adjudicated on a single occasion, when he was twelve years old. The juvenile probation officer assigned to Joe's case attributed his behavior to the fact that "he is easily influenced and associates with the wrong crowd." She observed that "[i]t is apparent that Joe is a very immature naive person who is a follower rather than a leader" and that he has the potential to "be a positive and productive individual."

Joe's record of mostly misdemeanor-level juvenile incidents—nearly all of which were nonviolent and which did not merit more than a single court adjudication in a two-year period—was viewed differently by the sentencing judge, who concluded that "the juvenile system has been utterly incapable of doing anything with Mr. Sullivan." The court concluded that Joe had been "given opportunity after opportunity to upright himself and take advantage of the second and third chances he's been given." In truth, Joe was never given a second, much less a third, chance to "upright himself," but he was nonetheless characterized at age thirteen as a "serial" or "violent recidivist" by prosecutors. The judge sentenced him to life imprisonment without the possibility of parole.

Despite numerous potentially meritorious grounds for appeal, Joe's appointed appellate counsel filed an *Anders* brief—indicating his belief that there were no legitimate grounds for appeal and no credible basis to complain about the conviction or sentence—and was permitted to withdraw from representing Joe. Joe, just one year into his own adolescence, was sent to adult prison, where an eighteen-year nightmare began. In prison, he was repeatedly raped and sexually assaulted. He attempted suicide on multiple occasions. He developed multiple sclerosis, which eventually forced him into a wheelchair. Doctors later concluded that his neurological disorder might have been triggered by trauma in prison.

Another inmate housed with Joe wrote to us and described him as disabled, horribly mistreated, and wrongfully condemned to die in prison for a non-homicide crime at thirteen. In 2007, we wrote to Joe and discovered that he had no legal assistance and had spent the previous eighteen years in prison with no one to help him challenge his conviction or sentence. When I received Joe's response to my letter, a scribbled note in the handwriting of a child, he could still only read at a third-grade level, despite the fact that he was thirty-one. He told me in his letter that he was "okay." Then he wrote, "If I didn't do anything, shouldn't I be able to go home now? Mr. Bryan, if this is true, can you please write me back and come get me?"

I wrote to Joe that we would look deeper into his case and that we were convinced that he had a credible claim of innocence. We attempted to prove his innocence through a motion for DNA testing, but because the state had destroyed the relevant biological evidence, the motion was denied. Disheartened, we decided to challenge Joe's death-in-prison sentence as unconstitutionally cruel and unusual punishment.

I drove from Montgomery through South Alabama to Florida and then along a tangle of wooded back roads to get to the Santa Rosa Correctional Facility in the town of Milton to meet Joe for the first time. Santa Rosa County borders the Gulf of Mexico at the western end of the Florida Panhandle and had long been known for agriculture. Between 1980 and 2000, the county's population doubled in size as the coastal areas attracted beach homes and resort properties. Many affluent families left Pensacola for Santa Rosa County, and military families from nearby Eglin Air Force Base settled there. But there was another industry in town—incarceration.

The Florida Department of Corrections built the prison to house 1,600 people in the 1990s, when America was opening prisons at a pace never before seen in human history. Between 1990 and 2005, a new prison opened in the United States every ten days. Prison growth and the resulting "prison-industrial complex"—the business interests that capitalize on prison construction—made imprisonment so profitable that millions of dollars were spent lobbying state legislators to keep expanding the use of incarceration to respond to just about any problem. Incarceration became the answer to everything—health care problems like drug addiction, poverty that had led someone to write a bad check, child behavioral disorders, managing the mentally disabled poor, even immigration issues generated responses from legislators that involved sending people to prison. Never before had so much lobbying money been spent to expand America's prison population, block sentencing reforms, create new crime categories, and sustain the fear and anger that fuel mass incarceration than during the last twenty-five years in the United States.

When I arrived at Santa Rosa, I didn't encounter any staff who were people of color, although 70 percent of the men incarcerated there were black or brown. This was a bit unusual; I frequently saw black and brown correctional officers at other prisons. I was subjected to an elaborate admission process and given a beeper to activate if I was ever threatened or distressed while inside the prison. I was escorted to a forty-by-forty-foot room where more than two dozen incarcerated men sat sadly while uniformed correctional staff buzzed in and out.

There were three six-foot-tall metal cages in the corner that couldn't have been more than four feet by four feet. In all my years of visiting prisons, I had never seen such small cages used to hold a prisoner inside a secure prison. I wondered what danger the caged men presented that they couldn't sit with the other incarcerated men on the benches. Two young men stood in each of the first two cages. In the third cage, which was wedged into the corner, sat a small man in a wheelchair. His wheelchair faced the back of the cage, so he could not look out into the room. I couldn't see his face, but I was certain it was Joe. A correctional officer was constantly walking into the room and calling out a name, prompting one of the men to get up from his bench and follow the officer down a hallway where he would meet with an assistant warden or whomever they were scheduled to see. Finally, the officer called out, "Joe Sullivan, legal visit." I walked over to the man and said that I was the attorney for the legal visit. He summoned two officers, who went to Joe's cage to unlock it. The cage was so small that when they tried to remove Joe's wheelchair, the spokes on the chair got caught on the cage, and they couldn't budge it.

I stood there watching for several minutes while more officers got involved in an increasingly elaborate effort to dislodge Joe's wheelchair from the tight cage. They pulled up on the wheelchair. Then they pushed down on the chair, raising the front off the ground, but this didn't work, either. They tugged at the chair with loud grunts and tried to force it free, but it was completely stuck.

Two inmate trusties who had been mopping the floor stopped to watch the officers struggle with the wheelchair and the cage. They finally offered to help out, even though no one had asked for their input. The officers silently accepted the assistance of the inmates, but none of them could come up with a solution. As the staff became more frustrated by their inability to get Joe out of the cage, there was talk of using pliers and hacksaws, of putting the cage on its side with Joe in it. Someone suggested trying to lift Joe from his wheelchair to remove him without the chair, but both Joe and the chair were packed so tightly into the cage that no one could get in to move him.

I asked the guards why he was in the cage in the first place, which prompted a brusque response: "Lifer. All lifers have to be moved with higher security protocols."

I couldn't see Joe's face while all of this was going on, but I could hear him crying. He occasionally made a whining sound, and his shoulders jerked up and down. When the staff proposed turning the cage on its side, he moaned audibly. Finally, the prisoner trusties suggested lifting the cage and tilting it slightly, which everyone agreed to try. The two trusties lifted and tilted the heavy cage, while three officers yanked Joe's chair with a violent pull that finally dislodged it. The guards gave each other high fives, the inmate trusties walked away silently, and Joe sat motionlessly in his chair in the middle of the room, looking down at his feet.

I walked over to him and introduced myself. His face was tear-stained, and his eyes were red, but he looked up at me and began clapping his hands giddily. "Yeah! Yeah! Mr. Bryan." He smiled and offered me both of his hands, which I took.

I wheeled Joe to a cramped office for our legal visit. He continued cheering quietly and kept clapping his hands in excitement. I had to argue with the attending prison guard for permission to close the door and talk confidentially with Joe. The officer eventually relented. Joe seemed to relax when I closed the door. Despite the terrifying start to the visit, he was extremely cheerful. I couldn't shake the feeling that I was talking to a young child.

I explained to Joe how disappointed we were that the State had destroyed the biological evidence that might have allowed us to prove he was innocent through DNA testing. We had discovered that both the victim and one of his co-defendants had died. The other co-defendant would not say anything about what had really happened, making it extremely difficult for us to challenge Joe's conviction. I then offered our new idea about challenging his sentence as unconstitutional, which might create another way for him to possibly go home. He smiled throughout my explanation, although it was clear he didn't understand all of it. He had a legal pad on his lap, and when I finished he told me that he had prepared some questions for our visit.

During the entire visit I kept thinking about how he was much more enthusiastic and excited than I had expected him to be, given his history. When he told me about the questions he had prepared for me, he was practically bubbling. He explained that if he ever got out of prison he might want to be a reporter so "I can tell people what's really going on." He spoke with great pride when he announced that he was ready to ask his questions.

"Joe, I'll be happy to answer your questions. Fire away."

He read with some difficulty.

"Do you have children?" He looked up at me expectantly.

"No, I don't have children. I have nieces and nephews, though."

"What is your favorite color?" He once again smiled eagerly.

I chuckled, since I don't have a favorite color. But I wanted to respond to him.

"Brown."

"Okay, my last question is the most important." He looked up at me briefly with big eyes and smiled. He then became serious and read his question.

"Who is your favorite cartoon character?" He was beaming when he looked at me.

"Please, tell the truth. I really want to know."

I couldn't think of anything and had to force myself to keep smiling. "Wow, Joe, I honestly don't know. Can I think about that and get back to you? I'll write you with my answer." He nodded enthusiastically.

Over the next three months I received a flood of scrawled letters from Joe, one almost every day. The letters were usually short statements about what he'd eaten that day or what show he'd seen on television. Sometimes they were just two or three Bible verses he had copied. He would always ask me to write him back and let him know if his handwriting was improving. Sometimes the letters contained only a few words or a single question like, "Do you have friends?"

We filed a petition to challenge Joe's sentence as unconstitutionally cruel and unusual punishment. We knew that there would be procedural objections to filing it nearly twenty years after his sentencing, but we thought the Supreme Court's recent decision banning the death penalty for juveniles could provide a basis for relief. In 2005, the Court recognized that differences between children and adults required that kids be shielded from the death penalty under the Eighth Amendment. My staff and I discussed how we might use the constitutional reasoning that banned the execution of children as a legal basis for challenging juvenile life-without-parole sentences.

We filed similar challenges to life-without-parole sentences in several other cases involving children, including Ian Manuel's case. Ian was still being held in solitary confinement in Florida. We filed cases in Missouri, Michigan, Iowa, Mississippi, North Carolina, Arkansas, Delaware, Wisconsin, Nebraska, and South Dakota. We filed a case in Pennsylvania to help Trina Garnett, the girl who had been convicted for arson. She was still struggling at the women's prison but was excited about the possibility of our doing something to change her sentence. We filed a case in California for Antonio Nuñez.

We filed two cases in Alabama. Ashley Jones was a fourteen-year-old girl who had been convicted of killing two family members when her older boyfriend tried to help her escape her family. Ashley suffered from a horrific history of abuse and neglect. When she was still a teenager serving her sentence at the Tutwiler Prison for Women, she started writing to me to ask about various legal decisions she'd read about in the newspaper. She never asked for legal assistance; she simply asked about what she'd read and expressed interest in the law and our work. She started sending notes congratulating me and EJI whenever we won a death penalty appeal. When we decided to challenge death-in-prison sentences imposed on children, I told her we might be able to finally challenge her sentence. She was thrilled.

Evan Miller was another fourteen-year-old condemned to die in prison in Alabama. Evan is from a poor white family in North Alabama. His difficult life was punctuated by suicide attempts that started at age seven when he was in elementary school. His parents were abusive and had drug addiction problems, so he was in and out of foster care, but he was living with his mother at the time of the crime. A middle-aged neighbor, Cole Cannon, had come over one night seeking to buy drugs from Evan's mother. The fourteen-year-old Evan and his sixteen-year-old friend went to the man's house with him to play cards. Cannon gave the teens drugs and played drinking games with them. At one point, he sent the boys out to buy more drugs. The boys returned and stayed over as it got later and later. Eventually the boys thought Cannon had passed out and tried to steal his wallet. Cannon was startled awake and jumped on Evan. The older boy responded by hitting the man in the head with a bat. Both boys started beating him and then set his trailer on fire. Cole Cannon died, and Evan and his friend were charged with capital murder. The older boy made a deal with prosecutors and got a parole-eligible life sentence, while Evan was convicted and sentenced to life imprisonment without parole.

I got involved in Evan's case right after his trial and filed a motion to reduce his sentence, even though it was the mandatory punishment for someone convicted of capital murder who was too young to be executed. At a hearing, I asked the judge to reconsider Evan's sentence in light of his age. The prosecutor argued, "I think he should be executed. He deserves the death penalty." He then lamented that the law no longer authorized the execution of children because he just couldn't wait to put this fourteen-year-old boy in the electric chair and kill him. The judge denied our motion.

When I visited Evan at the jail, we would have long talks. He loved to talk about anything he could think of when we were together to extend our visits. We talked about sports and exercise, we talked about books, we talked about his family, we talked about music, we talked about all the things he wanted to do when he grew up. He was usually animated and excited about something, although when he didn't hear from his family for a while or had to deal with some bad incident at the prison, he would become extremely depressed. He couldn't understand some of the hostile and violent behavior he saw from prisoners and the other people around him. He once told me that a guard had punched him in the chest just because he had asked a question about meal times. He started crying as he told me this because he just couldn't understand why the officer had done that.

Evan was sent to the St. Clair Correctional Facility, a maximum-security adult prison. Not long after he first arrived, he was attacked by another prisoner, who stabbed him nine times. He recovered without serious physical problems but was traumatized by the experience and disoriented by the violence. When he talked about his own act of violence, he seemed deeply confused about how it was possible he could have done something so destructive.

Most of the juvenile lifer cases we handled involved clients who shared Evan's confusion about their adolescent behavior. Many had matured into adults who were much more thoughtful and reflective; they were now capable of making responsible and appropriate decisions. Almost all of the cases involved condemned people marked by the tragic irony that they were now nothing like the confused children who had committed a violent crime; they had all changed in some significant way. This made them distinct from most of my clients who committed crimes as adults. That I was involved in the cases of teens who'd committed violent crimes was itself ironic.

I was sixteen years old, living in southern Delaware. I was headed outside one day when our phone rang. I watched my mother answer it as I strolled past her. A minute later I heard her scream inside the house. I ran back inside and saw her lying on the floor, sobbing, "Daddy, Daddy" while the phone's receiver dangled from its base. I picked it up; my aunt was on the line. She told me that my grandfather had been murdered.

My grandparents had been separated for many years, and my grandfather had for some time lived alone in the South Philadelphia housing projects. It was there that he was attacked and stabbed to death by several teens who had broken into his apartment to steal his black-and-white television set. He was eighty-six years old.

Our large family was devastated by his senseless murder. My grandmother, who had separated from my grandfather many years earlier, was especially unnerved by the crime and his death. I had older cousins who worked in law enforcement and sought information about the boys who committed the crime—I remember them being more astonished than vengeful about the immaturity and lack of judgment the juveniles had demonstrated. We all kept saying and thinking the same thing: *They didn't have to kill him.* There was no way an eighty-six-year-old man could have stopped them from getting away with their paltry loot. My mother could never make sense of it. And neither could I. I knew kids at school who seemed out of control and violent, but still I wondered how someone could be so pointlessly destructive. My grandfather's murder left us with so many questions.

Now, decades later, I was starting to understand. In preparing litigation on behalf of the children we were representing, it was clear that these shocking and senseless crimes couldn't be evaluated honestly without understanding the lives these children had been forced to endure. And, in banning the death penalty for juveniles, the Supreme Court had paid great attention to the emerging body of medical research about adolescent development and brain science and its relevance to juvenile crime and culpability.

Contemporary neurological, psychological, and sociological evidence has established that children are impaired by immature judgment, an underdeveloped capacity for self-regulation and responsibility, vulnerability to negative influences and outside pressures, and a lack of control over their own impulses and their environment. Generally considered to encompass ages twelve to eighteen, adolescence is defined by radical transformation, including the obvious and often distressing physical changes associated with puberty (increases in height and weight and sex-related changes) as well as progressive gains in the capacity for reasoned and mature judgment, impulse control, and autonomy. As we later explained to the Court, experts had come to the following conclusion:

"A rapid and dramatic increase in dopaminergic activity within the socioemotional system around the time of puberty" drives the young adolescent toward increased sensation-seeking and risk-taking; "this increase in reward seeking precedes the structural maturation of the cognitive control system and its connections to areas of the socioemotional system. A maturational process that is gradual, unfolds over the course of adolescence, and permits more advanced self-regulation and impulse control . . . The temporal gap between the arousal of the socioemotional system, which is an early adolescent development, and the full maturation of the cognitive control system, which occurs later, creates a period of heightened vulnerability to risk taking during middle adolescence."

These biological and psychosocial developments explain what is obvious to parents, teachers, and any adult who reflects on his or her own teenage years: Young teens lack the maturity, independence, and future orientation that adults have acquired. It seemed odd to have to explain in a court of law something so fundamental about childhood, but the commitment to harsh punishments for children was so intense and reactionary that we had to articulate these basic facts.

We argued in court that, relative to that of adults, young teenage judgment is handicapped in nearly every conceivable way: Young adolescents lack life experience and background knowledge to inform their choices; they struggle to generate options and to imagine consequences; and, perhaps for good reason, they lack the necessary self-confidence to make reasoned judgments and stick by them. We argued that neuroscience and new information about brain chemistry help explain the impaired judgment that teens often display. When these basic deficits that burden all children are combined with the environments that some poor children experience—environments marked by abuse, violence, dysfunction, neglect, and the absence of loving caretakers—adolescence can leave kids vulnerable to the sort of extremely poor decision making that results in tragic violence.

We were able to make persuasive arguments about the differences between children and adults, but that wasn't the only obstacle to relief. The Supreme Court's Eighth Amendment precedent requires not only that a particular sentence offend "evolving standards of decency" but also that it be "unusual." In the cases where the Supreme Court had previously granted relief under the Eighth Amendment, the number of sentences challenged usually totaled fewer than a hundred or so nationwide. In 2002, there were about a hundred people with mental retardation facing execution when the Court banned the death penalty for people with intellectual disability. In 2005, there were fewer than seventy-five juvenile offenders on death row when the Court banned the death penalty for kids. Even smaller numbers accompanied the Court's decisions banning the death penalty for non-homicide offenses.

Our litigation strategy was complicated by the fact that more than 2,500 children in the United States had been sentenced to life imprisonment without parole. We decided to focus on two subsets of kids to help the Court grant relief if it wasn't ready to ban all life sentences without parole for juveniles. We focused on the youngest kids, who were thirteen and fourteen. There were fewer than a hundred children under the age of fifteen who had been sentenced to life imprisonment without parole. We also focused on the children who, like Joe Sullivan, Ian Manuel, and Antonio Nuñez, had been convicted of non-homicide offenses. Most juveniles sentenced to life imprisonment without parole had been convicted of homicide crimes. We estimated there were fewer than two hundred juvenile offenders serving life without parole for non-homicide offenses.

We argued that the ban on the death penalty had implications because a death-in-prison sentence is also a terminal, unchangeable, once-and-for-all judgment on the whole life of a human being that declares him or her forever unfit to be part of civil society. We asked courts to recognize that such a judgment cannot rationally be passed on children below a certain age because they are unfinished products, human works in progress. They stand at a peculiarly vulnerable moment in their lives. Their potential for growth and change is enormous. Almost all of them will outgrow criminal behavior, and it is practically impossible to detect the few who will not. They are "the products of an environment over which they have no real control—passengers through narrow pathways in a world they never made," as we wrote in our brief.

We emphasized the incongruity of not allowing children to smoke, drink, vote, drive without restrictions, give blood, buy guns, and a range of other behaviors because of their well-recognized lack of maturity and judgment while simultaneously treating some of the most at-risk, neglected, and impaired children exactly the same as full-grown adults in the criminal justice system.

Initially, we had little success with these arguments. Joe Sullivan's judge ruled that our claims were "meritless." In other states, we were met with similar skepticism and resistance. Eventually we exhausted options provided by the state of Florida in Joe Sullivan's case and filed an appeal in the U.S. Supreme Court. In May 2009, the Supreme Court agreed to review the case. It felt like a miracle. Review in the Supreme Court is rare enough, but the possibility that the Court might create constitutional relief for children sentenced to die in prison made this opportunity even more thrilling. It was a chance to change the rules across the country.

The Court granted review in Joe's case and in another Florida case that involved a sixteen-year-old teen convicted of a non-homicide and sentenced to life with no parole. Terrance Graham was from Jacksonville, Florida, and had been on probation when he was accused of trying to rob a store. As a result of his new arrest, the judge revoked Terrance's probation and sentenced him to die in prison. Because both Joe's case and the Graham case involved non-homicides, it was likely that if we won a favorable ruling from the Court, it would only apply to life-without-parole sentences imposed on juveniles convicted of non-homicides, but that was an exciting possibility.

The cases generated a lot of national media attention. When we filed our brief in the U.S. Supreme Court, national organizations joined us and filed amicus briefs urging the Court to rule in our favor. We received support from the American Psychological Association, the American Psychiatric Association, the American Bar Association, the American Medical Association, former judges, former prosecutors, social workers, civil rights groups, human rights groups, even some victims' rights groups. Former juvenile offenders who had later become well-known public figures filed supporting documents, including very conservative politicians like former U.S. senator Alan Simpson from Wyoming. Simpson had spent eighteen years in the Senate, including ten as the Republican whip, the second-ranking senator in his party. He had also been a former juvenile felon. He had been adjudicated as a juvenile delinquent when he was seventeen, for multiple convictions for arson, theft, aggravated assault, gun violence, and, finally, assaulting a police officer. He later confessed: "I was a monster." His life didn't begin to change until he found himself imprisoned in "a sea of puke and urine" following another arrest. Senator Simpson knew firsthand that you cannot judge a person's full potential by his juvenile misconduct. Another brief was filed on behalf of former child soldiers whose terrifying behavior after being forced into violent African militias made the crimes of our clients seem much less aggravated by comparison. Yet these former child soldiers, rescued from their armies, had mostly recovered and been widely embraced at American colleges and universities, where many of them had thrived.

In November 2009, after the briefs were filed in Joe's case and the

Graham case, I went to Washington for my third U.S. Supreme Court oral argument. There was a lot more media attention and national news coverage than in any of my earlier cases. The Court was packed. There were hundreds of people outside the Court as well. A wide assortment of children's rights advocates, lawyers, and mental health experts were watching closely when we asked the Court to declare life-without-parole sentences imposed on children unconstitutional.

During the argument, the Court was feisty, and it was impossible to predict what the justices were going to do. I told the Court that the United States is the only country in the world that imposes life imprisonment without parole sentences on children. I explained that condemning children violates international law, which bans these sentences for children. We showed the Court that these sentences are disproportionately imposed on children of color. We argued that the phenomenon of life sentences imposed on children is largely a result of harsh punishments that were created for career adult criminals and were never intended for children—which made the imposition of such a sentence on juveniles like Terrance Graham and Joe Sullivan unusual. I also told the Court that to say to any child of thirteen that he is fit only to die in prison is cruel. I had no way of knowing if the Court had been persuaded.

I had promised Joe, whose name and case were constantly being discussed on television, that I would visit him after the argument in the Supreme Court. At first Joe was very excited by all the attention his case was generating, but then the guards and other prisoners started making fun of him and treating him more harshly than usual. They seemed to resent the attention he was getting. I told him that now that the argument was over, things would calm down.

For weeks he'd been working on memorizing a poem he said he'd written. When I asked if he had really written it, he acknowledged that another inmate had helped him, but his excitement about the poem was undiminished. He had repeatedly promised that he would recite it for me when I visited him after the argument. When I arrived at the prison, Joe was wheeled into the visitation area without any difficulty. I talked to him about the argument in Washington, but he was much more interested in preparing me to hear his poem. I could tell he was nervous about whether he'd be able to do it. I cut short my report about his case so I could hear his poem. He closed his eyes to concentrate and then began to recite the lines:

> *Roses are red, violets are blue.*
> *Soon I'll come home to live with you.*
> *My life will be better, happy I'll be,*
> *You'll be like my Dad and my family.*
> *We'll have fun with our friends and others will see,*
> *I'm a good person . . . uh . . . I'm a good person . . . I'm . . . a . . .*
> *good . . . person . . . uh . . .*

He couldn't remember the last line. He looked up at the ceiling, then at the floor straining to remember. He squeezed his eyes, trying to force the last words to mind, but they wouldn't come. I was tempted to supply him a line just to help him get through it—"so be happy for me" or "now people will see." But I realized that creating a line for him wasn't the right thing to do, so I just sat there.

Finally, he seemed to accept that he wouldn't remember the line. I thought he'd be upset, but when it was clear that he wouldn't remember the last line, he just started laughing. I smiled at him, relieved. For some reason it became funnier and funnier to him that he couldn't think of the last line—until he abruptly stopped laughing and looked at me.

"Oh, wait. I think the last line . . . actually, uh, I think the last line is just what I said. The last line is just 'I'm a good person.' "

He paused, and I looked at him skeptically for several seconds. I said it before I thought about it. "Really?"

I should have stopped, but I continued, "We'll have fun with our friends and others will see, I'm a good person?"

He looked at me for an instant with a serious expression, and then we both broke out simultaneously in wild laughter. I wasn't sure I should be laughing, but Joe was laughing, which made me think it was okay. Honestly, I couldn't help it. In a few seconds we were both in hysterics. He was rocking in his wheelchair from side to side with laughter, clapping his hands. I couldn't stop laughing, either; I was trying hard to stop but failing. We looked at each other as we laughed. I watched Joe, who laughed like a little boy, but I saw the lines in his face and even the emergence of a few prematurely gray hairs on his head. I realized even while I laughed that his unhappy childhood had been followed by unhappy, imprisoned teenage years followed by unhappy incarceration through young adulthood. All of a sudden it occurred to me what a miracle it was that he could still laugh. I thought about how wrong the world is about Joe Sullivan and how much I wanted to win his case.

We both finally calmed down. I tried to speak as sincerely as I could manage. "Joe, it's a very, very nice poem." I paused. "I think it's beautiful."

He beamed at me and clapped his hands.

Chapter Fifteen

Broken

Walter's decline came quickly. The moments of confusion got longer and longer. He started forgetting things he had done just a few hours earlier. The details of his business slipped away from him, and managing work became complicated in ways he couldn't understand, which depressed him. At some point I went over his records with him, and he'd been selling things at a fraction of their worth and losing a lot of money.

A film crew from Ireland came to Alabama to make a short documentary about the death penalty that would feature Walter's case and the cases of two other Alabama death row prisoners. James "Bo" Cochran had been released after spending nearly twenty years on Alabama's death row; a new trial was awarded after federal courts reversed his conviction because of racial bias during jury selection. At his new trial, a racially diverse jury found him not guilty of murder, and he was freed. The third man featured in the film, Robert Tarver, also adamantly maintained his innocence. The prosecutor later admitted that his jury had been illegally selected in a racially discriminatory manner, but courts refused to review the claim because the defense lawyer failed to make an adequate objection, so Tarver was executed.

We hosted a premiere of the film at our office, and I invited Walter and Bo to address the audience. About seventy-five people from the community gathered in EJI's meeting room, where we screened the film. Walter struggled. He was more terse than usual and looked at me frantically whenever someone asked him a question. I told him that he wouldn't have to do any more presentations. His sister told me that he'd started wandering in the evenings and getting lost. He began drinking heavily, something he'd never done before. He told me that he was anxious all the time and that the alcohol calmed his nerves. Then one day he collapsed. He was at a hospital in Mobile when they reached me in Montgomery. I drove down to speak with his doctor, who told me that Walter had advancing dementia, likely trauma-induced, and that he would need constant care. The doctor also said the dementia would progress and that Walter would likely become incapacitated.

We met with Walter's family at our office and agreed that he should move to Huntsville to live with a relative who could provide consistent care. It worked for a while, but Walter became agitated there, and he was out of money, so he moved back to Monroeville, where his sister Katie Lee agreed to watch him. For a while, he did much better in Monroeville, but then his condition began to deteriorate again.

Soon, Walter needed to be moved into the sort of facility that provided care for the elderly and infirm. Most places wouldn't take him because he had been convicted of a felony. Even when we explained that he was wrongfully convicted and later proved innocent, we couldn't get anyone to admit him. EJI now had a social worker on staff, Maria Morrison, who began working with Walter and his family to find a suitable placement for him. It was an extremely frustrating and maddening process. Maria eventually found a place in Montgomery that agreed to take Walter for a short stay—no longer than ninety days. He went there while we figured out what to do next.

The whole thing made me incredibly sad. Our workload was increasing too quickly. I had just argued Joe Sullivan's case at the U.S. Supreme Court, and I was anxiously awaiting that judgment. The Alabama Supreme Court had scheduled execution dates for several death row prisoners who had completed the appeals process. For years we'd been fearing what would happen when a sizable number of condemned prisoners exhausted their appeals. More than a dozen people were now vulnerable to execution dates, and we knew that it would be extremely difficult to block those executions given the current legal climate in Alabama, combined with the limits on federal court review in capital cases. I met with our staff, and we made the difficult decision to represent all of the people who were scheduled for execution and didn't have counsel.

A few weeks later, I found myself deeply distressed. I was worried about the execution dates that were set for every other month in Alabama. I was worried about what the U.S. Supreme Court would do with all of the children condemned to die in prison, now that it had the issue to consider. I was worried about our funding and whether we had enough staff and resources to meet the demands of our expanding docket. I was worried about several clients who were struggling. When I got to the Montgomery nursing home to see Walter a week after he'd arrived there, I felt like I had been worrying all day.

Walter sat in a common room with older, heavily medicated people watching TV. It was jarring to see him sitting in a hospital gown among people so compromised and infirm. I stopped before I walked into the room and looked at him; he hadn't seen me yet. He looked sleepy and unhappy slumped in a reclining chair, his head rested on his hand. He was staring in the general direction of the television, but it didn't seem like he was watching the program. He wasn't shaved, and something he'd eaten had crusted on his chin. There was a sadness in his eyes I had never seen before. Looking at him, I felt my heart sink; a part of me wanted to leave. A nurse saw me standing outside the room and asked if I was there to see someone. I told her I was, and she smiled sympathetically.

When the nurse escorted me into the room, I walked up to Walter and put my hand on his shoulder. He stirred and looked up, then gave me a broad smile.

"Hey, there he is!" He sounded cheerful, and suddenly he looked like himself. He started laughing and stood up. I gave him a hug. I was relieved; he hadn't recognized some family members recently.

"How you doing?" I asked him while he leaned on me slightly.

"Well, you know, I'm doing okay." We started walking to his room where we could talk privately.

"Are you feeling better?"

It was not a sensible question, but I was a little unnerved seeing Walter like this. He'd lost weight, and his gown wasn't tied in the back, which he didn't seem to notice. I stopped him.

"Wait, let me help you out."

I tied the strings on his gown and we continued to his room. He moved slowly and cautiously, sliding his feet in his slippers across the floor as if he'd forgotten how to pick them up. He grabbed my arm a few feet down the hall and leaned on me as we slowly made our way.

"Well, I told them people I got plenty of cars, plenty of cars." He spoke emphatically, with much more excitement than I'd heard from him in a while. "All different colors, shapes, and sizes. The man say, 'Your cars don't work.' I told him my cars do work, too." He looked at me. "You may have to talk to that man about my cars, okay?"

I nodded and thought of his field of metal. "You do have lots of cars—"

"I know!" He cut me off and started laughing. "See, I told them people, but they didn't believe me. I told them." He was smiling and chuckling now, but he looked confused and not himself. "Them people think I don't know what I'm talking about, but I know exactly what I'm talking about." He spoke defiantly. We reached his room, and he sat down on his bed while I pulled up a chair. He became still and quiet and suddenly looked very worried.

"Well, it looks like I'm back here," he said with a heavy sigh. "They done put me back on death row."

His voice was mournful.

"I tried, I tried, I tried, but they just won't let me be." He looked me in the eye. "Why they want to do somebody like they're doing me is something I'll never understand. Why are people like that? I mind my own business. I don't hurt nobody. I try to do right, and no matter what I do, people come along, put me right back on death row . . . for nothing. Nothing. I ain't done nothing to nobody. Nothing, nothing, nothing."

He was becoming agitated so I put my hand on his arm.

"Hey, it's okay," I said as gently as I could. "It's not as bad as it seems. I think—"

"You're going to get me out, right? You're going to get me off the row again?"

"Walter, this isn't the row. You haven't been feeling well, and so you're here so you can get better. This is a hospital."

"They've got me again, and you've got to help me."

He was starting to panic, and I wasn't sure what to do. Then he started crying. "Please get me out of here. Please? They're going to execute me for no good reason, and I don't want to die in no electric chair." He was crying now with a forcefulness that alarmed me.

I moved to the bed next to him and put my arm around him. "It's okay, it's okay. Walter, it's going to be all right. It's going to be all right."

He was trembling, and I got up so that he could lie down. He stopped crying as his head hit the pillow. I began talking to him softly about trying to make arrangements so he could stay at home and how we needed to find help, and that the problem was that it really wasn't safe for him to be alone. I could see his eyes drooping as I spoke, and within a matter of minutes he was sound asleep. I'd been with him less than twenty minutes. I pulled his blankets up and watched him sleep.

In the hallway, I asked one of the nurses how he'd been doing.

"He's really sweet," she said. "We love having him here. He's nice to the staff, very polite and gentle. Sometimes he gets upset and starts talking about prison and death row. We didn't know what he was talking about, but one of the girls looked him up on the Internet, and that's when we read what happened to him. Somebody said someone like that is not supposed to be here, but I told them that our job is to help anybody who needs help."

"Well, the State acknowledged that he didn't do anything wrong. He is innocent."

The nurse looked at me sweetly. "I know, Mr. Stevenson, but a lot of people here think that once you go to prison, whether you belong there or not, you become a dangerous person, and they don't want to have nothing to do with you."

"Well, that's a shame." It was all I could muster.

I left the facility shaken and disturbed. My cell phone rang as soon as I stepped outside. The Alabama Supreme Court had just scheduled another death row prisoner's execution. One of EJI's best lawyers was now serving as our deputy director. Randy Susskind interned with us as a law student when he was at Georgetown University and became a staff attorney right out of law school. He proved to be an outstanding litigator and an extremely effective project manager. I called Randy and we discussed what we would do to block the execution, although we both knew that it was going to be difficult to obtain a stay at this stage. I told Randy about my visit with Walter and how painful it had been to see him. We were silent on the phone for a while, something that happens a lot when we talk.

The increasing rate of executions in Alabama went against the national trend. Media coverage of all the innocent people wrongly convicted had an effect on the death-sentencing rate in America, which began to decline in 1999. But the terrorist attacks in New York City on September 11, 2001, and threats of terrorism and global conflict seemed to disrupt the progress toward a repeal of capital punishment. But then a few years later, rates of execution and death sentencing were once again decreasing. By 2010, the number of annual executions fell to less than half the number in 1999. Several states were seriously debating ending the death penalty. New Jersey, New York,

Illinois, New Mexico, Connecticut, and Maryland all took capital punishment off the books. Even in Texas, where nearly 40 percent of the nearly 1,400 modern-era executions in the United States had taken place, the death-sentencing rate had dropped dramatically, and the pace of executions had finally slowed. Alabama's death-sentencing rate had also dropped from the late 1990s, but it was still the highest in the country. By the end of 2009, Alabama had the nation's highest execution rate per capita.

Every other month someone was facing execution, and we were scrambling to keep up. Jimmy Callahan, Danny Bradley, Max Payne, Jack Trawick, and Willie McNair were executed in 2009. We had actively tried to block these executions, mostly by arguing about the way the executions were being carried out. In 2004, I argued a case at the U.S. Supreme Court that raised questions about the constitutionality of certain methods of execution. States had largely abandoned execution by electrocution, gas chamber, firing squad, and hanging in favor of lethal injection. Viewed as more sterile and serene, lethal injection had become the most common method for the sanctioned killing of people in virtually every death state. But questions about the painlessness and efficacy of lethal injection were emerging.

In the case I argued before the Court, we challenged the constitutionality of Alabama's protocols for lethal injection. David Nelson had very compromised veins. He was in his sixties and had been a drug addict earlier in his life, making access to his veins difficult. Members of the correctional staff were not able to insert an IV in his arm in order to carry out his execution without medical complications. The Hippocratic oath prevents doctors and medical personnel from participating in executions, so Alabama officials planned for untrained correctional staff to take a knife and make a two-inch incision in Mr. Nelson's arm or groin so that they could find a vein in which to inject him with toxins and kill him. We argued that without anesthesia, the procedure would be needlessly painful and cruel.

The State of Alabama had argued that procedural rules barred Mr. Nelson from challenging the constitutionality of the protocol.

The U.S. Supreme Court intervened. The legal question was whether condemned prisoners could file civil rights actions to challenge arguably unconstitutional methods of execution. Justice Sandra Day O'Connor was especially active during the oral argument, asking me lots of questions about the propriety of correctional staff engaging in medical procedures. The Court ruled unanimously in our favor, deciding that a condemned prisoner could challenge unconstitutional methods of execution by filing a civil rights case. David Nelson died of natural causes a year after we won relief.

Following the Nelson litigation, questions about the drug combination that most states used to carry out lethal injections arose. Many states were using drugs that had been banned for animal euthanasia because they caused a painful and torturous death. The drugs weren't readily available in the United States, and so states had started importing them from European manufacturers. When the news spread that the drugs were being used in executions in the United States, European producers stopped making them available. The drugs became scarce, which prompted state correctional authorities to obtain them illegally, without complying with FDA rules that regulate the interstate sale and transfer of drugs. Drug raids of state correctional facilities were a bizarre consequence of this surreal drug dealing to carry out executions. The U.S. Supreme Court, in *Baze v. Rees*, later held that the execution protocols and drug combinations weren't inherently unconstitutional. The executions would resume.

What that meant for Alabama death row prisoners and EJI staff was seventeen executions in thirty months. It happened at the same time that we were representing children sentenced to life without parole all over the country. I'd flown to South Dakota, Iowa, Michigan, Missouri, Arkansas, Virginia, Wisconsin, and California to argue cases on behalf of condemned children over the preceding months. The courts, procedures, and players were all different, and the travel was exhausting. We were still very actively litigating on behalf of condemned children in Mississippi, Georgia, North Carolina, Florida, and Louisiana—Southern states where we had litigated previously. And, of course, our Alabama docket had never been more jammed or demanding. In a two-week period, I had been in California visiting Antonio Nuñez at a remote prison in the middle of the state before arguing his case in an appellate court there, while also actively trying to win relief for Trina Garnett in Pennsylvania and Ian Manuel in Florida. I had visited Ian and Joe Sullivan in a Florida prison, and both of them were struggling. Prison officials weren't allowing Joe to have regular access to his wheelchair, and he had fallen repeatedly and injured himself. Ian was still in isolation. Trina's medical condition was worsening.

I was having an increasingly difficult time managing it all. At the same time, Walter's authorized length of stay at the Montgomery facility was up, so we frantically made arrangements for him to move back home, where his sister would do the best she could to take care of him. It was a worrisome situation for him and his family, for all of us.

By the time Jimmy Dill was scheduled for execution in Alabama, the entire EJI staff was exhausted. The execution date couldn't have come at a more difficult time. We had no prior involvement in Mr. Dill's case, which meant getting up to speed in the thirty days before his scheduled execution. It was an unusual crime. Mr. Dill was accused of shooting someone during the course of a drug deal after an argument erupted. The shooting victim did not die; Mr. Dill was arrested and charged with aggravated assault. He was in jail for nine months awaiting trial while the victim was released from the hospital and was recovering fine. But after several months of caring for him at home, the victim's wife apparently abandoned him and he became gravely ill. When he died, state prosecutors changed the charges against Mr. Dill from assault to capital murder.

Jimmy Dill suffered from an intellectual disability and had been sexually and physically abused throughout his childhood. He struggled with drug addiction until his arrest. He was appointed counsel who did very little to prepare the case for trial. Almost no investigation was done into the poor medical care the victim had received, care that constituted the actual cause of death. The state made a plea offer of twenty years, but it was never adequately communicated to Mr. Dill, so he went to trial, was convicted, and was sentenced to death. The appellate courts affirmed his conviction and sentence. He couldn't find volunteer counsel for his postconviction appeals, so most of his legal claims were procedurally barred because he had missed the filing deadlines.

When we first looked at Mr. Dill's case a few weeks before his scheduled execution, no court had reviewed critical issues about the reliability of his conviction and sentence. Capital murder requires an intent to kill, and there was a persuasive argument that there was no intent to kill in this case and that poor health care had caused the victim's death. Most gunshot victims don't die after nine months, and it was surprising that the state was seeking the death penalty in this case. And the U.S. Supreme Court had previously banned the execution of people with mental retardation, so Mr. Dill should have been shielded from the death penalty because of his intellectual disability, but no one had investigated or presented evidence in support of the claim.

Along with his other challenges, Mr. Dill had enormous difficulty speaking. He had a speech impediment that caused him to stutter badly. When he became excited or agitated, it got worse. Because he had not previously had a lawyer who would see him or speak to him, Mr. Dill saw our intervention as something of a miracle. I sent my young lawyers to meet with him regularly after we got involved, and Mr. Dill called me frequently.

We tried frantically to get the Courts to issue a stay based on the new issues we'd uncovered, to no avail. Courts are deeply resistant to reviewing claims once a condemned prisoner has completed the appeals process the first time. Even the claim of mental retardation was thwarted because no court would grant a hearing at such a late stage. Although I knew the odds were against us, Mr. Dill's severe disabilities had made me privately hopeful that maybe a judge would be concerned and at least let us present additional evidence. But every court told us, "Too late."

On the day of the scheduled execution, I once again found myself talking to a man who was about to be strapped down and killed. I had asked Mr. Dill to call throughout the day because we were waiting to hear the outcome of our final stay request at the U.S. Supreme Court. Early in the day he had sounded anxious, but he kept insisting that things would work out, and he told me he wasn't going to give up hope. He tried to express his gratitude for what we had done in the weeks leading up to his execution. He thanked me for sending staff down to visit him regularly. We had located family members with whom he had reconnected. We told him that we believed that he had been unfairly convicted and sentenced. Even though we hadn't yet persuaded a court to stay his execution, our efforts seemed to help him cope. But then the Supreme Court denied our final request for a stay of execution, and there was nothing else to do. He would be executed in less than an hour, and I had to tell him that the Court would not grant him a stay. I felt overwhelmed.

We spoke on the phone shortly before he was taken into the execution chamber. Listening to him was hard. He was stuttering worse than usual and having great difficulty getting his words out. The imminent execution had unnerved him, but he was trying valiantly to express his gratitude for our efforts. I sat for a long time holding the phone while he strained to speak. It was heartbreaking. At one point, I remembered something I had completely forgotten until that moment.

When I was a boy, my mother took me to church. When I was about ten years old, I was outside of our church with my friends, one of whom had brought a visiting relative to the service. The visiting child was a shy, skinny boy about my height who was clinging to his cousin nervously. He didn't say anything as the group of us chatted away. I asked him where he was from, and when this child tried to speak he stumbled horribly. He had a severe speech impediment and couldn't get his mouth to cooperate. He couldn't even say the name of the town where he lived. I had never seen someone stutter like that; I thought he must have been joking or playing around, so I laughed. My friend looked at me worriedly, but I didn't stop laughing. Out of the corner of my eye, I saw my mother looking at me with an expression

I'd never seen before. It was a mix of horror, anger, and shame, all focused on me. It stopped my laughing instantly. I'd always felt adored by my mom, so I was unnerved when she called me over.

When I got to her, she was very angry with me. "What are you doing?"

"What? I didn't do . . ."

"Don't you *ever* laugh at someone because they can't get their words out right. Don't you *ever* do that!"

"I'm sorry." I was devastated to be reprimanded by my mom so harshly. "Mom, I didn't mean to do anything wrong."

"You should know better, Bryan."

"I'm sorry. I thought . . ."

"I don't want to hear it, Bryan. There is no excuse, and I'm very disappointed in you. Now, I want you to go back over there and tell that little boy that you're sorry."

"Yes, ma'am."

"Then I want you to give that little boy a hug."

"Huh?"

"Then I want you to tell him that you love him." I looked up at her and, to my horror, saw that she was dead serious. I had reacted as apologetically as I possibly could, but this was way too much.

"Mom, I can't go over and tell that boy I love him. People will—" She gave me that look again. I somberly turned around and returned to my group of friends. They had obviously seen my mother's scolding; I could tell because they were all staring at me. I went up to the little boy who had struggled to speak.

"Look, man, I'm sorry."

I was genuinely apologetic for laughing and even more deeply regretful of the situation I had put myself in. I looked over at my mother, who was still staring at me. I lunged at the boy to give him a very awkward hug. I think I startled him by grabbing him like that, but when he realized that I was trying to hug him, his body relaxed and he hugged me back.

My friends looked at me oddly as I spoke.

"Uh . . . also, uh . . . I love you!" I tried to say it as insincerely as I could get away with and half-smiled as I spoke. I was still hugging the boy, so he couldn't see the disingenuous look on my youthful face.

It made me feel less weird to smile like it was a joke. But then the boy hugged me tighter and whispered in my ear. He spoke flawlessly, without a stutter and without hesitation.

"I love you, too." There was such tenderness and earnestness in his voice, and just like that, I thought I would start crying.

I was in my office, talking to Jimmy Dill on the night of his execution, and I realized I was thinking about something that had happened nearly forty years earlier. I also realized that I was crying. The tears were sliding down my cheeks—runaways that escaped when I wasn't paying attention. Mr. Dill was still laboring to get his words out, desperately trying to thank me for trying to save his life. As it got closer and closer to the time of his execution, it became harder for him to speak. The guards were making noise behind him, and I could tell he was upset that he couldn't get his words out right, but I didn't want to interrupt him. So I sat there and let the tears fall down my face.

The harder he tried to speak, the more I wanted to cry. The long pauses gave me too much time to think. He would never have been convicted of capital murder if he had just had the money for a decent lawyer. He would never have been sentenced to death if someone had investigated his past. It all felt tragic. His struggle to form words and his determination to express gratitude reinforced his humanity for me, and it made thinking about his impending execution unbearable. *Why couldn't they see it, too?* The Supreme Court had banned the execution of people with intellectual disability, but states like Alabama refused to assess in any honest way whether the condemned are disabled. We're supposed to sentence people fairly after fully considering their life circumstances, but instead we exploit the inability of the poor to get the legal assistance they need—all so we can kill them with less resistance.

On the phone with Mr. Dill, I thought about all of his struggles and all the terrible things he'd gone through and how his disabilities had broken him. There was no excuse for him to have shot someone, but it didn't make sense to kill him. I began to get angry about it. Why do we want to kill all the broken people? What is wrong with us, that we think a thing like that can be right?

I tried not to let Mr. Dill hear me crying. I tried not to show him that he was breaking my heart. He finally got his words out.

"Mr. Bryan, I just want to thank you for fighting for me. I thank you for caring about me. I love y'all for trying to save me."

When I hung up the phone that night I had a wet face and a broken heart. The lack of compassion I witnessed every day had finally exhausted me. I looked around my crowded office, at the stacks of records and papers, each pile filled with tragic stories, and I suddenly didn't want to be surrounded by all this anguish and misery. As I sat there, I thought myself a fool for having tried to fix situations that were so fatally broken. *It's time to stop. I can't do this anymore.*

For the first time I realized that my life was just full of brokenness. I worked in a broken system of justice. My clients were broken by mental illness, poverty, and racism. They were torn apart by disease, drugs and alcohol, pride, fear, and anger. I thought of Joe Sullivan and of Trina, Antonio, Ian, and dozens of other broken children we worked with, struggling to survive in prison. I thought of people broken by war, like Herbert Richardson; people broken by poverty, like Marsha Colbey; people broken by disability, like Avery Jenkins. In their broken state, they were judged and condemned by people whose commitment to fairness had been broken by cynicism, hopelessness, and prejudice.

I looked at my computer and at the calendar on the wall. I looked again around my office at the stacks of files. I saw the list of our staff, which had grown to nearly forty people. And before I knew it, I was talking to myself aloud: "I can just leave. Why am I doing this?"

It took me a while to sort it out, but I realized something sitting there while Jimmy Dill was being killed at Holman prison. After working for more than twenty-five years, I understood that I don't do what I do because it's required or necessary or important. I don't do it because I have no choice.

I do what I do because I'm broken, too.

My years of struggling against inequality, abusive power, poverty, oppression, and injustice had finally revealed something to me about myself. Being close to suffering, death, executions, and cruel punishments didn't just illuminate the brokenness of others; in a moment of anguish and heartbreak, it also exposed my own brokenness. You can't effectively fight abusive power, poverty, inequality, illness, oppression, or injustice and not be broken by it.

We are all broken by something. We have all hurt someone and have been hurt. We all share the condition of brokenness even if our brokenness is not equivalent. I desperately wanted mercy for Jimmy Dill and would have done anything to create justice for him, but I couldn't pretend that his struggle was disconnected from my own. The ways in which I have been hurt—and have hurt others—are different from the ways Jimmy Dill suffered and caused suffering. But our shared brokenness connected us.

Paul Farmer, the renowned physician who has spent his life trying to cure the world's sickest and poorest people, once quoted me something that the writer Thomas Merton said: We are bodies of broken bones. I guess I'd always known but never fully considered that being broken is what makes us human. We all have our reasons. Sometimes we're fractured by the choices we make; sometimes we're shattered by things we would never have chosen. But our brokenness is also the source of our common humanity, the basis for our shared search for comfort, meaning, and healing. Our shared vulnerability and imperfection nurtures and sustains our capacity for compassion.

We have a choice. We can embrace our humanness, which means embracing our broken natures and the compassion that remains our best hope for healing. Or we can deny our brokenness, forswear compassion, and, as a result, deny our own humanity.

I thought of the guards strapping Jimmy Dill to the gurney that very hour. I thought of the people who would cheer his death and see it as some kind of victory. I realized they were broken people, too, even if they would never admit it. So many of us have become afraid and angry. We've become so fearful and vengeful that we've thrown away children, discarded the disabled, and sanctioned the imprisonment of the sick and the weak—not because they are a threat to public safety or beyond rehabilitation but because we think it makes us seem tough, less broken. I thought of the victims of violent crime and the survivors of murdered loved ones, and how we've pressured them to recycle their pain and anguish and give it back to the offenders we prosecute. I thought of the many ways we've legalized vengeful and cruel punishments, how we've allowed our victimization to justify the victimization of others. We've submitted to the harsh instinct to crush those among us whose brokenness is most visible.

But simply punishing the broken—walking away from them or hiding them from sight—only ensures that they remain broken and we do, too. There is no wholeness outside of our reciprocal humanity.

I frequently had difficult conversations with clients who were struggling and despairing over their situations—over the things they'd done, or had been done to them, that had led them to painful moments. Whenever things got really bad, and they were questioning the value of their lives, I would remind them that each of us is more than the worst thing we've ever done. I told them that if someone tells a lie, that person is not *just* a liar. If you take something that doesn't belong to you, you are not *just* a thief. Even if you kill someone, you're not *just* a killer. I told myself that evening what I had been telling my clients for years. I am more than broken. In fact, there is a strength, a power even, in understanding brokenness, because embracing our brokenness creates a need and desire for mercy, and perhaps a corresponding need to show mercy. When you experience mercy, you learn things that are hard to learn otherwise. You see things you can't otherwise see; you hear things you can't otherwise hear. You begin to recognize the humanity that resides in each of us.

All of sudden, I felt stronger. I began thinking about what would happen if we all just acknowledged our brokenness, if we owned up to our weaknesses, our deficits, our biases, our fears. Maybe if we did, we wouldn't want to kill the broken among us who have killed others. Maybe we would look harder for solutions to caring for the disabled, the abused, the neglected, and the traumatized. I had a notion that if we acknowledged our brokenness, we could no longer take pride in mass incarceration, in executing people, in our deliberate indifference to the most vulnerable.

When I was a college student, I had a job working as a musician in a black church in a poor section of West Philadelphia. At a certain point in the service I would play the organ before the choir began to sing. The minister would stand, spread his arms wide, and say, "Make me to hear joy and gladness, that the bones which thou hast broken may rejoice." I never fully appreciated what he was saying until the night Jimmy Dill was executed.

I had the privilege of meeting Rosa Parks when I first moved to Montgomery. She would occasionally come back to Montgomery from Detroit, where she lived, to visit dear friends. Johnnie Carr was one of those friends. Ms. Carr had befriended me, and I quickly learned that she was a force of nature—charismatic, powerful, and inspiring. She had been, in many ways, the true architect of the Montgomery Bus Boycott. She had organized people and transportation during the boycott and done a lot of the heavy lifting to make it the first successful major action of the modern Civil Rights Movement, and she succeeded Dr. Martin Luther King Jr. as the president of the Montgomery Improvement Association. She was in her late seventies when I first met her. "Now Bryan, I'm going to call you from time to time and I'm going ask you to do this or that and when I ask you to do something you're going to say 'Yes, ma'am,' okay?"

I chuckled—and I said, "Yes, ma'am." She would sometimes call just to check in on me, and on occasion she would invite me over when Ms. Parks came to town.

"Bryan, Rosa Parks is coming to town, and we're going to meet over at Virginia Durr's house to talk. Do you want come over and listen?"

When Ms. Carr called me, she either wanted me to go some place to "speak" or to go some place to "listen." Whenever Ms. Parks came to town, I'd be invited to listen.

"Oh, yes, ma'am. I'd love to come over and listen," I'd always say, affirming that I understood what to do when I arrived.

Ms. Parks and Ms. Carr would meet at Virginia Durr's home. Ms. Durr was also a larger-than-life personality. Her husband, Clifford Durr, was an attorney who had represented Dr. King throughout his time in Montgomery. Ms. Durr was determined to confront injustice well into her nineties. She frequently asked me to accompany her to various places or invited me over to dinner. EJI started renting her home for our law students and staff during the summers when she was away.

When I would go over to Ms. Durr's home to listen to these three formidable women, Rosa Parks was always very kind and generous with me. Years later, I would occasionally meet her at events in other states, and I ended up spending a little time with her. But mostly, I just loved hearing her and Ms. Carr and Ms. Durr talk. They would talk and talk and talk. Laughing, telling stories, and bearing witness about what could be done when people stood up (or sat down, in Ms. Parks's case). They were always so spirited together. Even after all they'd done, their focus was always on what they still planned to do for civil rights.

The first time I met Ms. Parks, I sat on Ms. Durr's front porch in Old Cloverdale, a residential neighborhood in Montgomery, and I listened to the three women talk for two hours. Finally, after watching me listen for all that time, Ms. Parks turned to me and sweetly asked, "Now, Bryan, tell me who you are and what you're doing." I looked at Ms. Carr to see if I had permission to speak, and she smiled and nodded at me. I then gave Ms. Parks my rap.

"Yes, ma'am. Well, I have a law project called the Equal Justice Initiative, and we're trying to help people on death row. We're trying to stop the death penalty, actually. We're trying to do something about prison conditions and excessive punishment. We want to free people who've been wrongly convicted. We want to end unfair sentences in criminal cases and stop racial bias in criminal justice. We're trying to help the poor and do something about indigent defense and the fact that people don't get the legal help they need. We're trying to help people who are mentally ill. We're trying to stop them from putting children in adult jails and prisons. We're trying to do something about poverty and the hopelessness that dominates poor communities. We want to see more diversity in decision-making roles in the justice system. We're trying to educate people about racial history and the need for racial justice. We're trying to confront abuse of power by police and prosecutors—" I realized that I had gone on way too long, and I stopped abruptly. Ms. Parks, Ms. Carr, and Ms. Durr were all looking at me.

Ms. Parks leaned back, smiling. "Ooooh, honey, all that's going to make you tired, tired, tired." We all laughed. I looked down, a little embarrassed. Then Ms. Carr leaned forward and put her finger in my face and talked to me just like my grandmother used to talk to me. She said, "That's why you've got to be brave, brave, brave." All three women nodded in silent agreement and for just a little while they made me feel like a young prince.

I looked at the clock. It was 6:30 P.M. Mr. Dill was dead by now. I was very tired, and it was time to stop all this foolishness about quitting. It was time to be brave. I turned to my computer, and there was an email inviting me to speak to students in a poor school district about remaining hopeful. The teacher told me that she had heard me speak and wanted me to be a role model for the students and inspire them to do great things. Sitting in my office, drying my tears, reflecting on my brokenness, it seemed like a laughable notion. But then I thought about those kids and the overwhelming and unfair challenges that too many children in this country have to overcome, and I started typing a message saying that I would be honored to come.

On the drive home, I turned on the car radio, seeking news about Mr. Dill's execution. I found a station airing a news report. It was a local religious station, but in their news broadcast there was no mention of the execution. I left the station on, and before long a preacher began a sermon. She started with scripture.

Three different times I begged the Lord to take it away. Each time he said, "My grace is sufficient. My power is made perfect in your weakness." So now I am glad to boast about my weaknesses, so that the power of Christ may work through me. Since I know it is all for Christ's good, I am quite content with my weaknesses and with insults, hardships, persecutions and calamities. For when I am weak, then I am strong.

I turned off the radio station, and as I slowly made my way home I understood that even as we are caught in a web of hurt and brokenness, we're also in a web of healing and mercy. I thought of the little boy who hugged me outside of church, creating reconciliation and love. I didn't deserve reconciliation or love in that moment, but that's how mercy works. The power of just mercy is that it belongs to the undeserving. It's when mercy is least expected that it's most potent—strong enough to break the cycle of victimization and victimhood, retribution and suffering. It has the power to heal the psychic harm and injuries that lead to aggression and violence, abuse of power, mass incarceration.

I drove home broken and brokenhearted about Jimmy Dill. But I knew I would come back the next day. There was more work to do.

Chapter Sixteen

The Stonecatchers'
Song of Sorrow

On May 17, 2010, I was sitting in my office waiting anxiously when the U.S. Supreme Court announced its decision: Life imprisonment without parole sentences imposed on children convicted of non-homicide crimes is cruel and unusual punishment and constitutionally impermissible. My staff and I jumped up and down in celebration. Moments later we were inundated with a flood of calls from media, clients, families, and children's rights advocates. It was the first time the Court had issued a categorical ban on a punishment other than the death penalty. Joe Sullivan was entitled to relief. Scores of people, including Antonio Nuñez and Ian Manuel, were entitled to reduced sentences that would give them a "meaningful opportunity for release."

Two years later, in June 2012, we won a constitutional ban on mandatory life-without-parole sentences imposed on children convicted of homicides. The Supreme Court had agreed to review Evan Miller's case and the case of our client from Arkansas, Kuntrell Jackson. I argued both cases in March of that year and waited anxiously until we won a favorable ruling. The Court's decision meant that no child accused of any crime could ever again be automatically sentenced to die in prison. Over two thousand condemned people sentenced to life imprisonment without parole for crimes when they were children were now potentially eligible for relief and reduced sentences. Some states changed their statutes to create more hopeful sentences for child offenders. Prosecutors in many places resisted retroactive application of the Court's decision in *Miller v. Alabama,* but everyone now had new hope, including Ashley Jones and Trina Garnett.

We continued our work on issues involving children by pursuing more cases. I believe there should be a total ban on housing children under the age of eighteen with adults in jails or prisons. We filed cases seeking to stop the practice. I am also convinced that very young children should never be tried in adult court. They're vulnerable to all sorts of problems that increase the risk of a wrongful conviction. No child of twelve, thirteen, or fourteen can defend him- or herself in the adult criminal justice system. Wrongful convictions and illegal trials involving young children are very common.

A few years earlier, we won the release of Phillip Shaw, who was fourteen when he was improperly convicted and sentenced to life imprisonment without parole in Missouri. His jury was illegally selected, excluding African Americans. I argued two cases at the Mississippi Supreme Court in which the Court ruled that the convictions and sentences of young children were illegal. Demarious Banyard was a thirteen-year-old who had been bullied into participating in a robbery that resulted in a fatal shooting in Jackson, Mississippi. He was given a mandatory death-in-prison sentence after his jury was illegally told that he had to prove his innocence beyond a reasonable doubt and the State introduced impermissible evidence. He was resentenced to a finite term of years and now has hope for release.

Dante Evans was a fourteen-year-old child living in a FEMA trailer with his abusive father in Gulfport, Mississippi, after Hurricane Katrina. His dad, who had twice before nearly killed Dante's mother, was shot by Dante while he slept in a chair. Dante had repeatedly told school officials about his father's abuse, but no one ever intervened. I discussed Dante's prior diagnosis of post-traumatic stress disorder following the attempted murder of his mother in my oral argument before the Mississippi Supreme Court. The Court emphasized the trial court's refusal to permit introduction of this evidence and granted Dante a new trial.

Our death penalty work had also taken a hopeful turn. The number of death row prisoners in Alabama for whom we'd won relief reached one hundred. We had created a new community of formerly condemned prisoners in Alabama who had been illegally convicted or sentenced and received new trials or sentencing hearings. Most never returned to death row. Starting in 2012, we had eighteen months with no executions in Alabama. Continued litigation about lethal injection protocols and other questions about the reliability of the death penalty slowed the execution rate in Alabama dramatically. In 2013, Alabama recorded the lowest number of new death sentences since the resumption of capital punishment in the mid-1970s. These were very hopeful developments.

Of course, there were still challenges. I was losing sleep over another man on Alabama's death row, a man who was clearly innocent. Anthony Ray Hinton was on death row when Walter McMillian arrived in the 1980s. Mr. Hinton was wrongly convicted of two robbery-murders outside Birmingham after state forensic employees mistakenly concluded that a gun recovered from his mother's home had been used in the crimes. Mr. Hinton's appointed defense lawyer got only $500 from the court to retain a gun expert to confront the state's case, so he ended up with a mechanical engineer who was blind in one eye and who had almost no experience testifying as a gun expert.

The State's primary evidence against Mr. Hinton involved a third crime where a witness identified him as the assailant. But we found a half-dozen people and security records that proved that Mr. Hinton was locked inside a secure supermarket warehouse working as a night laborer fifteen miles away at the time of the crime. We got some of the nation's best experts to review the gun evidence, and they concluded the Hinton weapon could not be matched to the murders. I had hopes that the State might reopen the case. Instead they persisted in moving toward execution. The media was not interested in the story, citing "innocence fatigue." "We've done that story before," we heard again and again. We kept getting very close decisions from appellate courts denying relief, and Mr. Hinton remained on death row facing execution. It would soon be thirty years. He was always upbeat and encouraging when I met with him, but I was increasingly desperate to find a way to get his case overturned.

I was encouraged by the fact that nationwide the rate of mass incarceration had finally slowed. For the first time in close to forty years, the country's prison population did not increase in 2011. In 2012, the United States saw the first decline in its prison population in decades. I spent a lot of time in California that year supporting ballot initiatives and was encouraged that voters decided, by a huge margin, to end the state's "three strikes" law that imposed mandatory sentences on nonviolent offenders. The initiative won majority support in every county in the state. California voters also came very close to banning the death penalty; the ballot initiative lost by only a couple of percentage points. Almost banning the death penalty through a popular referendum in an American state would have been unimaginable just a few years earlier.

We were able to finally launch the race and poverty initiative I'd long been hoping to start at EJI. For years I'd wanted to implement a project to change the way we talk about racial history and contextualize contemporary race issues. We published a racial history calendar for 2013 and 2014. We started working with poor children and families in Black Belt counties across the South. We brought hundreds of high school students to our office for supplemental education and discussion about rights and justice. Also, we worked on reports and materials that seek to deepen the national conversation about the legacy of slavery and lynching and our nation's history of racial injustice.

I found the new race and poverty work extremely energizing. It closely connected to our work on criminal justice issues; I believe that so much of our worst thinking about justice is steeped in the myths of racial difference that still plague us. I believe that there are four institutions in American history that have shaped our approach to race and justice but remain poorly understood. The first, of course, is slavery. This was followed by the reign of terror that shaped the lives of people of color following the collapse of Reconstruction until World War II. Older people of color in the South would occasionally come up to me after speeches to complain about how antagonized they feel when they hear news commentators talking about how we were dealing with domestic terrorism for the first time in the United States after the 9/11 attacks.

An older African American man once said to me, "You make them stop saying that! We grew up with terrorism all the time. The police, the Klan, anybody who was white could terrorize you. We had to worry about bombings and lynchings, racial violence of all kinds."

The racial terrorism of lynching in many ways created the modern death penalty. America's embrace of speedy executions was, in part, an attempt to redirect the violent energies of lynching while assuring white southerners that black men would still pay the ultimate price.

Convict leasing was introduced at the end of the nineteenth century to criminalize former slaves and convict them of nonsensical offenses so that freed men, women, and children could be "leased" to businesses and effectively forced back into slave labor. Private industries throughout the country made millions of dollars with free convict labor, while thousands of African Americans died in horrific work conditions. The practice of re-enslavement was so widespread in some states that it was characterized in a Pulitzer Prize–winning book by Douglas Blackmon as *Slavery by Another Name.* But the practice is not well known to most Americans.

During the terror era there were hundreds of ways in which people of color could commit a social transgression or offend someone that might cost them their lives. Racial terror and the constant threat created by violently enforced racial hierarchy were profoundly traumatizing for African Americans. Absorbing these psychosocial realities created all kinds of distortions and difficulties that manifest themselves today in multiple ways.

The third institution, "Jim Crow," is the legalized racial segregation and suppression of basic rights that defined the American apartheid era. It is more recent and is recognized in our national consciousness, but it is still not well understood. It seems to me that we've been quick to celebrate the achievements of the Civil Rights Movement and slow to recognize the damage done in that era. We have been unwilling to commit to a process of truth and reconciliation in which people are allowed to give voice to the difficulties created by racial segregation, racial subordination, and marginalization. Because I was born during a time when the stigma of racial hierarchy and Jim Crow had real consequences for the ways my elders had to act or react to a variety of indignations, I was mindful of the way that the daily humiliations and insults accumulated.

The legacy of racial profiling carries many of the same complications. Working on all of these juvenile cases across the country meant that I was frequently in courtrooms and communities where I'd never been before. Once I was preparing to do a hearing in a trial court in the Midwest and was sitting at counsel table in an empty courtroom before the hearing. I was wearing a dark suit, white shirt, and tie. The judge and the prosecutor entered through a door in the back of the courtroom laughing about something.

When the judge saw me sitting at the defense table, he said to me harshly, "Hey, you shouldn't be in here without counsel. Go back outside and wait in the hallway until your lawyer arrives."

I stood up and smiled broadly. I said, "Oh, I'm sorry, Your Honor, we haven't met. My name is Bryan Stevenson, I am the lawyer on the case set for hearing this morning."

The judge laughed at his mistake, and the prosecutor joined in. I forced myself to laugh because I didn't want my young client, a white child who had been prosecuted as an adult, to be disadvantaged by a conflict I had created with the judge before the hearing. But I was disheartened by the experience. Of course innocent mistakes occur, but the accumulated insults and indignations caused by racial presumptions are destructive in ways that are hard to measure. Constantly being suspected, accused, watched, doubted, distrusted, presumed guilty, and even feared is a burden borne by people of color that can't be understood or confronted without a deeper conversation about our history of racial injustice.

The fourth institution is mass incarceration. Going into any prison is deeply confusing if you know anything about the racial demographics of America. The extreme overrepresentation of people of color, the disproportionate sentencing of racial minorities, the targeted prosecution of drug crimes in poor communities, the criminalization of new immigrants and undocumented people, the collateral consequences of voter disenfranchisement, and the barriers to re-entry can only be fully understood through the lens of our racial history.

It was gratifying to be able, finally, to address some of these issues through our new project and to articulate the challenges created by racial history and structural poverty. The materials we developed were generating positive feedback, and I became hopeful that we might be able to push back against the suppression of this difficult history of racial injustice.

I was also encouraged by our new staff. We were now attracting young, gifted lawyers from all over the country who are extremely skilled. We started a program for college graduates to work at EJI as Justice Fellows. Having a bigger staff with very talented people made meeting the new challenges created by our much broader docket seem possible.

A bigger staff, bigger cases, and a bigger docket also sometimes meant bigger problems. While exciting and very gratifying, the Supreme Court rulings on juveniles created all sorts of new challenges for us. Hundreds of people were now entitled to pursue new sentences, and most were in states where they had no clear right to counsel. In states like Louisiana, Alabama, Mississippi, and Arkansas, there were hundreds of people whose cases were affected by the recent decisions, but no lawyers were available to assist these condemned juvenile lifers. We ended up taking on almost one hundred new cases following the court's ban on life imprisonment without parole for kids convicted of non-homicide offenses. We then took on another hundred new cases after the decision banning mandatory life without parole for juveniles. In addition to the dozens of cases already on our juvenile docket, we were quickly overwhelmed.

The total ban on life-without-parole sentences for children convicted of non-homicides should have been the easiest decision to implement, but enforcing the Supreme Court's ruling was proving much more difficult than I had hoped. I was spending more and more time in Louisiana, Florida, and Virginia, which together had close to 90 percent of the non-homicide cases. The trial courts were often less sophisticated in thinking about the differences between children and adults than we had hoped, and we would often have to relitigate the basic unfairness of treating kids like adults that the Supreme Court had already recognized.

Some judges seemed to want to get as close to life expectancy or natural death as possible before they would create release opportunities for child offenders. Antonio Nuñez's judge in Orange County, California, replaced his sentence of life imprisonment without parole with a sentence of 175 years. I had to go back to an appellate court in California and argue to get that sentence replaced with a reasonable sentence. We met resistance in Joe Sullivan's and Ian Manuel's cases as well. Ultimately, we were able to get sentences that meant they could both be released after serving a few more years.

In some cases, clients had already been in prison for decades and had very few, if any, support systems to help them re-enter society. We decided to create a re-entry program to assist these clients. EJI's program was specifically developed for people who have spent many years in prison after being incarcerated when they were children. We were committed to providing services, housing, job training, life skills, counseling, and anything else people coming out of prison needed to succeed. We told the judges and parole boards we were committed to providing the assistance our clients required.

In particular, the Louisiana clients serving life without parole for non-homicides faced many challenges. We undertook representation of all sixty of those eligible for relief in Louisiana. Almost all of them were at Angola, a notoriously difficult place to do time, especially in the 1970s and 1980s when many had first arrived. For many years, violence was so bad at Angola that it was almost impossible to be incarcerated and not get disciplinaries—additional punishments or time tacked onto your sentence—due to conflicts with another inmate or staff. Prisoners were required to do manual labor in very difficult work environments or face solitary confinement or other disciplinary action. It was not uncommon for inmates to be seriously injured, losing fingers or limbs, after working long hours in brutal and dangerous conditions.

For years, Angola—a slave plantation before the end of the Civil War—forced inmates to work in the fields picking cotton. Prisoners who refused would receive "write-ups" that went into their files and face months of solitary confinement. The horrible conditions of confinement and their constantly being told that they would die in prison no matter how well they behaved meant that most of our clients had long lists of disciplinaries. At the resentencing hearings we were preparing, state lawyers were using these prior disciplinaries to argue against favorable new sentences.

Remarkably, several former juvenile lifers had developed outstanding institutional histories with very few disciplinaries, even though they did their time with no hope of ever being released or having their institutional history reviewed. Some became trustees, mentors, and advocates against violence among inmates. Others had become law librarians, journalists, and gardeners. Angola evolved over time to have some excellent programs for incarcerated people who stayed out of trouble, and many of our clients took full advantage.

We decided to prioritize resentencing hearings in Louisiana for the "old-timers," juvenile lifers who had been there for decades. Joshua

Carter and Robert Caston were the first two cases we decided to litigate. In 1963, when he was sixteen, Joshua Carter was accused of a rape in New Orleans and quickly given the death penalty. A condemned black child awaiting execution in those days had little reason to hope for relief. But to coerce a confession from him, police officers had beaten Joshua so brutally that even in 1965 the Louisiana Supreme Court felt the need to overturn his conviction. Mr. Carter was resentenced to life imprisonment without parole and sent to Angola. After struggling for years, he became a model prisoner and trustee. In the 1990s, he developed glaucoma and didn't get the medical care he needed, and he soon lost his sight in both eyes. We tried to persuade New Orleans prosecutors that Mr. Carter, blind and in his sixties, should be released after nearly fifty years in prison.

Robert Caston had been at Angola for forty-five years. He lost several fingers working in a prison factory and was now disabled as a result of his forced labor at Angola.

I traveled back and forth between the trial courts in Orleans Parish quite a bit on the Carter and Caston cases. The Orleans Parish courthouse is a massive structure with intimidating architecture. There are multiple courtrooms aligned down an enormous hallway with grand marble floors and high ceilings. Hundreds of people crowd the hallways, bustling between the various courtrooms each day. Hearings in the vast courthouse are never reliably scheduled. Frequently, there would be a date and time for the Carter and Caston resentencings, but it seemed to mean very little to anyone. I would arrive in court, and there would always be a stack of cases, and clients with lawyers gathered in an overcrowded courtroom, all waiting to be heard at the time of our hearings. Overwhelmed judges tried to manage the proceedings with bench meetings while dozens of young men—most of whom were black—sat handcuffed in standard jail-issued orange jumpsuits in the front of the court. Lawyers consulted with clients and family members scattered around the chaotic courtroom.

After three trips to New Orleans for sentencing hearings, we still did not have a new sentence for Mr. Carter or Mr. Caston. We met with the district attorney, filed papers with the judge, and consulted with a variety of local officials in an effort to achieve a new, constitutionally acceptable sentence. Because Mr. Carter and Mr. Caston had both been in prison for nearly fifty years, we wanted their immediate release.

A couple of weeks before Christmas, I was back in court for the fourth time trying to win the release of the two men. There were two different judges and courtrooms involved, but we felt if we won release for one it might then become easier to win release for the other. We were working with the Juvenile Justice Project of Louisiana, and their lawyer Carol Kolinchak had agreed to be our local counsel in all of the Louisiana cases. At this fourth hearing, Carol and I were busily trying to process papers and resolve the endless issues that had emerged to keep Mr. Carter and Mr. Caston incarcerated.

Mr. Carter had a large family that had maintained a close relationship with him despite the passage of time. In the aftermath of Hurricane Katrina, many family members had fled New Orleans and were now living hundreds of miles away. But a dozen or so family members would dutifully show up at each hearing, some traveling from as far away as California. Mr. Carter's mother was nearly a hundred years old. She had vowed to Mr. Carter for decades that she wouldn't die until he came home from prison.

Finally, it seemed like we were close to success. We got things resolved so that the Court could grant our motion and resentence Mr. Caston so that he would immediately be released from prison. The State usually wouldn't bring inmates from Angola to New Orleans for hearings but instead had them view proceedings on a video hookup at the prison. After I made our arguments in the noisy, frenetic courtroom, the judge granted our motion. She recited the facts about the date of Mr. Caston's conviction, and then something quite unexpected happened. As the judge spoke about Mr. Caston's decades in prison, the courtroom, for the first time in my multiple trips there, became completely silent. The lawyers stopped conferring, the prosecutors awaiting other cases paid attention, and family members ceased their chatter. Even the handcuffed inmates awaiting their cases had stopped talking and were listening intently. The judge detailed Mr. Caston's forty-five years at Angola for a non-homicide crime when he was sixteen. She noted that Caston had been sent to Angola in the 1960s. Then the judge pronounced a new sentence that meant Mr. Caston would immediately be released from prison.

I looked at Carol and smiled. Then the people in the silent courtroom did something I'd never seen before: They erupted in applause. The defense lawyers, prosecutors, family members, and deputy sheriffs applauded. Even the inmates applauded in their handcuffs.

Carol was wiping tears from her eyes. Even the judge, who usually tolerated no disruptions, seemed to embrace the drama of the moment. A number of my former students now worked with the public defender's office in New Orleans, and they, too, had come to court and were cheering. I had to speak with Mr. Caston by phone and explain what had happened, since he couldn't see everything from the video monitor. He was overjoyed. He became the first person to be released as a result of the Supreme Court's ban on death-in-prison sentences for juvenile lifers.

We went down the hall to Mr. Carter's courtroom and had another success, winning a new sentence that meant that he, too, would be released immediately. Mr. Carter's family was ecstatic. There were hugs and promises of home-cooked meals for me and the staff of EJI.

Carol and I busily began making arrangements for Mr. Caston's and Mr. Carter's releases, which would take place that evening. The protocol at Angola was to release prisoners at midnight and give them bus fare to New Orleans or a city of their choice in Louisiana. We dispatched staff to Angola, which was several hours away, to meet the men when they were released, sparing them the midnight bus trip.

Exhausted, I wandered the halls of the courthouse while we waited for one more piece of paper to be faxed and approved to clear the way for the release of Mr. Caston and Mr. Carter. An older black woman sat on the marble steps in the massive courthouse hallway. She looked tired and wore what my sister and I used to call a "church meeting hat." She had smooth dark skin, and I recognized her as someone who had been in the courtroom when Mr. Carter was resentenced. In fact, I thought I'd seen her each time I'd come to the courthouse in New Orleans. I assumed that she was related or connected to one of the clients, although I didn't remember the other family members ever mentioning her. I must have been staring because she saw me looking and waved at me, gesturing for me to come to her.

When I walked over to her she smiled at me. "I'm tired and I'm not going to get up, so you're going to have to lean over for me to give you a hug." She had a sweet voice that crackled.

I smiled back at her. "Well, yes, ma'am. I love hugs, thank you." She wrapped her arms around my neck.

"Sit, sit. I want to talk to you," she said.

I sat down beside her on the steps. "I've seen you here several times, are you related to Mr. Caston or Mr. Carter?" I asked.

"No, no, no, I'm not related to nobody here. Not that I know of, anyway." She had a kind smile, and she looked at me intensely. "I just come here to help people. This is a place full of pain, so people need plenty of help around here."

"Well, that's really kind of you."

"No, it's what I'm supposed to do, so I do it." She looked away before locking eyes with me again. "My sixteen-year-old grandson was murdered fifteen years ago," she said, "and I loved that boy more than life itself."

I wasn't expecting that response and was instantly sobered. The woman grabbed my hand.

"I grieved and grieved and grieved. I asked the Lord why he let someone take my child like that. He was killed by some other boys. I came to this courtroom for the first time for their trials and sat in there and cried every day for nearly two weeks. None of it made any sense. Those boys were found guilty for killing my grandson, and the judge sent them away to prison forever. I thought it would make me feel better but it actually made me feel worse."

She continued, "I sat in the courtroom after they were sentenced and just cried and cried. A lady came over to me and gave me a hug and let me lean on her. She asked me if the boys who got sentenced were my children, and I told her no. I told her the boy they killed was my child." She hesitated. "I think she sat with me for almost two hours. For well over an hour, we didn't neither one of us say a word. It felt good to finally have someone to lean on at that trial, and I've never forgotten that woman. I don't know who she was, but she made a difference."

"I'm so sorry about your grandson," I murmured. It was all I could think of to say.

"Well, you never fully recover, but you carry on, you carry on. I didn't know what to do with myself after those trials, so about a year later I started coming down here. I don't really know why. I guess I just felt like maybe I could be someone, you know, that somebody hurting could lean on." She looped her arm with mine.

I smiled at her. "That's really wonderful."

"It has been wonderful. What's your name again?"

"It's Bryan."

"It has been wonderful, Bryan. When I first came, I'd look for people who had lost someone to murder or some violent crime. Then it got to the point where some of the ones grieving the most were the ones whose children or parents were on trial, so I just started letting anybody lean on me who needed it. All these young children being sent to prison forever, all this grief and violence. Those judges throwing people away like they're not even human, people shooting each other, hurting each other like they don't care. I don't know, it's a lot of pain. I decided that I was supposed to be here to catch some of the stones people cast at each other."

I chuckled when she said it. During the McMillian hearings, a local minister had held a regional church meeting about the case and had asked me to come speak. There were a few people in the African American community whose support of Walter was muted, not because they thought he was guilty but because he had had an extramarital affair and wasn't active in the church. At the church meeting, I spoke mostly about Walter's case, but I also reminded people that when the woman accused of adultery was brought to Jesus, he told the accusers who wanted to stone her to death, "Let he who is without sin cast the first stone." The woman's accusers retreated, and Jesus forgave her and urged her to sin no more. But today, our self-righteousness, our fear, and our anger have caused even the Christians to hurl stones at the people who fall down, even when we know we should forgive or show compassion. I told the congregation that we can't simply watch that happen. I told them we have to be stonecatchers.

When I chuckled at the older woman's invocation of the parable, she laughed, too. "I heard you in that courtroom today. I've even seen you here a couple of times before. I know you's a stonecatcher, too."

I laughed even more. "Well, I guess I try to be."

She took my hands and rubbed my palms. "Well, it hurts to catch all them stones people throw." She kept stroking my hands, and I couldn't think of anything to say. I felt unusually comforted by this woman. It would take me nearly five hours to drive back to Montgomery once I got things settled for Mr. Caston and Mr. Carter. I needed to keep moving, but it felt nice sitting there with the woman now earnestly massaging my palms in a way that was so sweet, even though it seemed strange, too.

"Are you trying to make me cry?" I asked. I tried to smile.

She put her arm around me and smiled back. "No, you done good today. I was so happy when that judge said that man was going home. It gave me goose bumps. Fifty years in prison, he can't even see no more. No, I was grateful to God when I heard that. You don't have anything to cry about. I'm just gonna let you lean on me a bit, because I know a few things about stonecatching."

She squeezed me a bit and then said, "Now, you keep this up and you're gonna end up like me, singing some sad songs. Ain't no way to do what we do and not learn how to appreciate a good sorrow song.

"I've been singing sad songs my whole life. Had to. When you catch stones, even happy songs can make you sad." She paused and grew silent. I heard her chuckle before she continued. "But you keep sing-ing. Your songs will make you strong. They might even make you happy."

People buzzed down the busy corridors of the courthouse while we sat silently.

"Well, you're very good at what you do," I finally said. "I feel much better."

She slapped my arm playfully. "Oh, don't you try to charm me, young man. You felt just fine before you saw me. Them men are going home and you were fine walking around here. I just do what I do, nothing more."

When I finally excused myself, giving her a kiss on the cheek and telling her I needed to sign the prisoners' release papers, she stopped me. "Oh, wait." She dug around in her purse until she found a piece of wrapped peppermint candy. "Here, take this."

The gesture made me happy in a way that I can't fully explain.

"Well, thank you." I smiled and leaned down to give her another kiss on the cheek.

She waved at me, smiling. "Go on, go on."

Epilogue

Walter died on September 11, 2013.

  He remained kind and charming until the very end, despite his increasing confusion from the advancing dementia. He lived with his sister Katie, but in the last two years of his life he couldn't enjoy the outdoors or get around much without help. One morning he fell and fractured his hip. Doctors felt it was inadvisable to operate, so he was sent home with little hope of recovery. The hospital social worker told me that they would arrange home health and hospice care, which was sad but dramatically better than what he feared when he was on Alabama's death row. He lost a lot of weight and became less and less responsive to visitors after returning home from the hospital. He passed away quietly in the night a short time later.

  We held Walter's funeral at Limestone Faulk A.M.E. Zion Church near Monroeville on a rainy Saturday morning. It was the same pulpit where over twenty years earlier I had spoken to the congregation about casting and catching stones. It felt strange to be back there. Scores of people packed the church, and dozens more stood outside. I looked at the mostly poor, rural black people huddled together with their ungrieved suffering filling the sad space of yet another funeral,

made all the more tragic by the unjustified pain and unnecessary tor-
ment that had preceded it. I often had this feeling when I worked on
Walter's case, that if the anguish of all the stressed lives, the pain of all
of the oppressed people in all of the menaced spaces of Monroe
County could be gathered in some carefully constructed receptacle, it
could power something extraordinary, operate as some astonishing
alternative fuel capable of igniting previously impossible action. And
who knew what might come of it—righteous disruption or transfor-
mational redemption? Maybe both.

The family had a large TV monitor near the casket that flashed
dozens of pictures of Walter before the service. Almost all of the photos were taken on the day he was released from prison. Walter and I
stood next to each other in several of the photos, and I was struck by
how happy we both seemed. I sat in the church and watched the pictures with some disbelief about the time that had passed.

When Walter was on death row, he once told me how ill he had
become during the execution of one of the men on his tier. "When
they turned on the electric chair you could smell the flesh burning!
We were all were banging on the bars to protest, to make ourselves
feel better, but really it just made me sick. The harder I banged, the
more I couldn't stand any of it.

"Do you ever think about dying?" he asked me. It was an unusual
question for someone like Walter to pose. "I never did before, but now
I think about it all the time," he continued. He looked troubled. "This,
right here, is a whole 'nother kind of situation. Guys on the row talk
about what they're going to do before their executions, how they're
going to act. I used to think it was crazy to talk like that, but I guess
I'm starting to do it, too."

I was uncomfortable with the conversation. "Well, you should think
about living, man—what you're going to do when you get out of here."

"Oh, I do that, too. I do that a lot. It's just hard when you see people
going down that hall to be killed. Dying on some court schedule or
some prison schedule ain't right. People are supposed to die on God's
schedule."

Before the service began, I thought about all the time I had spent with Walter after he got out. Then the choir sang, and the preacher gave a rousing sermon. He spoke about Walter being pulled away from his family in the prime of his life by lies and bigotry. I told the congregation that Walter had become like a brother to me, that he was brave to trust his life to someone who was as young as I was then. I explained that we all owed Walter something because he had been threatened and terrorized, wrongly accused and wrongly condemned, but he never gave up. He survived the humiliation of his trial and the charges against him. He survived a guilty verdict, death row, and the wrongful condemnation of an entire state. While he did not survive without injury or trauma, he came out with his dignity. I told people that Walter had overcome what fear, ignorance, and bigotry had done to him. He had stood strong in the face of injustice, and his exonerated witness might just make the rest of us a little safer, slightly more protected from the abuse of power and the false accusations that had almost killed him. I suggested to his friends and family that Walter's strength, resistance, and perseverance were a triumph worth celebrating, an accomplishment to be remembered.

I felt the need to explain to people what Walter had taught me. Walter made me understand why we have to reform a system of criminal justice that continues to treat people better if they are rich and guilty than if they are poor and innocent. A system that denies the poor the legal help they need, that makes wealth and status more important than culpability, must be changed. Walter's case taught me that fear and anger are a threat to justice; they can infect a community, a state, or a nation and make us blind, irrational, and dangerous. I reflected on how mass imprisonment has littered the national landscape with carceral monuments of reckless and excessive punishment and ravaged communities with our hopeless willingness to condemn and discard the most vulnerable among us. I told the congregation that Walter's case had taught me that the death penalty is not about whether people deserve to die for the crimes they commit. The real question of capital punishment in this country is, *Do we deserve to kill?*

Finally and most important, I told those gathered in the church that Walter had taught me that mercy is just when it is rooted in hopefulness and freely given. Mercy is most empowering, liberating, and transformative when it is directed at the undeserving. The people who haven't earned it, who haven't even sought it, are the most meaningful recipients of our compassion. Walter genuinely forgave the people who unfairly accused him, the people who convicted him, and the people who had judged him unworthy of mercy. And in the end, it was just mercy toward others that allowed him to recover a life worth celebrating, a life that rediscovered the love and freedom that all humans desire, a life that overcame death and condemnation until it was time to die on God's schedule.

After the service, I didn't stay long. I walked outside and looked down the road and thought about the fact that no one was ever prosecuted for Ronda Morrison's murder after Walter's release. I thought about the anguish that must still create for her parents.

There were lots of people who came up to me who needed legal help for all sorts of things. I hadn't brought business cards, so I wrote my number down for each person and encouraged them to call my office. It wasn't likely that we could do much for many of the people who needed help, but it made the journey home less sad to hope that maybe we could.

Postscript

On a warm Good Friday morning in 2015, I walked out of a Birmingham jail with an innocent man who had been condemned on Alabama's death row for nearly thirty years. Anthony Ray Hinton had been locked down in solitary confinement for three decades at Holman Correctional Facility in a 5-by-7-foot cell just down the hall from the chamber where more than fifty condemned people were executed during his time on the row. In the electric chair years, he complained he could smell burning flesh after the midnight executions. Mr. Hinton arrived at Holman in the 1980s, *before* Walter McMillian was sent to death row. In 2000, we presented test results that confirmed Mr. Hinton's innocence, and I begged prosecutors to retest the gun evidence that was the sole basis for his conviction, but for fifteen years they refused. In February 2015, we finally won a unanimous ruling from the United States Supreme Court that compelled prosecutors to reexamine the evidence. The new tests confirmed his innocence and Anthony Ray Hinton became the 152nd person to be exonerated after being wrongly convicted and sentenced to death. His compelling story is the subject of a new book, *The Sun Does Shine*, and Mr. Hinton now works as a community educator at the Equal Justice Initiative in Montgomery, Alabama.

In November 2016, Florida finally released Ian Manuel. Imprisoned since he was thirteen years old, Ian spent most of his incarceration in solitary confinement. Upon his release, Ian was embraced by the woman he was convicted of shooting. They had dinner together before he came to Montgomery and joined our reentry program. A few months later, Ian performed one of his poems at EJI's annual event in New York City, where he now writes and performs spoken word poetry.

On December 1, 2017, an ecstatic Joe Sullivan, laughing and shouting in his wheelchair, was pushed out the door of a different Florida prison, thrilled to be free. Our staff embraced him and brought him to Montgomery, where he gave me five Father's Day cards because he couldn't decide which one he liked best. After eighteen months in our residential program, Joe moved to Joseph House, a home for formerly incarcerated people with significant disabilities, where he now resides. Ian and Joe are among dozens of clients sentenced to die in prison as children who are now free.

Trina Garnett has been resentenced and is now eligible for parole. She sings with a group of women serving life sentences at Muncy State Prison in Pennsylvania, where they recently performed a song titled "This Is Not My Home." We hope she will be paroled in the coming year. Soon, Antonio Nuñez will be eligible for release in California, where his reduced sentence has given him access to programming and educational opportunities that are denied to people serving life imprisonment without parole, even if they were arrested at fourteen.

In 2012, after I argued Kuntrell Jackson's case, *Jackson v. Hobbs*, and its companion case, *Miller v. Alabama*, at the United States Supreme Court, the Court banned mandatory life-without-parole sentences for all children seventeen and younger. Hundreds of people condemned to die in prison for crimes committed as children have been released across the country. Kuntrell was released in February 2017 and has started his career in the performing arts with an appearance in the film adaptation of *Just Mercy*.

Henry, the man I first met on death row as a law student, is no longer on death row and hopes to be released soon.

I am especially excited that we have been able to advance our work confronting America's history of racial inequality. We have produced groundbreaking reports on slavery, lynching, and segregation in the United States, and in April 2018, we opened the Legacy Museum: From Enslavement to Mass Incarceration and the National Memorial for Peace and Justice—the country's first comprehensive memorial dedicated to victims of racial terror lynching—in Montgomery, Alabama. I hope you will visit our museum and memorial to learn more about our work to create greater justice in the world.

I remain the Executive Director of EJI, which is a great privilege. With my amazing colleagues at EJI, I continue to represent people on death row, children prosecuted as adults, and incarcerated women, men, and children who have been wrongly convicted or unfairly sentenced. In February 2019, we won a landmark ruling from the United States Supreme Court banning the execution of condemned people who become incompetent as a result of dementia or neurological disease.

I continue to meet stonecatchers along the way who inspire me and make me believe that we can do better for the accused, convicted, and condemned among us—and that all of us can do better for one another. The work continues.

Acknowledgments

I want to thank the hundreds of accused, convicted, and imprisoned men, women, and children with whom I have worked and who have taught me so much about hope, justice, and mercy. I'm especially appreciative of and humbled by the people who appear in this book, victims and survivors of violence, criminal justice professionals, and those who have been condemned to unimaginably painful spaces and yet have shown tremendous courage and grace. All the names of people who appear in these pages are real with the exception of just a few whose privacy and security needed to be protected.

I'm extremely grateful to Chris Jackson, my extraordinary editor, for his thoughtful guidance and kind assistance. I feel very, very fortunate to have worked with an editor as insightful and generous. I'm also deeply thankful to Cindy Spiegel and Julie Grau whose tremendous support and feedback has genuinely inspired me in ways I never imagined. One of my great joys with this project has been the privilege of working with and learning from all my new friends at Spiegel & Grau and Random House who have been so wonderfully encouraging. I want to also thank Sharon Steinerman at New York University School of Law for her excellent research assistance for this project.

All my work is made possible by the exceptional staff of the Equal Justice Initiative, each of whom fearlessly contributes to the cause of justice every day with enough hope and humility to make me believe that we can do the things that must be done to serve the least of these. I want to especially thank Aaryn Urell and Randy Susskind for feedback and editing. Additionally, I'm grateful to Eva Ansley and Evan Parzych for research assistance. Finally, I cannot say enough about Doug Abrams, agent extraordinaire, who persuaded me to take on this project. Without his invaluable guidance, encouragement, and friendship, this book would not have been possible.

Author's Note

With more than two million incarcerated people in the United States, an additional six million people on probation or parole and an estimated sixty-eight million Americans with criminal records, there are endless opportunities for you to do something about criminal justice policy or help the incarcerated or formerly incarcerated. If you have interest in working with or supporting volunteer programs that serve incarcerated people, organizations that provide re-entry assistance to the formerly incarcerated or organizations around the globe that seek reform of criminal justice policy, please contact us at the Equal Justice Initiative in Montgomery, Alabama. You can visit our website at www.eji.org or email us at contact_us@eji.org.

Notes

INTRODUCTION

15   **One in every fifteen people born . . .**   Thomas P. Bonczar, "Prevalence of Imprisonment in the U.S. Population, 1974-2001," Bureau of Justice Statistics (August 2003), available at www.bjs.gov/index.cfm?ty=pbdetail&iid=836, accessed April 29, 2014.

15   **one in every three black male babies . . .**   Bonczar, "Prevalence of Imprisonment"; "Report of The Sentencing Project to the United Nations Human Rights Committee Regarding Racial Disparities in the United States Criminal Justice System," The Sentencing Project (August 2013), available at http://sentencing project.org/doc/publications/rd_ICCPR%20Race%20and%20Justice%20 Shadow%20Report.pdf, accessed April 29, 2014.

15   **Some states have no minimum age . . .**   In twenty-three states, there is no minimum age for which children can be tried as adults in at least some circumstances. Howard N. Snyder and Melissa Sickmund, "Juvenile Offenders and Victims: 2006 National Report," National Center for Juvenile Justice (March 2006), available at www.ojjdp.gov/ojstatbb/nr2006/downloads/NR2006.pdf, accessed April 29, 2014.

15   **There are more than a half-million people . . .**   "Fact Sheet: Trends in U.S. Corrections," The Sentencing Project (May 2012), available at www.sentencing project.org/doc/publications/inc_Trends_in_Corrections_Fact_sheet.pdf, accessed April 29, 2014; Marc Mauer and Ryan S. King, "A 25-Year Quagmire: The War on Drugs and Its Impact on American Society," *The Sentencing Project* (September 2007), 2, available at www.sentencingproject.org/doc/publications/dp _25yearquagmire.pdf, accessed April 29, 2014.

16   **We ban poor women . . .**   Federal law bars states from providing SNAP benefits, formerly known as food stamps, to those who have been convicted of a drug-related felony, although states may opt out or modify this ban. Currently thirty-two states have some sort of ban based on prior drug convictions, including ten states that have permanent bans. States may also evict or deny individuals from receiving federal benefits related to housing assistance, whether through the Section 8 program or placement in public housing, based on drug convictions. Maggie McCarty, Randy Alison Aussenberg, Gene Falk, and David H. Carpenter, "Drug Testing and Crime-Related Restrictions in TANF, SNAP, and Housing Assistance," Congressional Research Service (September 17, 2013), available at www.fas.org/sgp/crs/misc/R42394.pdf, accessed April 29, 2014.

16 **Some states permanently strip people . . .**   Twelve states permanently disenfranchise all or some felony offenders. Thirty-five prohibit parolees from voting, and thirty-one prohibit those on probation from voting. The Sentencing Project, "Felony Disenfranchisement Laws in the United States" (June 2013), available at www.sentencingproject.org/doc/publications/fd_Felony%20 Disenfranchisement%20Laws%20in%20the%20US.pdf, accessed April 30, 2014.

16 **as a result, in several Southern states . . .**   In Alabama, Mississippi, and Tennessee more than 10 percent of African Americans cannot vote. In Florida, Kentucky, and Virginia, more than one in five African Americans cannot vote. Christopher Uggen, Sarah Shannon, and Jeff Manza, "State-Level Estimates of Felon Disenfranchisement in the United States, 2010," The Sentencing Project (July 2012), available at http://sentencingproject.org/doc/publications/fd_ State_Level_Estimates_of_Felon_Disen_2010.pdf, accessed April 30, 2014.

16 **Scores of innocent people have been exonerated . . .**   The Death Penalty Information Center reports that 144 death row inmates have been exonerated since 1973. "The Innocence List," Death Penalty Information Center, available at www.deathpenaltyinfo.org/innocence-list-those-freed-death-row, accessed April 25, 2014.

16 **Hundreds more have been released . . .**   According to the Innocence Project, there have been 316 post-conviction DNA exonerations in the United States. Eighteen of the exonerated prisoners spent time on death row. "DNA Exonerations Nationwide," The Innocence Project, available at www.innocenceproject .org/Content/DNA_Exonerations_Nationwide.php, accessed April 25, 2014.

16 **Presumptions of guilt, poverty, racial bias . . .**   John Lewis and Bryan Stevenson, "State of Equality and Justice in America: The Presumption of Guilt," *Washington Post* (May 17, 2013).

16 **Spending on jails and prisons . . .**   In 2010, the latest year for which statistics are currently available, the cost of incarceration in America was about $80 billion. Attorney General Eric Holder, American Bar Association Speech (August 12, 2013); Tracey Kyckelhahn and Tara Martin, Bureau of Justice Statistics, "Justice Expenditure and Employment Extracts, 2010–Preliminary" (July 2013), available at www .bjs.gov/index.cfm?ty=pbdetail&iid=4679, accessed April 30, 2014. By comparison, that figure was about $6.9 billion in 1980. Bureau of Justice Statistics, "Justice

Expenditure and Employment Extracts—1980 and 1981 Data from the Annual General Finance and Employment Surveys" (March 1985), available at www.bjs .gov/index.cfm?ty=pbdetail&iid=3527, accessed April 30, 2014.

CHAPTER ONE: MOCKINGBIRD PLAYERS

24   **Thirteen of the state's sixteen pulp and paper mills . . .**   Conner Bailey, Peter Sinclair, John Bliss, and Karni Perez, "Segmented Labor Markets in Alabama's Pulp and Paper Industry," *Rural Sociology* 61, no. 3 (1996): 475–96.

28   **"The evil tendency of the crime" . . .**   *Pace & Cox v. State,* 69 Ala. 231, 233 (1882).

29   **The State of Idaho banned interracial marriage . . .**   U.S. Census Office, *Fourteenth Census of Population* (Washington, D.C.: Government Printing Office, 1920).

29   **It wasn't until 1967 . . .**   When the Virginia legislature passed the Racial Integrity Act in 1924, authorizing the forced sterilization of black women thought to be defective or dangerous and criminalizing marriage between a black person and white person, people in Caroline County took these pronouncements very seriously. Decades later, when a young white man, Richard Loving, fell in love with a black woman named Mildred Jeter, the young couple decided to get married after learning that Mildred was pregnant. They went to Washington, D.C., to "get legal," knowing that it wouldn't be possible in Virginia. They tried to stay away but got homesick and returned to Caroline County after the wedding to be near their families. Word about the marriage got out, and some weeks later the sheriff and several armed deputies stormed into their home in the middle of the night to arrest Richard and Mildred for miscegenation. Jailed and humiliated, they were forced to plead guilty and were told that they should be grateful that their prison sentences would be suspended as long as they agreed to leave the county and not return for "at least twenty-five years." They fled the state again but this time decided to fight the law in court with a lawsuit filed with the assistance of the American Civil Liberties Union. In 1967, after years of defeats in lower courts, the U.S. Supreme Court struck down miscegenation laws, declaring them unconstitutional.

29   **"The legislature shall never pass any law" . . .**   Even though the restriction could not be enforced under federal law, the state ban on interracial marriage in Alabama continued into the twenty-first century. In 2000, reformers finally had the votes to get the issue on the statewide ballot, where a majority of voters chose to eliminate the ban, although 41 percent voted to keep it. A 2011 poll of Mississippi Republicans found that 46 percent supported a legal ban on interracial marriage, 40 percent opposed such a ban, and 14 percent were undecided.

30   **Nearly a dozen people had been lynched . . .**   The names of the people

lynched are as follows: October 13, 1892: Burrell Jones, Moses Jones/Johnson, Jim Packard, and one unknown (brother of Jim Packard). Tuskegee University, "Record of Lynchings in Alabama from 1871 to 1920," compiled for the Alabama Department of Archives and History by the Tuskegee Normal and Industrial Institute, Alabama Dept. of Archives and History Digital Collections, available at http://digital.archives.alabama.gov/cdm/singleitem/collection/voices/id/2516, accesssed September 18, 2009; also, "Four Negroes Lynched," *New York Times* (October 14, 1892); Stewart Tolnay, compiler, "NAACP Lynching Records," Historical American Lynching Data Collection Project, available at http://people.uncw.edu/hinese/HAL/HAL%20Web%20Page.htm#Project%20HAL, accessed April 30, 2014.

> October 30, 1892: Allen Parker. Tuskegee University Archives; Tolnay, "NAACP Lynching Records."
> August 30, 1897: Jack Pharr. Tuskegee University Archives; Tolnay, "NAACP Lynching Records."
> September 2, 1897: Unknown. Tuskegee University Archives.
> August 23, 1905: Oliver Latt. Tuskegee University Archives.
> February 7, 1909: Will Parker. Tuskegee University Archives.
> August 9, 1915: James Fox. Tuskegee University Archives; "Negro Lynched for Attacking Officer," *Montgomery Advertiser* (August 10, 1915). Tuskegee University Archives; Tolnay, "NAACP Lynching Records."
> August 9, 1943: Willie Lee Cooper. "NAACP Describes Alabama's Willie Lee Case as Lynching," *Journal and Guide* (September 8, 1943); "NAACP Claims Man Lynched in Alabama," *Bee* (September 26, 1943); "Ala. Workman 'Lynched' After Quitting Job," *Afro-American* (September 18, 1943). Tuskegee University Archives.
> May 7, 1954: Russell Charley. "Violence Flares in Dixie," *Pittsburgh Courier* (June 5, 1954); "Suspect Lynching in Ala. Town," *Chicago Defender* (June 12, 1954); "Hint Love Rivalry Led to Lynching," *Chicago Defender* (June 19, 1954); "NAACP Probes 'Bama Lynching," *Pittsburgh Courier* (June 26, 1954). Tuskegee University Archives.

CHAPTER TWO: STAND

37 **Suicide, prisoner-on-prisoner violence ...**   The Bureau of Justice Statistics reports that throughout the 1980s, several hundred incarcerated individuals died each year of suicide, homicide, and other "unknown" reasons. Christopher J. Mumola, "Suicide and Homicide in State Prisons and Local Jails," Bureau of Justice Statistics (August 2005), available at www.bjs.gov/index.cfm?ty=pbdetail &iid=1126, accessed April 30, 2014; Lawrence A. Greenfield, "Prisons and Pris-

oners in the United States," Bureau of Justice Statistics (April 1992), available at www.bjs.gov/index.cfm?ty=pbdetail&iid=1392.

43   **I found Bureau of Justice statistics . . .**   In 1978, black people were eight times more likely than whites to be killed by police officers. Jodi M. Brown and Patrick A. Langan, "Policing and Homicide, 1976-1998: Justifiable Homicide by Police, Police Officers Murdered by Felons," Bureau of Justice Statistics (March 2001), available at www.bjs.gov/index.cfm?ty=pbdetail&iid=829, accessed April 30, 2014.

43   **By the end of the twentieth century . . .**   By 1998, black people were still four times more likely to be killed by the police than white people. Brown and Langan, "Policing and Homicide, 1976–1998."

43   **the problem would get worse . . .**   In states with "Stand Your Ground" laws, the rate of "justifiable" homicides of blacks more than doubled between 2005 and 2011, the period when the majority of these laws were enacted. The rate of such homicides against whites also rose, but only slightly, and the homicide rate against whites was much lower to begin with. "Shoot First: 'Stand Your Ground' Laws and Their Effect on Violent Crime and the Criminal Justice System," joint press release from the National Urban League, Mayors Against Illegal Guns, and VoteVets.org (September 2013), available at http://nul.iamempowered.com/content/mayors-against-illegal-guns-national-urban-league-votevets-release-report-showing-stand-your, accessed April 30, 2014.

CHAPTER THREE: TRIALS AND TRIBULATION

48   **"We're going to keep all you niggers" . . .**   *McMillian v. Johnson,* Case No. 93-A-699-N, P. Exh. 12, Plaintiff's Memorandum in Opposition to Defendant's Motion for Summary Judgment (1994).

55   **"At 8:40 P.M., a third charge of electricity" . . .**   *Glass v. Louisiana,* 471 U.S. 1080 (1985), denying cert. to 455 So.2d 659 (La. 1984) (J. Brennan, dissenting).

58   **In 1987, all forty . . .**   Ruth E. Friedman, "Statistics and Death: The Conspicuous Role of Race Bias in the Administration of Death Penalty," *Berkeley Journal of African-American Law and Policy* 4 (1999): 75. See also Danielle L. McGuire and John Dittmer, *Freedom Rights: New Perspectives on the Civil Rights Movement* (Lexington: University of Kentucky, 2011).

59   **In 1945, the Supreme Court upheld a Texas statute . . .**   *Akins v. Texas,* 325 U.S. 398 (1945).

59   **Local jury commissions used statutory requirements . . .**   David Cole, "Judgment and Discrimination," in *No Equal Justice: Race and Class in the American Criminal Justice System* (New York: New Press, 1999), 101–31.

59   **In the 1970s, the Supreme Court ruled . . .**   *Duren v. Missouri,* 439 U.S. 357 (1979); *Taylor v. Louisiana,* 419 U.S. 522 (1975).

60   In the mid-1960s, the Court held . . .   *Swain v. Alabama,* 380 U.S. 202 (1965).

60   The practice of striking all . . .   "Illegal Racial Discrimination in Jury Selection: A Continuing Legacy," Equal Justice Initiative (2009), available at www.eji.org/files/EJI%20Race%20and%20Jury%20Report.pdf, accessed April 30, 2014.

CHAPTER FOUR: THE OLD RUGGED CROSS

70   In 91 percent of these cases . . .   "The Death Penalty in Alabama: Judge Override," Equal Justice Initiative (2011), 4, available at http://eji.org/eji/files/Override_Report.pdf, accessed April 30, 2014.

70   Alabama elects all of its judges . . .   Billy Corriher, "Partisan Judicial Elections and the Distorting Influence of Campaign Cash," Center for American Progress (October 25, 2012), available at www.americanprogress.org/issues/civil-liberties/report/2012/10/25/42895/partisan-judicial-elections-and-the-distorting-influence-of-campaign-cash/, accessed July 8, 2013.

70   Judge overrides are an incredibly potent . . .   In November 2013, U.S. Supreme Court Justice Sonia Sotomayor wrote a blistering critique of Alabama's continued use of judicial override to impose death sentences in a dissent from the Court's decision to not review the issue. Joined by Justice Breyer, the Justices found serious constitutional defects in both the politics surrounding judge override and the way it undermines the role of the jury. *Woodward v. Alabama* (2013).

70   it's not surprising that judge overrides . . .   "The Death Penalty in Alabama," 5.

71   As peculiar as the practice is . . .   *Harris v. Alabama,* 513 U.S. 504 (1995); *Spaziano v. Florida,* 468 U.S. 447 (1984).

71   Mr. Dunkins suffered from intellectual disabilities . . .   See *Penry v. Lynaugh,* 492 U.S. 302 (1989).

71   Thirteen years later . . .   *Atkins v. Virginia,* 536 U.S. 304 (2002), explaining that a national consensus had been reached against executing the mentally ill after state legislatures adopted new laws limiting the practice following *Penry.*

72   They killed him . . .   Peter Applebome, "2 Electric Jolts in Alabama Execution," *New York Times* (July 15, 1989), available at www.nytimes.com/1989/07/15/us/2-electric-jolts-in-alabama-execution.html, accessed April 30, 2014; see also "Two Attempts at Execution Kill Dunkins," *Gadsden Times* (July 14, 1989), available at http://news.google.com/newspapers?id=02cfAAAAIBAJ&sjid=3NQEAAAAIBAJ&pg=3122%2C1675665, accessed April 30, 2014.

78   The Court decided to bar claims . . .   *Rose v. Lundy,* 455 U.S. 509 (1982).

78   the Court rejected a constitutional challenge . . .   *Stanford v. Kentucky,* 492 U.S. 361 (1989); *Penry,* 492 U.S. at 305; *McCleskey v. Kemp,* 481 U.S. 279 (1987).

78   "Let's get on with it" . . .   Bryan Stevenson, "The Hanging Judges," *The Nation* (October 14, 1996), 12.

84   "Mr. Stevenson, I'm calling to let you know" . . .   *Richardson v. Thigpen*, 492 U.S. 934 (1989).

88   I thought about the botched execution . . .   Applebome, "2 Electric Jolts in Alabama Execution."

CHAPTER FIVE: OF THE COMING OF JOHN

94   Monroe County is a "dry county" . . .   Monroe County is now technically considered "moist." The city of Monroeville and Frisco have approved laws permitting the sale of some alcoholic beverages.

CHAPTER SIX: SURELY DOOMED

115   Alabama had more juveniles sentenced to death . . .   Victor L. Streib, *Death Penalty for Juveniles* (Bloomington: Indiana University Press, 1987).

116   While the Supreme Court had upheld . . .   *Stanford v. Kentucky*, 492 U.S. 361 (1989); *Thompson v. Oklahoma*, 487 U.S. 815 (1988); *Wilkins v. Missouri* was consolidated with the *Stanford* decision.

CHAPTER SEVEN: JUSTICE DENIED

131   We found court records revealing . . .   *Giglio v. United States*, 405 U.S. 150 (1972); *Mooney v. Holohan*, 294 U.S. 103 (1935).

140   Some states authorized the family . . .   Peggy M. Tobolowsky, "Victim Participation in the Criminal Justice Process: Fifteen Years after the President's Task Force on Victims of Crime," *New England Journal on Criminal and Civil Confinement* 25 (1999): 21, available at http://heinonline.org/HOL/Page?handle=hein .journals/nejccc25&div=7&g_sent=1&collection=journals, accessed April 30, 2014.

140   Thirty-six states enacted laws . . .   *Booth v. Maryland*, 482 U.S. 496, 509n12 (1987).

141   The Court agreed . . .   *Booth v. Maryland*, 482 U.S. 496, 506n8 ("We are troubled by the implication that defendants whose victims were assets to their community are more deserving of punishment than those whose victims are perceived to be less worthy").

141   The Court's decision was widely criticized . . .   *Payne v. Tennessee*, 501 U.S. 808, 827 (1991) ("A State may legitimately conclude that evidence about the victim and about the impact of the murder on the victim's family is relevant to the jury's decision as to whether or not the death penalty should be imposed").

141 States found countless ways . . .   Tobolowsky, "Victim Participation," 48–95.

141 Some states made executions . . .   Michael Lawrence Goodwin, "An Eyeful for an Eye—An Argument Against Allowing the Families of Murder Victims to View Executions," *Brandeis Journal of Family Law* 36 (1997): 585, available at http://heinonline.org/HOL/Page?handle=hein.journals/branlaj36&div=38&g _sent=1&collection=journals, accessed April 30, 2014.

141 Megan's Law, for example . . .   Scott Matson and Roxanne Lieb, "Megan's Law: A Review of State and Federal Legislation," Washington State Institute for Public Policy (October 1997), available at www.wsipp.wa.gov/rptfiles/ meganslaw.pdf, accessed June 13, 2013.

142 Press coverage hyped the personal nature . . .   Chris Greer and Robert Reiner, "Mediated Mayhem: Media, Crime, Criminal Justice," in *The Oxford Handbook of Criminology*, ed. Mike Maguire, Rodney Morgan, and Robert Reiner (New York: Oxford University Press, 2002), 245–78.

142 The study conducted for that case . . .   *McCleskey v. Kemp*, 481 U.S. 279, 286 (1987), citing David C. Baldus et al., "Comparative Review of Death Sentences: An Empirical Study of the Georgia Experience," *Journal of Criminal Law and Criminology* 74 (1983): 661.

142 In Alabama, even though 65 percent . . .   American Bar Association, "Evaluating Fairness and Accuracy in State Death Penalty Systems: The Alabama Death Penalty Assessment Report" (June 2006), available at www.americanbar.org/ content/dam/aba/migrated/moratorium/assessmentproject/alabama/report .authcheckdam.pdf, accessed June 14, 2013.

142 Black defendant and white victim pairings . . .   *McCleskey v. Kemp*, 481 U.S. 286–87, citing Baldus et al., "Comparative Review"; U.S. General Accounting Office, *Death Penalty Sentencing: Research Indicates Pattern of Racial Disparities*, 1990, GAO/GGD-90-57 ("In 82 percent of the studies, race of victim was found to influence the likelihood of being charged with capital murder or receiving the death penalty, i.e., those who murdered whites were found to be more likely to be sentenced to death than those who murdered blacks").

CHAPTER EIGHT: ALL GOD'S CHILDREN

148 The extraordinarily high rates . . .   The Chester Upland school district has in the past two decades often ranked as the worst in the Commonwealth of Pennsylvania. James T. Harris III, "Success amid Crisis in Chester," Philly.com (February 16, 2012), available at http://articles.philly.com/2012-02-16/news/ 31067474_1_school-district-curriculum-parents-and-guardians, accessed April 30, 2014.

148 Close to 46 percent . . .   In 2012, it was estimated by the Census Bureau that 45.6 percent of Chester's residents under the age of eighteen lived below the

federal poverty level. U.S. Census Bureau, 2008–2012 American Community Survey, Chester city, Pennsylvania.

150 **Defendants who are deemed incompetent . . .**   50 Pennsylvania Consolidated Statutes § 7402.

150 **Pennsylvania sentencing law was inflexible . . .**   Until 2012, anyone convicted of first- or second-degree murder automatically received a sentence of life imprisonment without the possibility of parole. 18 Pennsylvania Consolidated Statutes § 1102; 61 Pennsylvania Consolidated Statutes § 6137. Life imprisonment without parole is possible, though no longer mandatory, for juveniles convicted of first- or second-degree murder. 18 Pennsylvania Consolidated Statutes § 1102.1.

150 **"This is the saddest case I've ever seen" . . .**   Liliana Segura, "Throwaway People: Teens Sent to Die in Prison Will Get a Second Chance," *The Nation* (May 28, 2012).

150 **For a tragic crime committed at fourteen . . .**   Segura, "Throwaway People"; *Commonwealth v. Garnett*, 485 A.2d 821 (Pa. Super. Ct. 1984).

151 **It wasn't until 2008 that most states . . .**   The Federal Bureau of Prisons adopted a policy in 2008 that restricts the shackling of pregnant inmates. Federal Bureau of Prisons, "Program Statement: Escorted Trips, No. 5538.05" (October 6, 2008), available at www.bop.gov/policy/progstat/5538_005.pdf, accessed April 30, 2014. Currently twenty-four states have laws or policies that prevent or restrict the shackling of pregnant inmates or inmates giving birth. Dana Sussman, "Bound by Injustice: Challenging the Use of Shackles on Incarcerated Pregnant Women," *Cardozo Journal of Law and Gender* 15 (2009): 477; "State Standards for Pregnancy-Related Health Care and Abortion for Women in Prison," American Civil Liberties Union, available at www.aclu.org/maps/state-standards-pregnancy-related-health-care-and-abortion-women-prison-map, accessed April 28, 2014.

151 **The guard appealed . . .**   *Garnett v. Kepner*, 541 F. Supp. 241 (M.D. Pa. 1982).

151 **She is one of nearly five hundred people . . .**   Paula Reed Ward, "Pa. Top Court Retains Terms for Juvenile Lifers," *Pittsburgh Post-Gazette* (October 30, 2013); "Juvenile Life Without Parole (JLWOP) in Pennsylvania," Juvenile Law Center, available at http://jlc.org/current-initiatives/promoting-fairness-courts/juvenile-life-without-parole/jlwop-pennsylvania, accessed April 26, 2014.

152 **The correctional staff at the prison . . .**   Meg Laughlin, "Does Separation Equal Suffering?" *Tampa Bay Times* (December 17, 2006).

152 **Juveniles housed in adult prisons . . .**   In enacting the Prison Elimination Act of 2003, Congress found that juveniles in adult facilities are five times more likely to be sexually assaulted. 42 U.S.C. § 15601(4).

153 **As he sank deeper into despair . . .**   Laughlin, "Does Separation Equal Suffering?"

153 **By 2010, Florida had sentenced . . .**   Florida had sentenced a total of seventy-seven juveniles to life imprisonment without parole for non-homicide offenses. Brief of Petitioner, *Graham v. Florida*, U.S. Supreme Court (2009); Paolo G. Annino, David W. Rasmussen, and Chelsea B. Rice, *Juvenile Life without Parole for Non-Homicide Offenses: Florida Compared to the Nation* (2009), 2, table A.

153 **several of whom were thirteen years old . . .**   Two thirteen-year-olds in Florida, including Joe Sullivan, had been sentenced to life imprisonment without parole for non-homicide offenses. Annino, Rasmussen, and Rice, *Juvenile Life without Parole for Non-Homicide Offenses,* chart E (2009).

154 **All of the youngest . . .**   "Cruel and Unusual: Sentencing 13- and 14-Year-Old Children to Die in Prison," Equal Justice Initiative (2008), available at http://eji.org/eji/files/Cruel%20and%20Unusual%202008_0.pdf, accessed April 30, 2014.

154 **Florida had the largest population . . .**   The United States is the only country in the world that sentences juveniles to die in prison for non-homicide offenses, and Florida has sentenced far more such offenders to life without parole than any other state. Annino, Rasmussen, and Rice, *Juvenile Life without Parole for Non-Homicide Offenses,* chart E.

154 **"He was excited to take his picture" . . .**   *In re Nunez*, 173 Cal.App. 4th 709, 720 (2009).

155 **He got his hands on a gun . . .**   *In re Nunez*, 173 Cal.App. 4th 709, 720–21 (2009).

156 **Many adults convicted of attempted murder . . .**   "Violent Crimes," Florida Department of Corrections, available at www.dc.state.fl.us/pub/timeserv/annual/section2.html, accessed January 9, 2014; Matthew R. Durose and Patrick A. Langan, "Felony Sentences in State Courts, 2004," Bureau of Justice Statistics (July 2007), available at www.bjs.gov/content/pub/pdf/fssc04.pdf; "State Court Sentencing of Convicted Felons 2004—Statistical Tables," Bureau of Justice Statistics (2007), available at www.bjs.gov/content/pub/html/scscf04/scscf04mt.cfm, accessed January 10, 2013.

157 **For instance, in the infamous . . .**   James Goodman, *Stories of Scottsboro* (New York: Pantheon Books, 1994), 8.

158 **Within hours of announcing . . .**   David I. Bruck, "Executing Teen Killers Again: The 14-Year-Old Who, in Many Ways, Was Too Small for the Chair," *Washington Post* (September 15, 1985).

158 **Despite appeals from the NAACP . . .**   Bruck, "Executing Teen Killers Again."

159 **Witnesses to the execution . . .**   Bruck, "Executing Teen Killers Again."

159 **Recently, an effort has been launched . . .**   George Stinney's family members are now seeking a new trial or exoneration for Stinney through the court system. Hearings were held in a South Carolina court in January 2014. Alan Blinder,

"Family of South Carolina Boy Put to Death Seeks Exoneration 70 Years Later," *New York Times* (January 22, 2014); Eliott C. McLaughlin, "New Trial Sought for George Stinney, Executed at 14," CNN.com (January 23, 2014).

159 **Influential criminologists predicted . . .** "Super-predator" language was commonly used in conjunction with dire predictions that a vast increase in violent juvenile crime was occurring or about to occur. See Office of Juvenile Justice and Delinquency Prevention, U.S. Department of Justice, "Juvenile Justice: A Century of Change" (1999), 4–5, available at www.ncjrs.gov/pdffiles1/ojjdp/178993.pdf, accessed April 30, 2014. See, for example, Sacha Coupet, "What to Do with the Sheep in Wolf's Clothing: The Role of Rhetoric and Reality About Youth Offenders in the Constructive Dismantling of the Juvenile Justice System," *University of Pennsylvania Law Review* 148 (2000): 1303, 1307; Laura A. Bazelon, "Exploding the Superpredator Myth: Why Infancy Is the Preadolescent's Best Defense in Juvenile Court," *New York University Law Review* 75 (2000): 159. Much of the frightening imagery was racially coded; see, for example, John J. DiIulio, "My Black Crime Problem, and Ours," *City Journal* (Spring 1996), available at www.city-journal.org/html/6_2_my_black.html, accessed April 30, 2014 ("270,000 more young predators on the streets than in 1990, coming at us in waves over the next two decades . . . as many as half of these juvenile super-predators could be young black males"); William J. Bennett, John J. DiIulio Jr., and John P. Walters, *Body Count: Moral Poverty—And How to Win America's War Against Crime and Drugs* (New York: Simon and Schuster, 1996), 27–28.

159 **Sometimes expressly focusing on black . . .** John J. DiIulio Jr., "The Coming of the Super-Predators," *Weekly Standard* (November 27, 1995), 23.

159 **Panic over the impending crime . . .** Bennett, DiIulio, and Walters, *Body Count*, 27. See also Office of Juvenile Justice and Delinquency Prevention, "Juvenile Justice."

160 **The juvenile population in America increased . . .** See, for example, Elizabeth Becker, "As Ex-Theorist on Young 'Superpredators,' Bush Aide Has Regrets," *New York Times* (February 9, 2001), A19.

160 **In 2001, the surgeon general . . .** U.S. Surgeon General, *Youth Violence: A Report of the Surgeon General* (2001), ch. 1, available at www.ncbi.nlm.nih.gov/books/NBK44297/#A12312, accessed April 30, 2014; see also U.S. Department of Justice, Office of Juvenile Justice and Delinquency Prevention, "Challenging the Myths" (2001), 5, available at www.ncjrs.gov/pdffiles1/ojjdp/178995.pdf, accessed April 30, 2014 ("[A]nalysis of juvenile homicide arrests also leads to the conclusion that juvenile superpredators are more myth than reality").

161 **We decided to publish a report . . .** "Cruel and Unusual."

CHAPTER NINE: I'M HERE

171 "Me, I can simply look" . . . *McMillian v. Alabama*, CC-87-682.60, Testimony of Ralph Myers During Rule 32 Hearing, April 16, 1992.

CHAPTER TEN: MITIGATION

187 In the 1960s and 1970s . . . In these decades, legislative and judicial reforms tightened the procedures by which individuals where subject to involuntary commitment. Stanley S. Herr, Stephen Arons, and Richard E. Wallace Jr., *Legal Rights and Mental Health Care* (Lexington, MA: Lexington Books, 1983). In 1978, the United States Supreme Court raised the burden on states seeking to have individuals involuntarily committed to mental health hospitals from the low "preponderance of the evidence" standard to a more difficult "clear and convincing evidence" standard. *Addington v. Texas*, 441 U.S. 418 (1978).

188 Today, over 50 percent of prison . . . Doris J. James and Lauren E. Glaze, "Mental Health Problems of Prison and Jail Inmates," Special Report, Bureau of Justice Statistics (September 2006), available at http://bjs.gov/content/pub/pdf/mhppji.pdf, accessed July 2, 2013. This number breaks down to 56 percent percent of state prisoners, 45 percent of federal prisoners, and 64 percent of local jail prisoners. In total, that accounts for an estimated 1,264,300 inmates. This study is the most comprehensive recent study available and yet was conducted in 2005, so numbers may have changed in more recent years. However, current sources (2012–13) still cite this study, so I feel comfortable concluding that it is still the most comprehensive and up-to-date source on the subject.

188 Nearly one in five prison . . . The category of "serious mental illness" includes schizophrenia, schizophrenia spectrum disorder, schizoaffective disorder, bipolar disorder, brief psychotic disorder, delusional disorder, and psychotic disorders not otherwise specified. This is distinguished from the more general category of "mental illness," which encompasses serious mental illness as well as other forms of mental illness. E. Fuller Torrey, Aaron D. Kennard, Don Eslinger, Richard Lamb, and James Pavle, "More Mentally Ill Persons Are in Jails and Prisons Than Hospitals: A Survey of the States," Treatment Advocacy Center (May 2010), available at www.treatmentadvocacycenter.org/storage/documents/final_jails_v_hospitals_study.pdf, accessed July 2, 2013.

188 In fact, there are more than three . . . Torrey et al., "More Mentally Ill Persons," 1.

190 They began squabbling with each other . . . The dispute is discussed in George's subsequent appeals. *Daniel v. State*, 459 So. 2d 944 (Ala. Crim. App. 1984); *Daniel v. Thigpen*, 742 F. Supp. 1535 (M.D. Ala. 1990).

191 George was convicted . . . *Daniel v. State*, 459 So. 2d 944 (Ala. Crim. App. 1984).

191 **We eventually won a favorable ruling** . . .   *Daniel v. Thigpen,* 742 F. Supp. 1535 (M.D. Ala. 1990).

193 **Confederate Memorial Day was declared a state holiday** . . .   Confederate Memorial Day was first celebrated in Alabama in 1901. See *The World Almanac and Encyclopedia 1901* (New York: Press Publishing Co., 1901), 29; "Confederate Memorial Day," Encyclopedia of Alabama, available at www.encyclopediaof alabama.org/face/Article.jsp?id=h-1663, accessed April 28, 2014. The holiday remains in the state code today. Ala. Code § 1-3-8.

193 **When black veterans returned** . . .   The 1948 platform of the Dixiecrat party stated, in part: "We stand for the segregation of the races and the racial integrity of each race; the constitutional right to choose one's associates; to accept private employment without governmental interference, and to earn one's living in any lawful way. We oppose the elimination of segregation, the repeal of miscegenation statutes, the control of private employment by Federal bureaucrats called for by the misnamed civil rights program." "Platform of the States Rights Democratic Party, August 14, 1948," The American Presidency Project, available at www.presidency.ucsb.edu/ws/index.php?pid=25851#axzz1iGn93BZz, accessed April 28, 2014.

193 **In fact, it was in the 1950s** . . .   Alabama, Georgia, and South Carolina all began to fly the Confederate battle flag in symbolic opposition to the *Brown* decision. James Forman Jr., "Driving Dixie Down: Removing the Confederate Flag from Southern State Capitols," *Yale Law Journal* 101 (1991): 505.

CHAPTER ELEVEN: I'LL FLY AWAY

209 **In a landmark ruling,** *New York Times v. Sullivan* . . .   *New York Times Co. v. Sullivan,* 376 U.S. 254 (1964).

210 **When he was first arrested** . . .   Several local newspapers highlighted the sodomy charge. Mary Lett, "McMillian Is Charged with Sodomy," *Monroe Journal* (June 18, 1987); "Myers Files Sodomy Charges Against McMillan [*sic*]," *Evergreen Courant* (June 18, 1987); Bob Forbish, "Accused Murderer Files Sodomy Charges Against His Accomplice," *Brewton Standard* (June 13–14, 1987).

210 **"Those entering the courtroom"** . . .   Dianne Shaw, "McMillian Sentenced to Death," *Monroe Journal* (September 22, 1988).

210 **Despite all of the evidence** . . .   On the same day it published an article on the ongoing hearings in the McMillian case, the *Mobile Press Register* reminded readers in another article that Walter McMillian had been arrested and charged with the Pittman murder. Connie Baggett, "Ronda Wasn't Only Girl Killed," *Mobile Press Register* (July 5, 1992). A *Monroe Journal* article about the McMillian proceedings also mentioned Walter McMillian's indictment in the Pittman murder.

Marilyn Handley, "Tape About Murder Played at Hearing for the First Time," *Monroe Journal* (April 23, 1992).

210 **"Convicted Slayer Wanted in East Brewton"** . . .   "Convicted Slayer Wanted in EB Student Murder," *Brewton Standard* (August 22, 1988).

210 **"Myers and McMillian were part"** . . .   Connie Baggett, "Infamous Murder Leaves Questions," *Mobile Press Register* (July 5, 1992).

211 **"Too many of these [out-of-town] writers"** . . .   Editorial, "'60 Minutes' Comes to Town," *Monroe Journal* (June 25, 1992).

212 **The *Journal* added that Chapman offered** . . .   Marilyn Handley, "CBS Examines Murder Case," *Monroe Journal* (July 8, 1992).

212 **The local writers complained** . . .   Connie Baggett, "DA: TV Account of Mc-Millian's Conviction a 'Disgrace,'" *Mobile Press Register* (November 24, 1992).

218 **The attorney general's motion** . . .   Motion from State to Hold Case in Abeyance, *McMillian v. State*, 616 So. 2d 933 (Ala. Crim. App. 1993), filed February 3, 1993.

219 **But Havel had said that these** . . .   Václav Havel, "Never Hope Against Hope," *Esquire* (October 1993), 68.

CHAPTER TWELVE: MOTHER, MOTHER

230 **Cook, who worked at the elementary school** . . .   *State v. Colbey*, 2007 WL 7268919 (Ala. Cir. Ct. 2007) (No. 2005-538), 824.

230 **Enstice had a history of prematurely** . . .   *State v. Colbey*, 2007, 1576.

231 **The pathologist subsequently performed an autopsy** . . .   *State v. Colbey*, 2007, 1511–21.

231 **She not only concluded** . . .   *State v. Colbey*, 2007, 1584.

231 **In fact, nationwide, most women** . . .   "Case Summaries for Current Female Death Row Inmates." Death Penalty Information Center, available at www.deathpenaltyinfo.org/case-summaries-current-female-death-row-inmates, accessed August 13, 2013.

231 **She testified that her conclusion** . . .   *State v. Colbey*, 2007, 1585.

231 **Dr. McNally testified that Mrs. Colbey's** . . .   *State v. Colbey*, 2007, 1129, 1133.

231 **Enstice's conclusion was** . . .   *State v. Colbey*, 2007, 1607.

232 **Police investigators went into her home** . . .   *State v. Colbey*, 2007, 1210, 1271, 1367.

232 **Ms. Colbey consistently maintained** . . .   *State v. Colbey*, 2007, 1040, 1060.

232 **Ms. Colbey rejected the State's offer** . . .   Supplemental Record at *State v. Colbey*, 155.

232 ***Time* magazine called the prosecution** . . .   John Cloud, "How the Casey Anthony Murder Case Became the Social-Media Trial of the Century," *Time* (June 16, 2011).

233 **The criminalization of infant mortality . . .**   This phenomenon of charging women, particularly poor women and women of color, who give birth to still-born babies or children who live only a short time, now seems commonplace to a casual observer of current events. Michelle Oberman, "The Control of Pregnancy and the Criminalization of Femaleness," *Berkeley Journal of Gender, Law, and Justice* 7 (2013): 1; Ada Calhoun, "The Criminalization of Bad Mothers," *New York Times* (April 25, 2012).

233 **This new information led the prosecutor . . .**   Stephanie Taylor, "Murder Charge Dismissed in 2006 Newborn Death," *Tuscaloosa News* (April 9, 2009).

234 **We won her freedom after establishing . . .**   Carla Crowder, "1,077 Days Later, Legal Tangle Ends; Woman Free," *Birmingham News* (July 18, 2002).

234 **In time, the Alabama Supreme Court . . .**   Ex parte Ankrom, 2013 WL 135748 (Ala. January 11, 2013); Ex parte Hicks, No. 1110620 (Ala. April 18, 2014).

235 **Some jurors indicated that they found . . .**   Supplemental Record, *State v. Colbey*, 2007, 516–17, 519–20, 552.

235 **Several revealed that they had . . .**   Supplemental Record, *State v. Colbey*, 2007, 426–27, 649.

235 **Another juror admitted trusting . . .**   Supplemental Record, *State v. Colbey*, 2007, 674.

236 **Approximately 75 to 80 percent . . .**   Angela Hattery and Earl Smith, *Prisoner Reentry and Social Capital: The Long Road to Reintegration* (Lanham, MD: Lexington, 2010).

CHAPTER FOURTEEN: CRUEL AND UNUSUAL

257 **Joe was made to say in court . . .**

> DEFENSE COUNSEL: All right. If you can't identify me, then I may not have to kill you.
>
> DEFENDANT: If you cannot identify me, I maybe won't kill you.
>
> WITNESS: It sounds—there's a tone in your voice that's just like that, only *you said it very loud to me that time* in a belligerent way.
>
> PROSECUTOR: I don't want to argue about it. Are you able to say that's the voice of the person?
>
> WITNESS: There's a tone in that voice that makes me know it's that person.
>
> PROSECUTOR: So you are saying the person who just spoke to you is the person that said that to you that day?
>
> WITNESS: *It sounds like the voice.*
>
> PROSECUTOR: All right.
>
> WITNESS: It's been six months. *It's hard, but it does sound similar.* But it's

said in a different way. See, the tone—it was said to me very belligerent in a loud voice.

Tr. I 86–88 (emphasis added).

259 **Despite numerous potentially meritorious grounds . . .**   See *Anders v. California*, 386 U.S. 738, 744 (1967). The brief asserted that counsel could perceive no issues worthy of appellate consideration.

268 **"A rapid and dramatic increase" . . .**   Brief of Petitioner, *Sullivan v. Florida*, U.S. Supreme Court (2009). Charles Geier and Beatriz Luna, "The Maturation of Incentive Processing and Cognitive Control," *Pharmacology, Biochemistry, and Behavior* 93 (2009): 212; see also L. P. Spear, "The Adolescent Brain and Age-Related Behavioral Manifestations," *Neuroscience and Biobehavioral Reviews* 24 (2000): 417 ("[A]dolescence is of its essence, a period of transitions rather than a moment of attainment."); also 434 (discussing radical hormonal changes in adolescence). Laurence Steinberg et al., "Age Differences in Sensation Seeking and Impulsivity as Indexed by Behavior and Self-Report," *Develpmental Psychology* 44 (2008): 1764; Laurence Steinberg, "Adolescent Development and Juvenile Justice," *Annual Review of Clinical Psychology* 5 (2009): 459, 466.

269 **We argued in court that, relative to . . .**   See B. Luna, "The Maturation of Cognitive Control and the Adolescent Brain," in *From Attention to Goal-Directed Behavior,* ed. F. Aboitiz and D. Cosmelli (New York: Springer, 2009), 249, 252–56 (cognitive functions that underlie decision-making are undeveloped in early teens: processing speed, response inhibition, and working memory do not reach maturity until about the age of fifteen); Elizabeth Cauffman and Laurence Steinberg, "(Im)maturity of Judgment in Adolescence: Why Adolescents May Be Less Culpable than Adults," *Behavioral Science and Law* 18 (2000): 741, 756 (significant gains in psychosocial maturity take place after the age of sixteen); Leon Mann et al., "Adolescent Decision-Making," *Journal of Adolescence* 12 (1989): 265, 267–70 (thirteen-year-olds show less knowledge, lower self-esteem as decision-makers, produce less choice options, and are less inclined to consider consequences than fifteen-year-olds); Jari-Erik Nurmi, "How Do Adolescents See Their Future? A Review of the Development of Future Orientation and Planning," *Develpmental Review* 11 (1991): 1, 12 (planning based on anticipatory knowledge, problem definition, and strategy selection used more frequently by older adolescents than younger ones).

270 **"the products of an environment" . . .**   *Sullivan v. Florida*, Brief of Petitioner, filed July 16, 2009.

271 **Former juvenile offenders who had later become . . .**   Brief of Former Juvenile Offenders Charles S. Dutton, Former Sen. Alan K. Simpson, R. Dwayne Betts, Luis Rodriguez, Terry K. Ray, T. J. Parsell, and Ishmael Beah as Amici Curiae in Support of Petitioners, *Graham v. Florida / Sullivan v. Florida*, U.S. Supreme Court (2009).

CHAPTER FIFTEEN: BROKEN

275 James "Bo" Cochran had been released . . .   *Cochran v. Herring,* 43 F.3d 1404 (11th Cir. 1995).

280 But then a few years later, rates of execution . . .   "Facts About the Death Penalty." Death Penalty Information Center (May 2, 2013), available at www .deathpenaltyinfo.org/FactSheet.pdf, accessed August 31, 2013.

280 By 2010, the number of annual executions . . .   There were 46 executions in 2010 compared to 98 in 1999."Executions by Year Since 1976," Death Penalty Information Center, available at www.deathpenaltyinfo.org/executions-year, accessed April 29, 2014.

280 New Jersey, New York, Illinois . . .   Act of May 2, 2013, ch. 156, 2013 Maryland laws; Act of April 25, 2012, Pub. Act No. 12-5, 2012 Connecticut Acts (Reg. Sess.); 725 Illinois Comp. Stat. 5/119-1 (2011); Act of March 18, 2009, ch. 11, 2009 New Mexico laws; Act of December 17, 2007, ch. 204, 2007 New Jersey laws.

281 Even in Texas, where nearly 40 percent . . .   In 2010, eight people were sentenced to death in Texas, following a recent trend in the state of eight to fourteen death sentences per year. In the 1990s, however, Texas routinely sentenced between twenty-four and forty people to death each year. "Death Sentences in the United States from 1977 by State and by Year," Death Penalty Information Center, available at www.deathpenaltyinfo.org/death-sentences-united-states--1977-2008, accessed August 31, 2013.

281 Alabama's death-sentencing rate . . .   "Alabama's Death Sentencing and Execution Rates Continue to Be Highest in the Country," Equal Justice Initiative (February 3, 2011), available at www.eji.org/node/503, accesssed August 31, 2013.

282 The Court ruled unanimously in our favor . . .   *Nelson v. Campbell,* 541 U.S. 637 (2004).

282 Many states were using drugs . . .   Ty Alper, "Anesthetizing the Public Conscience: Lethal Injection and Animal Euthanasia," *Fordham Urban Law Journal* 35 (2008): 817.

282 When the news spread that the drugs . . .   In early 2011, Hospira, Inc., the sole U.S. producer of the lethal injection drug sodium thiopental, halted production of the drug due to concerns of its use in lethal injections. Nathan Koppel, "Drug Halt Hinders Executions in the U.S.," *Wall Street Journal* (January 22, 2011). Similarly, Danish company Lundbeck stopped selling execution drug pentobarbital to prisons in states that carry out the death penalty. Jeanne Whalen and Nathan Koppel, "Lundbeck Seeks to Curb Use of Drug in Executions," *Wall Street Journal* (July 1, 2011).

282 Drug raids of state correctional facilities . . .   Kathy Lohr, "Georgia May Have Broken Law by Importing Drug," NPR (March 17, 2011), available at www.npr.org/2011/03/17/134604308/dea-georgia-may-have-broken-law-by-importing-lethal-injection-drug, accessed August 31, 2013; Nathan Koppel,

"Two States Turn Over Execution Drug to U.S.," *Wall Street Journal* (April 2, 2011), available at http://online.wsj.com/article/SB10001424052748703806304 576236931802889492.html, accessed August 31, 2013.

282 The U.S. Supreme Court, in *Baze v. Rees* . . .   *Baze v. Rees,* 553 U.S. 35 (2008).

CHAPTER SIXTEEN: THE STONECATCHERS' SONG OF SORROW

295 On May 17, 2010, I was sitting . . .   *Graham v. Florida,* 560 U.S. 48 (2010).

295 Two years later, in June 2012 . . .   *Miller v. Alabama,* 132 S. Ct. 2455 (2012).

296 His jury was illegally selected . . .   *Shaw v. Dwyer,* 555 F. Supp. 2d 1000 (E.D. Mo. 2008).

296 He was given a mandatory . . .   *Banyard v. State,* 47 So. 3d 676 (Miss. 2010).

297 The Court emphasized the trial court's . . .   *Evans v. State,* 109 So. 3d 1044 (Miss. 2013).

299 I believe that there are four institutions . . .   Alex Carp, "Walking with the Wind: Alex Carp Interviews Bryan Stevenson," *Guernica* (March 17, 2014), available at www.guernicamag.com/interviews/walking-with-the-wind/, accessed April 30, 2014.

302 I had to go back to an appellate court . . .   *People v. Nunez,* 195 Cal.App. 4th 404 (2011).

304 But to coerce a confession from him . . .   *State v. Carter,* 181 So. 2d 763 (La. 1965).

Index